Recognizing Adult ADHD

What Donald Trump Can Teach Us About Attention Deficit Hyperactivity Disorder

John Kruse M.D., Ph.D.

Copyright © 2019 by John Kruse M.D., Ph.D.
All rights reserved.

No part of this publication may be reproduced, stored in a retrieval system, or transmitted in any form or by any means, electronic, mechanical, scanning, recording, photocopying, or otherwise, without the prior written permission of the author.

Limit of Liability/Disclaimer of Warranty: This publication is designed to provide accurate and authoritative information in regard to the subject matter covered. It is sold with the understanding that neither the author nor the publisher is engaged in rendering legal, medical, investment, accounting or other professional services. While the publisher and author have used their best efforts in preparing this book, they make no representations or warranties with respect to the accuracy or completeness of the contents of this book and specifically disclaim any implied warranties of merchantability or fitness for a particular purpose. No warranty may be created or extended by sales representatives or written sales materials. The advice and strategies contained herein may not be suitable for your situation. You should consult with a professional when appropriate. Neither the publisher nor the author shall be liable for any loss of profit or any other commercial damages, including but not limited to special, incidental, consequential, personal, or other damages.

An important note: This book is not intended as a substitute for the medical recommendation of physicians or other health-care providers. Rather, it is intended to offer information to help the reader cooperate with physicians and health professionals in a mutual quest for optimum well-being. The author has not directly treated Donald Trump. Some identities have been changed to protect patient confidentiality.

Recognizing Adult ADHD
What Donald Trump Can Teach Us About Attention Deficit Hyperactivity Disorder
By Dr. John Kruse
1. PSY022010 - Attention-Deficit Disorder (ADD-ADHD)
2. PSY000000– Psychology, General
3. PSY036000 – Psychology, Mental Health
Paperback ISBN: 978-1-949642-22-3
Hardcover ISBN: 978-1-949642-24-7
Ebook ISBN: 978-1-949642-23-0
Library of Congress Control Number: 2019909839

Cover design by Lewis Agrell
Printed in the United States of America

Authority Publishing
11230 Gold Express Dr. #310-413
Gold River, CA 95670
www.AuthorityPublishing.com

DEDICATION

Dedicated to the patients who have shared so much with me, and who have taught me so much over the years.

TABLE OF CONTENTS

INTRODUCTION. 1

SECTION I. DONALD TRUMP: ADULT ADHD POSTER BOY

Chapter 1   ADULT ADHD ISN'T FAKE NEWS 15

Chapter 2   ADHD IS A BRAIN CONDITION—
            "AND I'VE GOT A REALLY GOOD BRAIN". . . 28

Chapter 3   THE FORMAL DSM-5 CRITERIA
            FOR ADHD (TRUMP SCORES BIGLY) 49

Chapter 4   BUT WAIT, THERE'S MORE!
            ADHD AND CO-MORBIDITY 63

Chapter 5   FAKING ADHD? ACTING OUT
            OR JUST ACTING? 86

Chapter 6   A STIMULATING DISCUSSION ABOUT
            TREATING ADHD 95

SECTION II. (CHIEF) EXECUTIVE FUNCTION DISORDER

Chapter 7   BEYOND DSM-5: ADHD AS EXECUTIVE
            FUNCTION DISORDER 117

Chapter 8	PERSISTENTLY INCONSISTENT: EXECUTIVE DYSFUNCTIONS EXPLAIN ADHD SYMPTOMS	125
Chapter 9	NOTHING SUCCEEDS LIKE EXCESS—POSITIVE ASPECTS OF ADHD	139

SECTION III. THE CHANGING WHIRLED OF ADHD: ETHICS AND POLITICS OF DIAGNOSING ADHD

Chapter 10	THROWING COLD WATER ON THE GOLDWATER RULE	149
Chapter 11	FOCUSING ON DAMAGE CONTROL WHEN CONTROL OF FOCUS IS DAMAGED	160
Chapter 12	IS THE ADHD LABEL LIABLE TO LIBEL SOMEONE? STIGMA AND ADHD	175
Chapter 13	BIG DATA TO THE RESCUE? TECHNOLOGY ALTERS ADHD ASSESSMENT AND TREATMENT	186
Chapter 14	IS ADHD CONTAGIOUS? CULTURAL APPROPRIATION OF THE ADHD COMMUNITY	202

ACKNOWLEDGMENTS.................................. 225
APPENDIX A: OFFICIAL DSM-5 CRITERIA FOR ADHD.. 229
APPENDIX B: LINKS TO ADHD SELF-ASSESSMENTS.... 233
BIBLIOGRAPHY 235

INTRODUCTION

The ADHD Problem

Attention Deficit Hyperactivity Disorder, or ADHD, derails careers, destroys relationships, damages self-esteem, and even kills people. It substantially increases the risk for incarceration, drug abuse, serious accidents, and suicide. Because ADHD symptoms often respond quickly and dramatically to medications and other treatments, we can avert tragedies by accurately identifying and treating adult ADHD.

You might be one of the almost ten million adults already receiving effective therapy for ADHD. Or perhaps you're among the tens of millions of family members, friends, and co-workers overwhelmed by the chaos, inconsistencies, and contradictions produced by someone in your life with ADHD. You might not even be aware you have it or are affected by those who do, since millions of adults with ADHD remain undiagnosed and untreated. Even if none of these groups applies to you, we live in a society growing evermore ADHD-like, which pushes us to react in ways that more closely resemble ADHD-driven behaviors. This book aims to teach you to recognize and understand ADHD in yourself and others, and provides coping strategies for addressing ADHD-driven behaviors.

When I started my psychiatric practice a quarter century ago, very few people recognized that adults could have ADHD. Even now, understanding of the condition remains superficial despite the proliferation of books and blogs about adult ADHD. We often dismiss ADHD as merely indicating distractibility ("There's a squirrel!") or fidgetiness, leading to the incorrect conclusion that failing to identify the condition harms nobody. We all need to learn more about ADHD in order to cope with this condition at individual, relational, and societal levels.

A Presidential Problem?

A conversation with one of my adult patients with ADHD, in the midst of the 2016 presidential campaign, inspired me to write this book. We were sitting in my San Francisco office a few days after the second presidential debate between Hillary Clinton and Donald Trump. Fiercely intelligent, Cassandra devoted little time or energy to politics, but watching the split screen images contrasting Mrs. Clinton's calm, methodical, and coherent presentation with Trump's frequent interruptions, unfinished thoughts, rambling sentences, and incessant motion had jolted Cassandra into recognizing her own ADHD behaviors splashed across the television screen. Suddenly, she saw how her symptoms might appear to others.

At that point, I had been treating Cassandra for ADHD and associated depression and anxiety for fifteen years. (I have altered the names and occasional details of the individual patients discussed in this book in order to protect anonymity.) Blonde, slim, and six feet tall, with high cheekbones, she still turns heads on the streets of San Francisco at well past forty. Her ADHD, however, and the failure of those around her to grasp the impact of ADHD on her behaviors and relationships, had repeatedly damaged her career and her romantic life, despite her intelligence, charisma, and good looks. Careers in television, hotel management, and veterinary medicine had all eluded her. Several years ago, she was simultaneously embroiled in two marriages and one divorce. Even after combining awareness of her ADHD with hard work and helpful medications, she still struggled. She summed it up with, "I don't know how to put it all together and make a life."

Another comment by Cassandra towards the end of that session galvanized me to work on improving our collective recognition of what adult ADHD looks like, and how it harms individuals and society. "The best thing Trump could do for me would be to come out as having ADHD!" She perceived that by publicizing ADHD's effect on a powerful, prominent person like Donald Trump, she could increase societal understanding of, and acceptance for, this brain condition, and that doing so might improve her own life.

The more the media covered Trump's actions and utterances, the more my patients with ADHD exclaimed some version of: "He has ADHD, doesn't he?" As a psychiatrist specializing in adult ADHD, I had privately concurred that Trump's behavior seemed to fit the diagnosis, but the sheer volume of comments on this topic led me to examine the issue in more detail. In addition to reviewing definitions of ADHD and standards for diagnosis [1,2], I watched numerous video appearances of Trump, some going back forty years, and read accounts by his friends, associates, and collaborators about how his mind works. My investigations, as described in this book, confirmed that Trump does indeed fulfill the criteria for an ADHD diagnosis. Moreover, I found myself agreeing with Cassandra about the importance of not squandering this teachable moment, but instead utilizing it to foster a greater understanding of ADHD, and of Trump himself.

Rather than seeing Trump as a jumble of unusual traits juxtaposed into a single and singular man, the lens of ADHD focuses our attention on how this condition provides a unifying explanation for so many of his aberrant and contradictory behaviors. While the ADHD label enshrines the symptoms of distractibility and hyperactivity, problems with attention and physical restlessness represent just two islands of impairment in the expanse of potential problems created by this condition. ADHD affects a broad range of what we call executive functions [3]. Executive functions describe the "command and control operations" of the brain, including how we direct, alter, and maintain our attention; use working memory; manage time; prioritize; plan for the future; suppress impulses; and regulate emotions [4]. Impairments in executive functions explain why people with ADHD display so many different problems, and can present them so inconsistently.

The impaired executive functions of the brains of individuals with ADHD produce a wide range of real-world problems. ADHD contributes, in Trump and others, to a variety of dysfunctional behaviors that can include: directly contradicting comments made minutes earlier; uttering verifiably untrue statements; focusing on appearances rather than substance (judging women by how they look; showing enthusiasm for military parades but not military planning); obsessively returning to topics when others have moved on (inaugural crowd size, electoral victory); blurting out inappropriate comments ("shit-hole countries"; having a "bigger button" than Kim Jung-un); anger outbursts; and not preparing for important events (ignoring security briefings; not preparing for debates or negotiations). We simplify and clarify the task of trying to comprehend the behavior of someone with ADHD when we understand that ADHD manifests in all of these seemingly disparate ways. Furthermore, realizing that all of these ostensibly unrelated issues are part of a larger problem allows us to be less distracted by each individual action and less perturbed by each unconventional utterance, and also informs us regarding effective ways to address these problems.

On an almost daily basis for several years, Trump has amazed America and puzzled pundits with his unconventional, ill-informed, impulsive, childish, disorganized, rude, uncouth, untruthful, and self-centered behaviors. Comments from a single article in *The New Yorker* [5] include how Trump "lacks self-restraint," said things that were "considered scandalous and disqualifying," made "outlandish and often incompatible claims," exhibits "crudeness" and "more than occasional intemperance." The near ubiquitous description in the media of his ADHD traits contrasts vividly with the stark absence of acknowledgment that these problems could all be manifestations of his ADHD. Transfixed by details, almost nobody is addressing the bigger picture. Hundreds of articles describe his lying, narcissism, sociopathy, pettiness, poor manners, and short temper. (There are too many to cite, but for a few vivid, articulate, and pertinent articles, see the bibliography [6-10]. Out of this vast cornucopia of commentary only a few authors mention that ADHD might be one of Trump's mental health issues [11, 12].

A Solution?

The world remains unaware of, or dismisses as trivial, Trump's ADHD, despite its contribution to substantive dysfunction. Similarly, millions of individuals impaired by ADHD don't recognize their own condition, and therefore don't seek treatment. I have tied these twin tragedies together in this book with the hope that we can 1) improve our recognition of adult ADHD whether it presents in presidents or the general population, 2) promote more effective treatment for ADHD, and 3) develop skilled coping strategies for dealing with individuals who have ADHD. The president, due to the prominence of his position and the severity of his ADHD, intrudes constantly into our consciousness. Because he reaches a far broader audience than any sports hero or entertainment celebrity, he has inadvertently cast himself as the "poster boy" for adult ADHD—an ideal agent to educate us about this condition.

Objections to the Solution

Over the years, I've detected three different rationales for why people avoid evaluation and treatment for ADHD. Because all of these people are *ach*ing, I categorize them as the not-aw*ake* group, the mist*ake* group and the fors*ake* group. Those "not-awake" remain unaware that they display ADHD symptoms or that ADHD is a serious and potentially treatable condition. Members of the "mistake" group, including their families, therapists, and doctors, confuse ADHD with other mental health problems and neglect to address the ADHD behaviors. Individuals of the "forsake" group know that they have ADHD but shun treatment out of fear of either stimulant medications or stigmatization for seeking mental health treatment.

Difficulties in directing and sustaining attention can render those with ADHD less aware of their own performances, and of how their inattentiveness, impulsiveness, or additional ADHD traits affect others. As one example, I've met many individuals with ADHD who consider themselves punctual, but then chronically arrive ten to twenty minutes late for appointments. Those oblivious to a problem remain unlikely to seek treatment for it. In addition to ADHD fostering reduced awareness regarding one's own behavior, an incomplete understanding of ADHD blocks many from entering treatment. In dozens of evaluations I've heard people proclaim that their friends had labeled them "spacey," "not really present," or had even suggested they had ADHD, "But I dismissed it because I thought it wasn't really a thing." Those in the "not-awake" group often need repetitive, descriptive, non-condemning feedback about their ADHD in order to grasp that their problematic behaviors have a common origin and are potentially treatable.

Symptoms of anxiety, depression, bipolar disorder, substance abuse, and personality disorders often obscure underlying ADHD and create a barrier to effective diagnosis and treatment. Family members, therapists, and even psychiatrists can become so distracted by these other problems that they miss the underlying ADHD. In addition to these situations of co-occurring or "co-morbid" conditions where an individual simultaneously displays symptoms of *both* ADHD and another mental health condition, another problem exists: Observers sometimes misattribute symptoms as stemming from other causes in people who actually *only* have ADHD. For example, in some individuals we misidentify the restlessness and the rapid, ricocheting repartee produced by ADHD, falsely labeling these behaviors as a product of anxiety. Inaccurate diagnoses stymie our ability to provide targeted help to individuals with "mistake" group ADHD. Educating the public about what ADHD does and does not entail will help more people seek appropriate treatment.

Trump highlights how other conditions often overshadow or obscure ADHD. The media and mental health community emphasize his "malignant narcissism," while perpetuating silence about his ADHD. However, his ADHD explains why someone so concerned with projecting power and competence acts so consistently to undermine this image with blatantly untrue statements, inconsistencies, temper tantrums, and lack of planning. When I have pointed out Trump's ADHD to many of my astute, seasoned, and thoughtful psychiatrist friends, so often I hear a version of, "Oh my god, you're right! I was so distracted by all of his personality issues, I never saw the ADHD!"

Beyond ignorance and confusion, fear fashions the third set of social barriers to discourage those with ADHD from seeking an evaluation. Worries about stigmatization or the adverse effects of treatment encourage avoidance of the mental health care system. Public discussions about ADHD—and in particular, addressing ADHD's origins in the brain, reminding people about how frequently it persists into adulthood, and identifying specific individuals who display the condition—all help to reduce stigma. Education also works to lessen fears regarding treatment. Some of those with "forsake" group ADHD might opt for treatment if they learned that the serious adverse effects of stimulants are rarer than imagined, or that numerous non-stimulant medications and non-medication approaches can significantly reduce ADHD symptoms and improve functioning and life satisfaction.

Given that Trump robustly displays ADHD behavior—he walks like a duck, talks like a duck, and even tweets like a duck—why do we duck the issue and avoid talking about his ADHD? Although ignorance about adult ADHD contributes mightily to this silence, Trump's powerfully polarizing personality presents other obstacles to a free and open discussion about his ADHD. The ADHD community fears that the diagnosis will be further stigmatized if people identify it too closely with the president. The president's allies feel that any psychiatric label must be derogatory. His political enemies voice concern that a diagnosis might humanize him when they feel he should be demonized. And organized psychiatry proclaims that ethical reasons forbid discussions about Trump's mental health.

A friend of mine, a mental health practitioner with ADHD himself, captured the fear that associating Trump with ADHD would stigmatize the whole diagnosis when he insisted that I should subtitle this book *…And Not Everyone with ADHD Is an Idiot or an Asshole*. I believe I can advance that message more effectively without stooping to name-calling. As I discuss in Chapter 12, we reduce stigma by talking openly about conditions and categories. We lessen the potential harm that might arise from associating ADHD with this president by educating people that ADHD informs us about how Trump absorbs, processes, and utilizes information, but does not dictate his policies or the content of his utterances.

Furthermore, ADHD, important and influential as it can be, is always only one aspect of any individual, not the whole picture. Factors including age, intelligence, other character traits, childhood experiences, socioeconomic status, and family attitudes all have profound impacts on how any particular adult manifests symptoms of ADHD [13-16]. A white, privileged, 20th century, New York City household, run by a multi-millionaire father who was both demanding and not particularly supportive [17] produced Trump, and these forces that shaped him continue to influence the content of his ADHD-driven behaviors. We cannot attribute his apparently racist, sexist, xenophobic, authoritarian comments to his ADHD, even if they explain part of why he blurts them out rather than keeping them to himself.

People with ADHD, even though they share important traits, do not all appear or act identically [18, 19]. We don't expect all blondes, all blind people, or all those from blended families to be similar in other aspects of their lives. As noted above, although we require an understanding of ADHD to decipher how Trump's mind works, we cannot blame ADHD for the content of his verbalizations or the policies he proclaims. Thus, while knowing that someone has ADHD helps us predict they will speak in a rambling, non-linear, emotionally driven manner, it does not dictate what items or topics that individual will fixate on, nor the direction of the next pivot.

Trump also helps with destigmatization because he demonstrates that even severe ADHD does not preclude societal success, and indeed much of his appeal—his spontaneity, unconventionality, and energetic presentations—are all attributes of his ADHD. Furthermore, his prominence could even encourage a healthy discussion about psychiatry's role in society, the significance of a mental health diagnosis, and evolving stances towards privacy and which aspects of our leaders' lives are pertinent in a democracy.

To those who worry that I am using ADHD as a cudgel to attack Trump, I aver that this diagnostic label describes his behavior far more accurately and empathetically than the phrases millions of others have already employed, including calling him a f***ing moron, a child, crazy, a pathological liar, and deranged [20-24].

To those who object that ADHD excuses Trump's behavior, I remind them that an explanation differs from an excuse. Possessing a framework for how he takes in information, processes it, and responds to it helps in understanding his decision-making process but does not exonerate him of responsibility for his actions. Furthermore, an accurate assessment of how his brain functions aids those who wish to craft an effective resistance to his statements and actions.

To organized psychiatry, as I discuss further in Chapter 3, the official definition of ADHD, uniquely among our common mental health conditions, depends entirely on observable behaviors. Thus, the trove of behavioral information in the public record pertaining to Trump provides a superior data set, compared to an in-person evaluation, in order to reliably determine that he fulfills diagnostic criteria for ADHD. No violations of confidentiality occur by describing Trump's ADHD. Remaining silent about Trump's ADHD causes more harm than does an informed discussion of how we can identify and respond to his condition.

Outline of the Book

I have organized *Recognizing Adult ADHD* into three sections, each challenging a certain dogma. The first section addresses the old, and largely refuted dogma that ADHD is not real, and in particular, that ADHD doesn't exist in adults. I review evidence for the brain's involvement in ADHD, address treatment issues, and discuss diagnostic criteria and co-morbidity confusion, using the example of Trump to clarify many of these topics. In the second section of the book I employ the concept of executive functions to help refute the dogma that ADHD is a trivial condition that doesn't warrant attention or treatment. The third section tackles social aspects of discussing ADHD, including directly rebutting the dogma that psychiatrists must avoid speaking about the mental health problems of important public figures. ADHD's interference with Trump's abilities demands that we discuss this topic openly, substantively, and transparently regarding the basis of our assertions. I hope that my attempts to teach old dogmas new tricks are successful.

Disclaimers

This disclosure of Trump's ADHD contains several additional disclaimers:

I am not attempting a full psychiatric diagnosis of Trump, which would have to include a comprehensive account of all his other mental health problems. This book focuses on his ADHD because of its primary role in explaining his actions and utterances. Only an in-person evaluation could determine whether he actually manifests the attitudes, feelings, thoughts, and behaviors required to diagnose almost all other psychiatric illnesses.

Although I provide the recipe by which we currently diagnose ADHD, my intention is to increase awareness about ADHD, not to encourage home-cooking enthusiasts towards self-diagnosis. If you remain hungry after reading this book, additional excellent sources of information about ADHD exist at libraries, bookstores, and online. My favorite references for digging more deeply into learning about and coping with adult ADHD include Gina Pera's book *Is It You, Me or Adult ADHD?* [25], Russel Barkley's book *Taking Charge of Adult ADHD* [26], and Jessica McCabe's YouTube channel *How to ADHD* [27]. Just as we inform the public about signs of heart attacks and strokes—not for the purpose of self-diagnosis, but so that people will seek professional help in a timely manner if they display symptoms of these serious medical problems—we hope ADHD sufferers will seek professional help. If you have concerns that ADHD affects you or a loved one, find a mental health professional experienced with ADHD to confirm or rule out the diagnosis and, if needed, map out treatment strategies.

While pharmaceutical companies have occasionally provided me with meals, potentially influencing my opinions on certain topics, I have attempted to find objective information to substantiate all factual statements in this book. I also strive to identify those claims that are my own conjectures and not established facts.

This book does not contain any insider gossip about the president. I direct commentary to the ADHD-driven behaviors that shape his policy-making decisions, rather than focus on the politics and policies themselves.

Introduction

I use the term ADHD (Attention Deficit Hyperactivity Disorder) throughout this book, rather than ADD. Colloquially many people use the two terms interchangeably, although some use "ADD" to indicate inattentive ADHD and "ADHD" to mean hyperactive ADHD. Officially the ADHD label encompasses inattentive ADHD, hyperactive ADHD, and a combined-type ADHD.

I consider adult ADHD to be a real, pervasive, misunderstood, and under-treated condition that harms people, their loved ones, and our whole society [28-30]. Improving our understanding about ADHD will reduce barriers to treatment, and thereby lessen the direct and indirect havoc that ADHD wreaks [25, 31]. We should talk about Trump's ADHD because, in and of itself, it harms him, harms the presidency, harms the US, and harms the world. We should talk about ADHD because millions of American adults suffer and are less productive because of undiagnosed and untreated ADHD [32]. We should talk about adult ADHD because recognizing and treating this condition will reduce human misery [25, 31, 33] and help millions achieve more in their lives [34].

SECTION I

DONALD TRUMP: ADULT ADHD POSTER BOY

CHAPTER 1

ADULT ADHD ISN'T FAKE NEWS

The Reality of Adult ADHD

You may already feel that articles in print and online oversaturate us with information about ADHD. However, much of the past decade's coverage centers around the increasing use, misuse, and abuse of stimulant medications, including how these substances destroy lives, and can even be lethal [35, 36]. Stimulant addiction and amphetamine-induced psychosis are uncommon but very serious potential adverse effects of treatment of ADHD, and that is why I always discuss these risks with my patients, and offer treatment options that include non-stimulant medications and other modalities.

However, we have been neglecting the other half of the ADHD story. Millions of American adults with ADHD have never received an accurate diagnosis, and thus remain unaware of their own condition. Only a portion of those diagnosed with ADHD have received treatment. And only a fraction of those who have been treated are receiving sustained and adequate treatment [31, 37]. Because ADHD can cause great suffering and dysfunction [38], and because in many cases treatment quickly and significantly improves aspects of the condition [39, 40], the ongoing under-recognition and under-treatment of ADHD in adults contributes to serious societal and individual distress, functional impairment, and financial loss [32, 38, 41, 42].

I first learned about adult ADHD almost a quarter century ago from one of my patients. Frank was in his mid-forties and had just finished six years of therapy with an experienced psychoanalyst. That therapy had led to no improvements in Frank's depression or anxiety, and had failed to help Frank make any lasting changes in his life. Despite being intelligent, friendly, and willing to work, Frank had briefly held more than a hundred different jobs, and was on permanent disability for mental health reasons. He had even been fired from a job as a grocery store cashier. While making change for customers, Frank would start chatting about the interesting cowboy jacket or colorful shoes the customer was wearing, and would then have no recollection as to whether the customer had handed him some singles, or whether he had been handing them back to the customer as change. Consequently, Frank's checkout lane was always far slower than the others, and at the end of the day, Frank's till was always short several dollars. Even though employers liked how amiable he was and admired his ability to interact with customers, his inability to follow directions—to stay on track and complete a task—repeatedly led to his being fired.

Frank's psychoanalyst referred him to a respected academic center to find a new therapist and for an evaluation to see if ADHD explained why he never carried out his intended goals. The university psychologists tested Frank for several long days, only to conclude, as they referred him to me, "It looks like maybe he has ADHD, but that doesn't exist in adults." So I started working with Frank without any clear diagnosis. Although Frank was enthusiastic during our sessions and appeared to enjoy the interaction, he often showed up late. He would amble down the hallway, loudly berating himself for his tardiness, and for having stopped to chat with strangers even though he knew he was running late. Often he would spend the first few minutes pacing around the room, shouting further imprecations at himself for his inability to keep track of time. The later he was, the more upset at himself he became, and consequently he would consume even more of the remaining session with this self-directed venom.

Once seated, he was capable of talking almost non-stop during the sessions. His attention was like a honeybee, nuzzling against one blossom, vibrating with excitement, then buzzing over to a distant, more attractive bloom, humming intently there for a few seconds and then moving on, but never methodically plodding from one adjacent flower to another. Occasionally Frank would interject that he knew he wasn't giving me time to respond. And despite how animated and energetic he was while talking, one of his foremost complaints was how tired he was and how "low energy" he perceived himself to be, and how, as soon as he got home, he would collapse into a chair; simple tasks like washing dishes or taking out the garbage would remain undone for weeks. Had Frank been eight years old, nobody would have questioned whether he had ADHD [1,2].

The prevailing view that I heard throughout the clinical mental health world in the early 1990s was that anyone who had ADHD as a child outgrew it by the end of adolescence. In my four years of psychiatric residency training during that era, there was not a single mention in any lecture or presentation that adults could have ADHD, although childhood ADHD was presented as a standard and common diagnosis. However, even back then, a few clinicians and researchers recognized and were promoting adult ADHD as a valid diagnosis [43,44]. Published reports from decades before that era described adults with ADHD but used a variety of older names and diagnostic titles, such as "minimal brain dysfunction" [45-48], a label that had also been used to describe children with ADHD [49]. However, at the time, those reports drew little attention and had almost no impact on how the mental health world evaluated and treated adult patients.

We now know that childhood ADHD can have three different trajectories, with roughly a third showing no improvement in ADHD symptoms into adulthood, the middle third showing some improvement, and the remaining third no longer displaying symptoms of ADHD. The respective sizes of these three groups are approximations, in part because different studies have looked at somewhat different populations, and even more crucially, have used different cut-off criteria for how many symptoms must persist for ADHD to be considered completely in remission, partially remitted, or not at all in remission [50]. While awareness of ADHD in adults has become more widespread clinically [34] and in popular culture [51], comprehension of what adult ADHD actually entails remains incomplete and is a topic of ongoing research [31, 52, 53], with "still much to be done in the area of ADHD in adulthood" [54].

Under-Diagnosis and Under-Treatment of ADHD

The lack of awareness of adult ADHD twenty-five years ago that led to confusion about what my patient, Frank, was dealing with, seems eerily replicated today by the lack of public discussion of Mr. Trump's ADHD. While many of my patients bring up the possibility of Mr. Trump having ADHD, and some individuals with ADHD have offered such observations online, there has been a dearth of high profile op-eds, articles or other commentary about Mr. Trump's ADHD (for several, see [11, 12]). I continue to be amazed and disappointed in the lack of discussion of Mr. Trump's ADHD, because it so powerfully and pervasively influences his behavior. The few times I have heard mention of the possibility, commentators offer dismissive comments such as, "Who really knows what he has?" or "It's so obvious that he has ADHD," but without any acknowledgment regarding how profoundly ADHD drives a broad range of the president's behaviors.

Judging from my clinical practice, there are two major reasons why ADHD in adults remains under-diagnosed, and both may be pertinent to the lack of public recognition of Mr. Trump's ADHD. Virtually every month for the past two decades I have seen people in my San Francisco psychiatry office who are negatively affected by ADHD but who were not previously diagnosed with it. The first group includes those whose partners, family members, and co-workers have "jokingly" said for years that the individual has ADHD, but their comments were not taken seriously enough to seek an evaluation, because ADHD was not regarded as a legitimate diagnosis. Often their ADHD contributed to substantial deficits in completing education or training programs, holding down jobs, advancing along a career path, or building and maintaining relationships. Even if their lives were not disasters, they invariably performed below the level one would expect based on their intelligence, efforts, creativity, and other talents.

Sometimes they even rationalized to themselves, that since they were managing to function in society, albeit struggling or distressed, that they couldn't really have ADHD.

The other group consists of patients who have circulated through the mental health system for years, treated by numerous therapists and psychiatrists who completely missed or ignored the underlying ADHD. These individuals usually have had years or decades of ineffective treatments for depression, bipolar disorder, anxiety, OCD, PTSD, substance abuse, or other mental health problems. Often the other conditions were not just co-occurring with the ADHD but were actually either symptoms of, or direct consequences of, ADHD. Some of these patients had been labeled "self-sabotaging," "lazy," "irrational," or "contrary," and many had failed to consistently follow their therapists' recommendations. These unproductive and negative experiences in treatment often deepened the patients' sense of defectiveness and failure. In scores of cases, I have seen that correctly identifying ADHD creates the possibility of successfully addressing and resolving problems that have not been helped by decades of misguided treatment.

A brief anecdote highlights how easy it is to overlook ADHD. Mark was referred to me by a skillful therapist to evaluate and prescribe medicine for his depression and anxiety. A tall, gangly, energetic, and engaging tech worker in his late twenties, Mark spoke of how he felt overworked and that his computer coding job "crushed" his creativity and individuality. He longed to do "more artsy but less prestigious" web-design work. He displayed substantive symptoms of both depression and anxiety that had not resolved with psychotherapy, and so we discussed medication options before starting him on duloxetine. He had a robust, positive response, with resolution of his depression. We stretched our follow-up visits to several months apart. He moved into a work position that better suited his interests, where he thrived.

At a check-in almost a year after the initial visit, he spoke about how well his life was going, but he retained a jangly, restless presence that he felt was his "baseline anxiety." Delving more deeply into this "anxiety" he revealed he no longer had worrisome thoughts about his job or partner, and no concerns of future disasters, just that his mind constantly flitted all over, and he had a restless, leg-bouncing energy.

Even before he mentioned that his older sister had just been diagnosed with ADHD, I realized that Mark himself had ADHD! It had been submerged under symptoms of genuine depression and anxiety when I first met him, but also lay hidden because his own understanding of his ADHD was entirely encompassed by the inaccurate label of "anxiety." We reviewed a range of ADHD symptoms, which he agreed were pervasive in his life, and confirmed the ADHD diagnosis. Several times his face flickered with insight, as previously incomprehensible behavior patterns suddenly made sense to him using this new ADHD framework. A few months later, with further education about ADHD and a change in his medication regimen, Mark felt more functional, happier, and more self-aware; he appreciated himself more than he ever had. While I was glad I'd helped him attain this life satisfaction, I remain abashed that despite having already written a rough draft of this book, and being attuned to the problem of under-diagnosis of ADHD, it took me almost a year to pick up on this patient's underlying ADHD.

The vast majority of adults I see with a new diagnosis of ADHD have expressed huge relief at finally understanding the source of many of their problems, and many go on to obtain significant help navigating life's difficulties once their ADHD is properly diagnosed. As Cassandra said: "All of those years I struggled getting my stuff together, and now I know why." For many people the diagnosis of ADHD, in and of itself, changes their lives, because they can shift from believing "I'm a messed-up failure" to "This is something my brain does that I can learn to manage."

So what epidemiological evidence supplements my clinical observations, to support the claim that we under-diagnose adult ADHD and fail to take it seriously enough? Research shows that about 5%-15% of children meet full criteria for ADHD [34, 55] and another approximately 5% are somewhere on the ADHD spectrum [56]. These findings are consistent across countries and studies [55], provided the same evaluation criteria and testing conditions are used. Furthermore, depending somewhat on where the lines are drawn, approximately 15%-33% of those children maintain full-blown ADHD into adulthood, with an additional 33%-50% carrying a substantial and impairing degree of "subclinical" ADHD into adulthood [57, 58]. Thus, of the 250 million adult Americans, the most conservative estimate suggests at least 2%, or 5 million individuals, have full ADHD, but more expansively 16%, or 40 million individuals, are on the ADHD spectrum [59]. A widely accepted study placed the total adult US rate of ADHD at 4.4%, or approximately 11 million individuals [60].

A useful gauge of how many Americans are being treated for ADHD comes from a study that used a database consisting of private health insurance records for approximately half the country (146 million people) [60]. The study, which was actually designed to document how treatment of ADHD with stimulant medications lowers the likelihood of motor vehicle accidents, found only 1.54 million adults diagnosed with ADHD. Broadly extrapolating to the total population would suggest that roughly 3 million adults have been diagnosed with ADHD, well below even the very lowest estimates. However, I believe we have good evidence that extrapolating from only those with private health insurance to the whole US population minimizes the problem, for two reasons: Those with private coverage probably have both a lower rate of occurrence of ADHD than the total population and a higher rate of detection and treatment of ADHD among individuals who display it. Support for these claims rests on the assertion that lower socio-economic groups are under-represented among those with private health insurance; evidence suggests these lower socio-economic groups actually have higher rates of ADHD than does the general population [61, 62]. ADHD itself directly contributes to being less likely to have private insurance due to adverse effects on employment, income, and increased rates of incarceration [33, 60, 63]. Furthermore, populations lacking private insurance have lower rates of utilizing medical and mental health care [64], which is why the rate of detection of ADHD is likely to be lower in this population, even though ADHD itself is more prevalent. Given these factors, we can speculate that more cases of ADHD are being missed in the general population than in the privately insured population. The available evidence confirms that we are still missing the diagnosis in millions with adult ADHD, and we are not providing sufficient treatment to many who have been accurately diagnosed.

Attempts to determine how many people are being treated for ADHD by looking at stimulant medication prescriptions provide estimates, rather than precise information. Such studies will miss those being treated with non-stimulant medications or with treatments that involve no medications at all [31]. Secondly, those individuals taking stimulants for reasons other than for ADHD will be misclassified as having ADHD; off-label indications for stimulant medications include depression [65]; weight loss [66] (one of the earliest medically-approved uses of stimulants [67]); low energy, fatigue, or narcolepsy [68]; and traumatic brain injury-induced "brain fog" [69]. Those who have falsely claimed ADHD in order to obtain stimulant medication will also contribute to the size of this group. While some authors suggest that those faking an ADHD diagnosis in order to obtain stimulants constitute a major public health concern [36], studies indicate that many of those who "falsely" claim to have ADHD or who misappropriate and use others' ADHD medications do actually fall somewhere on the ADHD spectrum, and are using the medications to treat their symptoms, not just for pleasure or to "get high" [70, 71].

Further lines of evidence bolstering the claim that we are under-treating adult ADHD derives from additional studies showing that only a minority of children with carefully diagnosed ADHD who are followed into adulthood accurately self-report ongoing ADHD symptoms and continue to receive treatment [65, 66]. Thus, many adults who were medicated for ADHD as children, and who continue to have ADHD, are not getting treatment. In the last year I treated two twenty-year-olds who had had extensive treatment for childhood ADHD, who continued to display severe symptoms of ADHD in adulthood, but whose parents (including doctors in both families) insisted they no longer had ADHD! Finally, individuals born before 1980 grew up in an era with much less awareness of ADHD in either childhood or adulthood; as a result, they are more likely than younger cohorts to remain undiagnosed, untreated, and even unaware that ADHD exists in adults.

Some providers do diagnose ADHD when it is not present; over-diagnosis, particularly of children, appears to occur more often in some regions than in others [72]. The medical community, the general public, and investigative reporters should continue to explore for and expose over-diagnosis, particularly if such practices arise from either attempts at social control (instances where schools insist that children with problematic behavior, most often boys, and especially boys of color, need to be medicated to remain in a classroom), or through practitioner avarice [72]. Over-treatment with stimulants becomes dangerous because of the very serious (but uncommon) risks of these medications, including sudden cardiac death, addiction, and amphetamine-induced psychosis [73, 74]. Part of the task of correcting the problems of over-diagnosis and over-treatment involves increasing awareness of what ADHD actually entails. When more patients, parents, teachers, and practitioners become aware of the symptoms of ADHD, and appropriate treatment for it, we increase the likelihood of detecting inaccurate diagnoses and inappropriate medication regimens. However, finding and publicizing isolated cases of incorrectly diagnosed ADHD adds little to our understanding that, at a national level, we so often miss it when it is present.

Combating the Trivialization of Adult ADHD

Distinct from the issue of whether over-diagnosis of ADHD is more prevalent than under-diagnosis, those arguing against over-diagnosis often trivialize the missing of an ADHD diagnosis, implying that it isn't a particularly serious problem while trumpeting that over-diagnosis often results in horrifically damaged or lost lives [36]. However, missing a diagnosis of ADHD risks substantial adverse effects, and can even be lethal [75]. People with ADHD are more likely to die at a young age than those without ADHD [34, 63]. Compared to the general population, people with ADHD have more than twice the rate of motor vehicle accidents [76], double the divorce rate [77], and substantially higher rates of being imprisoned [78, 79], developing substance abuse problems [63], or not finishing high school or college [77]. Effective recognition and treatment of ADHD symptoms have been demonstrated to lower the likelihood of these damaging outcomes [63, 76, 80]. Given these statistics and the potential for reduction of harm with effective treatment, identifying and treating more people with ADHD will lead to less suffering and fewer disrupted and derailed lives. Untreated ADHD can also contribute to feelings of failure, and to feeling defective, deficient, or different; the result is pervasive negative impact on self-esteem and achievement, and an increased risk for other mental health problems including depression, anxiety disorders, and substance abuse [25, 31, 32].

Much of the media coverage regarding the claims that ADHD is widely and wildly over-diagnosed relies on stories of horrendous cases of sloppy diagnosis, over-zealous prescribing, and careless follow-up [36, 81]. The portrayal of these patients' histories provokes strong emotional responses, which dry statistics regarding the rates of incidence and treatment of ADHD fail to elicit. As an antidote to those anecdotes, I provide two brief clinical examples, demonstrating that under-diagnosis and under-treatment can also lead to disastrous outcomes. These cases represent extremes in the range of treatment outcomes, but are drawn from my own practice in just the last few years. I offer them in the hope that greater awareness of ADHD, and greater availability of effective treatment, will help prevent similar tragedies in the future.

I first evaluated Lucy for admission to an outpatient medication group connected with a psychotherapy clinic after several months of talk therapy had not allayed her depression and anxiety. Her speech was loud and rapid, cartwheeling from topic to topic, often veering into subjects that brought up in her strong feelings of anger, sadness, frustration, and disgust. She had been fired from several jobs for missing deadlines, disagreeing vociferously with colleagues, and poor attention to details, despite otherwise being perceived as hardworking, intelligent, and energetic. At the end of the evaluation I suggested that her distractibility, inattention, and emotional volatility all could be part of ADHD, but she adamantly rejected the diagnosis and denied that any of these symptoms had been present in her childhood. It was not until the fourth group session, when several group members commented on her ADHD symptoms, that she conceded she had been treated with Ritalin for ADHD in childhood, but had felt so coerced and stigmatized by the treatment that she did not want to repeat any aspect of it. Her group experience helped show her that even if she wanted to ignore or to try to hide her ADHD symptoms, they were causing difficulties in her interactions with others (both in the group and in her life). She decided that it made sense to make another attempt at directly treating her ADHD with medications. We tried non-stimulant medications that partially helped with her ADHD, mood, and anxiety symptoms; we also used cognitive behavioral therapy techniques adapted for ADHD. Over the course of two years she was able to find a job that was a better match for her interests, and to strengthen several friendships. In the medication group she was calmer, more able to appropriately wait her turn to speak, and more adept at modulating her emotions.

Lucy moved out of state, stopped her medications, and was unable to replicate much of the structure and social support that had helped her stay on track. Years later, feeling defeated by the simultaneous terminations of another job and of a romantic relationship, she flew back to San Francisco without a plan other than going to an emergency room. She was hospitalized because of her suicidal thoughts. The psychiatric inpatient staff informed me of the hospitalization and that they were treating her for mania. I repeatedly described to the staff that Lucy had displayed these patterns of rapid, scattered speech, volatile emotions, and distractibility, at every one of my sessions with her, across a decade, and that her family, teachers, and co-workers corroborated that she presented this way on a daily basis for more than forty years. Furthermore, in the hospital she was not speaking in ways that were grandiose, silly, or delusional, she was sleeping for six hours or more each night, and was not acting in ways that were bizarre, delusional, or particularly impulsive. I explained that Lucy had ongoing, severe ADHD, exacerbated now by a life crisis, and that she was not in the midst of a manic episode.

Nevertheless, they sedated her with increasing doses of a potent antipsychotic medication, in an attempt to "stabilize her mood." They reported that her speech did slow down (to the point of being slurred) and her emotions flattened out during her stay, but also that she remained "oppositional" to their treatment plan and "defiant" in her insistence that they address her ADHD, all of which they took as further confirmation of her mania. After a few days of overwhelming sedation, the hospital discharged her. Within a day, still despairing, and feeling profoundly misunderstood, she jumped off the Golden Gate Bridge. For Lucy, identifying and treating her ADHD had provided only partial relief during her life, and the failure to identify ADHD in her final weeks killed her.

Paul was the son of one of my patients. Concerns about his mental health arose at age twelve when he hit his mother over the head with a skateboard during an argument and both of them were taken to the emergency room. Because of gross administrative inadequacies, his managed-care mental health system scheduled his first follow-up, with a social worker, a full six weeks after the ER visit. A child psychiatrist did not see him until another month had passed. At his first in-depth evaluation, seventy-five days after the initial crisis, the doctor determined that Paul had ADHD. However, since the doctor was about to depart on a lengthy vacation, no treatment was initiated for yet another two months. The intermittent, delayed, and partial treatment served to convey to Paul and his family that his ADHD was not important enough to address.

Paul almost failed out of school, started using street drugs, and began a life of petty crime. He was only on ADHD medication for brief periods, during which his school performance would improve, he would communicate more effectively with family members, and he would stop using meth and marijuana. Many factors contributed to the fragmented and inadequate treatment of his ADHD, including the managed-care company's trivialization of mental health, the disorganization in Paul's household, and his own ADHD—which contributed to missed appointments, inconsistencies in filling and taking medication, and decreasing Paul's awareness of how his behavior alienated others and led to poor decision making.

Paul was in and out of jail during his twenties for selling drugs, fencing stolen goods, and petty scams. One afternoon he returned to his car in a shopping mall parking lot, unaware that it had been staked-out by police as a stolen vehicle. He did know that he had an outstanding warrant for arrest because of a minor parole violation. When uniformed cops approached the car, Paul impulsively slammed the car into reverse, even though there was no open avenue for escape. His car hit one of the officers and Paul died in the ensuing fusillade of police bullets. His untreated ADHD contributed to the impulsive reaction that triggered his death, as it had to many of the rash decisions that propelled him along the path that ended in that parking lot. Extrapolating from Paul's positive experiences on prescription stimulants, it is likely that if he had stayed on his medication he would be alive today.

Missing the diagnosis of ADHD in adults, or under-treating it, kills people. The premature deaths of those with ignored or poorly treated ADHD are certainly tragic, but are only the prominent tip of the proverbial iceberg of suffering caused by inadequately treated ADHD. Adult ADHD not only wreaks havoc over the lives of sufferers; it also affects everyone around them [28, 30, 31, 82]. When ADHD leads to people being late for appointments, missing deadlines, impulsively blurting out hurtful comments, ignoring loved ones or business colleagues, abruptly changing plans or not completing tasks, the repercussions sometimes hurt others more than the individual with ADHD.

Returning to the national stage, I believe Mr. Trump's undiagnosed and untreated ADHD causes him to betray political allies (domestically and abroad) with his inconsistencies, to confuse the public with his contradictions, to alienate many with his intemperate outbursts, and to increase anxiety among the general population and even his supporters. Will his impulsiveness and poor judgment lead to nuclear war? Will his lack of preparation or his lack of adherence to principles derail any agenda he has started to act on? By propelling Trump's adult ADHD into the public conversation, I hope that a wider audience will become familiar with this serious diagnosis, and that people who might benefit from treatment of ADHD, including the president, find it sooner than they otherwise might.

CHAPTER 2

ADHD IS A BRAIN CONDITION—"AND I'VE GOT A REALLY GOOD BRAIN"

ADHD exists as a brain-based neurodevelopmental condition [83]. More than 20,000 scientific articles have been written about ADHD in the last ten years alone [84], establishing the validity of the diagnosis, exploring its underpinnings in the brain, and discovering genetic factors that contribute to its origins. Although the brain contributes fundamentally to the origins of ADHD, family, cultural, and experiential factors influence how these biologic seeds germinate and grow for each individual with a propensity for ADHD [85]. Exploring the biologic origins of adult ADHD also pushes us to confront the question of why we even make psychiatric diagnoses. I will address some of the problems inherent in categorizing human conditions, particularly mental health conditions. Moving from the general to the particular, I will then use this discussion to frame the importance of addressing Mr. Trump's ADHD.

Neuroanatomy of ADHD

Scores of studies have used MRI or other brain imaging techniques to compare and contrast the size of brain structures in individuals with

ADHD versus those who don't have the condition (see [86] among others). We lack complete uniformity in the results of various studies because of differences in patient and control populations, and in how researchers measured and analyzed brain regions. These brain studies repeatedly find differences in areas of the brain that we currently understand to be related to directing attention or controlling impulses or hyperactivity. However, from these anatomical studies the most that we can currently say is that these brain differences are correlated with ADHD, rather than having certainty that they cause the symptoms of ADHD. Correlational studies cannot determine whether differences in the size of brain regions cause ADHD, or whether ADHD causes the brain differences, or whether a third factor leads to both ADHD and altered brains.

Neuroscientists generally concur that in ADHD there is a reduction of gray matter (nerve cell bodies) in parts of the right basal ganglia, as well as in parts of the frontal cortex connected to the basal ganglia [86, 87], and also in specific regions of the cerebellum [88]. Increased thickness of the occipital cortex (i.e., gray matter density) has also been noted [87], along with connectivity differences of the visual attention network [89], which may be a factor in why visual information is often so salient to people with ADHD. However, some studies have found reduced volume in the visual cortex [90] [91]. Deficiencies in some of the white matter tracts connecting different brain regions have also been noted [92, 93], which fits in with ADHD being related to altered coordination between parts of the brain [93].

Prevalent fears that stimulant medications cause brain damage to youngsters with ADHD present a major barrier to some families in seeking treatment, or even evaluation, of their children with ADHD [94]. However, a meta-analysis report looked at more than two dozen neuro-imaging studies that examined the brains of three groups of children: 1) ADHD children with a history of stimulant medication treatment, 2) ADHD children who never consumed stimulant medications, and 3) healthy controls without ADHD and without any exposure to stimulant medication. In measures of both anatomy and brain activation, the brains of the stimulant-treated ADHD children were substantially *more* likely to resemble the brains of the healthy controls [95]. Rather than damaging the brains of children with

ADHD, the stimulants appear to "normalize" them. Thus, we may be contributing to long-term adverse brain alterations from ADHD by *not* treating children with medication. We know much less about whether the brains of adults with newly diagnosed ADHD can also undergo such changes in response to treatment with stimulant medications; given the evidence for stimulants "normalizing" the brains of ADHD children, similar results remain a possibility for adults with ADHD. We need to be investigating this important question.

When we look not just at the size of brain structures but at measures of brain activity in individuals with ADHD, we see differences compared to the brains of people without ADHD. In general, areas of the frontal cortices appear under-activated at rest [96], which is thought to correlate with less impulse control and decreased ability to guide attention and other aspects of behavior [97]. Other studies suggest that in brains of individuals with ADHD, certain tasks more extensively activate nerve cells throughout the brain, with less shutting down of activity in extraneous regions demonstrated by non-ADHD brains. This increased diffuse activation may lead to more distractibility [3] and to greater creativity (more unusual patterns of connectivity are being made) [98,99] seen in individuals with ADHD. Roughly 20% of the oxygen and 25% of the glucose consumed by the human body are used by the brain, despite the brain making up only ~2% of the body's total weight [100]; the brain uses more energy than any major muscle group in the body. Given the high metabolic demands of the brain, this diffuse hyperactivation with certain tasks may explain why so many people with ADHD persistently complain of fatigue after bouts of intellectual or social activity. Those with ADHD may have actually utilized far more calories to execute a given task, resulting in physiologic fatigue, not just some metaphorical sense of being psychologically tired. At least one study has indicated that the stimulant methylphenidate can decrease glucose utilization during a cognitive task, compared to a placebo group; the stimulant appears to help the ADHD brain perform certain cognitive tasks more efficiently [101,102].

Recent studies suggest that for children who have had ADHD, in comparison to non-ADHD children, differences in the activity of the caudate nucleus (part of the deeper brain regions of the basal ganglia) during an inhibition task persist into adulthood, whether or not the child outgrows the ADHD [103, 104]. In contrast, the cortical and cerebellar areas that are under-activated in children with ADHD while performing this inhibition task, improve towards normal levels in those who outgrow their ADHD, while remaining under-active in those whose ADHD persists into adulthood [104]. (Inhibition tasks require subjects to inhibit, or not respond to, a particular, expected stimulus and are among the more sensitive psychological tests for revealing ADHD tendencies.) Thus, we may have separate markers for ever having had ADHD (under-activation of the caudate), and for ADHD that resolves with age (normalization of under-active cortical and cerebellar regions). These findings suggest that treatments in childhood that work on cortical or cerebellar regions may have greater likelihood of changing the brain than those treatments that target the basal ganglia.

Rather than being localized to one part of the brain, ADHD is best understood as patterns of aberrant connectivity between brain regions, with resultant over-activation and under-activation of different networks, and with the regions most affected including the frontal cortex, the caudate nucleus of the striatum, and cerebellar circuitry.

Genetics of ADHD

A multitude of studies show that there is a large genetic component to ADHD [105, 106], with a heritability of approximately 80%, comparable in strength to the robust genetic influence on height [107], or schizophrenia [108], and stronger than the genetic component to depression (heritability estimates between 40-60% [109]). Although in a few rare families one specific gene mutation may predispose to ADHD [110], for most individuals with ADHD, a multitude of genes, each with small effects, appear to contribute to development of the condition [111]. Outside of those rare families, no single, determinative ADHD gene exists that we can test for. Although individual studies have suggested that more than twenty candidate genes (i.e., genes that are investigated because they are hypothesized to play a role in ADHD) are involved in the development of ADHD, the most consistent findings across studies have implicated variations of dopamine-related genes in contributing to the risk for ADHD. These dopamine-related genes include those that code for dopamine receptors, dopamine transporters that recycle dopamine from the synapse, and enzymes that break down dopamine [85]. The involvement of genes controlling the dopamine system as risk factors for ADHD is not surprising, given that many of the effective ADHD medications promote dopamine neurotransmission.

In comparison to candidate gene studies, more recent studies have used a "hypothesis-free" investigation of the entire genome, looking for possible genes linked to ADHD in an unbiased manner (genome wide association studies (GWAS)). Genes that have been detected using this method are known to play a role in the growth and movement of brain cells during development, cell maintenance, speech and language, and intellectual disability [105][111]. Additional studies have linked genes involved in setting the rhythmicity of the circadian clock [112], and influencing brain lateralization [113], to adult ADHD.

In addition to the genetic studies, we know that exposure of developing fetuses to a host of intrauterine toxins (alcohol, cigarette smoke, certain pesticides) and even prematurity itself, are associated with increased risks of developing ADHD [85]. A biologic basis for ADHD is also supported by the finding that when ADHD is assessed using standardized psychometric tools, similar rates of ADHD appear to be found across cultures [114]. We know from over 100 worldwide studies, approximately 5%-15% of children manifest symptoms of ADHD such as disrupted attention, greater impulsivity, and hyperactivity compared to age-matched children in their own culture [55]. Different cultures certainly respond differently to children with ADHD. Whereas in the United States and much of Europe we focus on medications and other tools to make the child's behavior more in line with societal norms, some cultures, both within the US and worldwide, focus much more strongly on changing educational and other systems to accommodate their ADHD populations [115][116]. Given the dearth of studies on the subject, it is not clear whether the medical-model approach compared to the social-accommodation approach to children with ADHD results in any significant differences by adulthood in the prevalence of ADHD, or in the severity, adaptive functioning, or contentment of individuals with ADHD. Given the potential importance of the subject, we should be engaging in such research.

Although ADHD is strongly shaped by both genetic and intrauterine factors, we know that how it develops and manifests in a given individual is also shaped by familial and cultural factors. As with almost every aspect of human behavior, it is a question of nature *and* nurture, not nature *or* nurture.

ADHD - Biologically Based but No Good Test

If ADHD is really a brain-based biological problem, and we have studies showing differences in the sizes of brain structures and in the activity of certain parts of the brain in people with ADHD compared to the control group, why don't we already have several biological tests to show who has ADHD? While scientists and clinicians search for potential tests for ADHD, one barrier to their development lies in understanding the difference between being able to find group differences and having a definitive test for a condition.

An analogy helps explain why differences between groups do not in themselves provide a definitive test: We can measure human height consistently and precisely, and on average, men are taller than women. If I said that a given individual is six feet tall, the best guess is that this is a man, but it is certainly possible that it could be a woman. Identifying group differences is not enough for making diagnoses about specific individuals when there is overlap in the range of distributions of the two groups. As we learn more about the brain, we may confirm chemical or physiological markers that allow us to distinguish individuals with ADHD from all others, but we are not quite there yet.

Despite the scientific consensus that the currently available brain research robustly demonstrates a biological basis for ADHD, and that this evidence is stronger than the evidence supporting a biological basis for depression, there remains substantial public reluctance to accept the existence of ADHD. Three issues are behind this reluctance. 1) Individuals without ADHD, at least some of the time, look like they have ADHD. 2) People with ADHD, at least some of the time, look like they don't have it. 3) The standard treatments for ADHD are medications that have uncommon, but not rare, risks for the very serious problems of addiction [117] and psychosis [118]. I will address the first (spectrum issue) and second (the inconsistency issue) topics here, and reserve the third topic for Chapter 6 on treatment of ADHD.

ADHD Exists on a Spectrum

ADHD lacks a pathognomonic trait—a behavior that is specifically characteristic of the condition. Actually, many of our psychiatric diagnoses lack pathognomonic behaviors, e.g., someone hearing voices might have a condition other than schizophrenia, someone who hoards every scrap of paper might have a condition other than obsessive-compulsive disorder. However, none of the characteristics of ADHD is particularly bizarre or relegated only to people with the condition, and virtually all "normal" individuals at least occasionally have lapses of attention, act impulsively, or behave restlessly. We diagnose ADHD based on a person displaying certain distracted, impulsive, and hyperactive behaviors to an excessive degree in multiple settings over a period of time. The fact that ADHD itself occurs on a spectrum of severity further complicates the difficulty of making a diagnosis: While it may be easy to identify people at the extreme ends of ADHD behavior who are interrupting others, misplacing items, or daydreaming far more often than "the norm," milder cases become more difficult to assess because of questions regarding where to place the line between "normal" and clearly excessive [119, 120].

We often consider psychiatry distinct from the rest of medicine, which purportedly deals with clear-cut categories: You are either pregnant or not, you have a broken bone or not, you have cancer or not, you have hypertension or not. All of these dichotomies are false, or are oversimplifications. Is an ectopic pregnancy implanted in the abdominal wall and never potentially capable of producing a full-term infant, a pregnancy? Is a developing blastocyst with a severe chromosomal abnormality that miscarries after a few weeks of growth a pregnancy? Is pseudocyesis—a condition in which the patient has all signs and symptoms of pregnancy without the presence of a fetus—a pregnancy? While a compound fracture is undoubtedly a broken bone, how about a hairline fracture, or a stress fracture, or that very same bone the week, day, hour, or second before a stress fracture "occurs"? There is ongoing controversy regarding whether many of the tiny tumors, particularly of the thyroid or breast, which seem destined to never become malignant, should be reclassified as non-cancers [121, 122]. And the numeric guidelines for what is hypertensive or not have gone back and forth during my lifetime, so that someone who had "normal" blood pressure a generation ago, with identical readings now would be classified as hypertensive [123]. Although human brains are "wired" for a propensity to categorize [124], nature can't always be "carved at the joints" into neat groupings, and human behaviors are even harder to sort out. Does the existence of intersex individuals mean that our concepts of male and female don't really exist, as some provocative thinkers propose? I maintain that there is some usefulness to retaining categories even if they fail to capture all the nuances and variability expressed in human lives.

That ADHD occurs on a spectrum of severity also causes controversy regarding whom we should be treating. Opposition to treating "pre-diabetes" or borderline hypertension is far more limited than to treating "subclinical" depression or ADHD. In part this is because we employ quantifiable numeric scales to record blood glucose levels or blood pressure, whereas our measures of severity of mental health conditions are much less precise. Also, pre-diabetes and borderline hypertension are more readily seen as potentially progressive conditions, so that treatment in early stages may prevent worse disease, whereas mental health conditions are often considered categorical by the general public: You're depressed or not, you have ADHD or not. However, the "hard" numbers we have for blood glucose or blood pressure may be more misleading than the fuzzy numbers we obtain from a depression or ADHD scale. Recent food intake, exercise, and circadian factors influence both blood glucose and blood pressure (posture also strongly influences blood pressure), yet we commonly use a single number to capture what we think of as important information regarding an individual's body. In essence, the numbers lull us into the delusion of reification: Because we can measure it easily, we feel that we know what blood pressure or blood sugar "is" when neither of these actually is a simple "thing." The vagueness inherent in our mental-health scales may more closely reflect our limited ability to capture an aspect of the human condition in a single number than the false precision of our measurements of physiology.

The notion that we may prevent more serious disease by treating earlier stages, pre-conditions or sub-syndromal states, is as germane to mental health as it is to physical conditions. With depression, since many individuals do traverse the scale of severity during the course of an episode, it is clear that treating a milder case may well prevent a severe, incapacitating suicidal depression [125, 126]. Also, with depression, we have extensive evidence that the longer the time one spends depressed, the more likely one is to fall back into depression in the future [127], increasing the long-term imperative to treat depression aggressively when it is present. For most depressed patients, episodes of depression last a limited amount of time [128]. In contrast, ADHD is not an episodic condition [2], and the "severity" or "degree" of ADHD displayed by an individual appears to be largely fixed by young adulthood [129]. Certainly, the relative stability of adult ADHD is what I have seen in my clinical practice over the years; it is what we would expect given that changes in brain structures and connectivity occur most actively during childhood and adolescence.

The studies demonstrating that childhood stimulant treatment makes the brains of children with ADHD more closely resemble brains that never had ADHD [95] strongly suggests that early treatment may well reduce or even eliminate the risk in some children with ADHD for continuing to have the condition as adults. Furthermore, even if the course or severity of ADHD itself is not altered by childhood treatment in some individuals, we can clearly improve the lives of many of these children even if we are not permanently improving the underlying ADHD. ADHD disrupts learning, disrupts performance, and disrupts socialization [3, 130]. Early treatment of ADHD could preserve access to various educational, career, and friendship options that might be precluded if the ADHD is not treated [80], even in cases where the ADHD is not severe. Might Trump be less defensive, less sensitive to perceived slights, and more attuned to the nuances of diplomacy or policy if his ADHD had been more effectively addressed in childhood?

Two decades ago, Peter Kramer's *Listening to Prozac* popularized the concept of cosmetic psychiatry [131], addressing some of the relevant issues regarding using medications to treat depression or anxieties on the milder end of the spectrum. Many modern critics go even further, suggesting that it is almost criminal to be providing medications to anyone whose ADHD does not meet full diagnostic criteria [36]. This is a particularly relevant issue because of the research indicating that many of the college students who obtain stimulant medications without a prescription are using the drugs primarily for performance—e.g., to help them study for exams or power through presentations—and that these individuals actually do have substantial symptoms of ADHD, even if they fall into a "sub-clinical range" or have not received a formal diagnosis [71, 132]. (This is not to deny that some of this clandestine use is to get "high" or achieve some other feeling of euphoria [71].) The "cosmetic psychopharmacology" issue becomes far murkier with stimulant medications because unlike the serotonin-reuptake inhibitor antidepressants, which seem to have minimal beneficial impact on "normal" non-depressed individuals [133], even someone without any trace of ADHD is likely to feel more focused and alert [134], and have an uplift in mood during occasional use of stimulant medications [135].

My own belief is that any adult on the ADHD spectrum, who suffers from the effects of their condition and desires treatment, merits a thorough evaluation and consideration of the full range of treatment options. I am specifically not addressing either adults without ADHD or children with ADHD, because ethical, political, and legal issues complicate those situations. It seems neither reasonable nor fair to deprive an adult with a condition, sub-clinical or not, of a treatment that helps improve performance and a sense of well-being. We don't arbitrarily say that if your vision is only 20-40, you can't have corrective lenses, and we will make eyeglasses available only to those whose vision is 20-80 or worse. Any individual who suffers or has impairment because of his or her condition, in consultation with a physician who has listened to and understands the individual and is informed about the condition and the treatment options, should be allowed to determine which treatments are appropriate. And potential ADHD treatments should include psychotherapy approaches as well as medications—stimulants or otherwise. This stance adheres to the ethical concepts of autonomy (a patient's right to make reasoned decisions), non-maleficence (not causing harm), and beneficence (helping others) [136].

Inconsistency of ADHD Symptoms

People frequently ask me why, if ADHD really is biologically based, do individuals with ADHD express the hallmark traits so inconsistently over time. I witnessed a vivid example of this inconsistency when I chaperoned a week-long class trip for my daughters' elementary school. One of the boys, Mark, inadvertently dropped both of his mittens on the dozen steps between the sledding hill and the classroom door, couldn't find his sandwich in his cluttered backpack (although it eventually turned up there, three days later, none the better for aging), was so distracted while eating that he sprayed a penumbra of crumbs and food debris around his lunch space, and fidgeted so much that he stood up and paced around his desk during science class. At the end of the trip, his teacher, a wise and experienced woman, asked me if I thought Mark had a mental health problem. She was sure that he couldn't have ADHD—because he was so focused and attentive during the math class that he loved. I explained to her that Mark's inconsistency was actually classic ADHD—i.e., ADHD does not mean that someone never pays attention; it indicates someone who has **difficulty in controlling attention** [3].

Children or adults with ADHD focus on what is interesting to them in the moment, rather than attending to what others consider to be important in a situation. The inconsistency of attentiveness does not disprove ADHD; it is characteristic of ADHD. Such inconsistency in behavior is part of what makes it frustrating to those who have ADHD and to those around them: How can they be spot-on with some tasks, while daydreaming or distracted or procrastinating for decades with other activities? Furthermore, unless an observer knows what tasks interest someone with ADHD, they will have difficulty predicting how attentive someone with ADHD will be in a given situation. The observer may think that closely watching fifteen minutes of cat videos requires as much attentiveness as spending a quarter hour recording expense report items, but for someone with ADHD one of these tasks may be excruciatingly more difficult to execute than the other.

Even when we understand and accept that ADHD is more about the control of attention than the inability to be attentive in all situations, many people still have trouble reconciling the inconsistency of performance with a biological basis for the behavior. We have a tendency to think that if a trait has a biological basis then it is hard-wired and invariant across different environments—like height, or the presbyopia I have developed in the last few years, in which the decreased flexibility of my lenses makes it harder to see close objects (i.e., far-sightedness requiring reading glasses). However, if I go spelunking and am stooped over in a cave, hasn't my height changed, even if temporarily? I can solve crossword puzzles in bright sunlight without reading glasses, but I struggle to read the exact same clues in a dim room—and in complete darkness I can't read anything at all! Is my presbyopia different in each of these three conditions? Clearly, expression of biologically based traits always depends on an interaction between the body and the world. Thus, we should expect those with a biologically/brain-based origin for their ADHD who are interacting with a complex, multifaceted world to manifest symptoms differently when attempting different tasks at different times. If ADHD impairs your ability to direct your attention, you might display highly distracted, flitting-about focus; bored and unfocused behavior; or hyper-focused behavior, depending on whether the environment provided multiple points of interest, no points of interest, or one strong point of interest to you. Your behavior will be different in each situation, even though each is reflecting your ADHD. And all of these behaviors will be particularly confusing to an observer who may not have any idea what your brain considers interesting.

Adult Onset ADHD?

The variability of ADHD symptoms over time also frames another controversial topic regarding adult ADHD [130]. Although it is widely accepted that some children can outgrow their ADHD by adulthood [137], there is much more disagreement about the reverse pattern: Can children who didn't have ADHD develop it as adults? Whether we put the cut-off at seven years (the previous definition) [1] or twelve years (currently) [2], we require the presence of ADHD symptoms in childhood in order to diagnose it in adulthood [2]. However, some provocative studies have concluded that substantial numbers of adults have symptoms of ADHD without having had the condition as a child [138-140]. Those objecting to this conclusion basically contend that these studies either misdiagnosed ADHD or misdiagnosed the onset of ADHD symptoms. Many of the new adult "ADHD" cases may be more accurately explained by other co-morbid conditions [141], including substance abuse or head trauma [142]. And many of the "new" adult ADHD cases may actually have displayed ADHD symptoms as adolescents. We know that the ability of adults to recall the severity of their childhood ADHD symptoms is often inconsistent and inaccurate [143, 144]. I have seen many adults fail to recall or report treatment for ADHD even when we have records of such treatment in their childhood. Many ADHD researchers do not believe that meaningful numbers of individuals just start having ADHD as adults.

My own clinical experience suggests that such cases are extremely rare. I checked my records sequentially, going back in time until I had gathered information from 100 individuals, all of whom robustly displayed ADHD symptoms as adults, but none of whom recalled any *diagnosis* of ADHD in childhood. (I specifically excluded those adults with ADHD who were clearly diagnosed with ADHD in childhood.) These adults ranged from college-aged to their early seventies. With one exception (a woman who hit her head ice skating in her forties) all of the other individuals clearly could report patterns of ADHD related difficulties before they reached adulthood—excessive daydreaming, constant restlessness, chronic lateness and procrastination with assignments, piling up vast numbers of parking tickets, or losing their house key or cell phone repeatedly. Particularly for some of my older patients, or those from rural or non-Western cultures, the delay until adulthood in diagnosing ADHD was due to when or where they grew up. In their childhoods, ADHD was not recognized, even among children, and they grew up feeling different but weren't able to say precisely why. Others lived in times and places where ADHD was acknowledged, but for various individual and family reasons, they slipped through the system. In my practice, new *onset* adult ADHD is extremely rare, but newly *diagnosed* adult ADHD is quite common. So what I see in my own practice coincides with published reports [145], that most adults who are correctly given a new diagnosis of adult ADHD have actually suffered with ADHD symptoms since childhood or adolescence. In Chapter 4, I address in more detail the topic of ADHD co-existing or being confused with other mental health conditions.

My clinical experience also agrees with published reports suggesting that personal, familial, and situational factors explain most cases of newly diagnosed adult ADHD, or more precisely, delayed diagnosis of ADHD. Personal factors include other strengths that compensated for those individuals' ADHD at earlier ages [146]. Some children with ADHD are bright enough to pass all of their classes without ever studying or handing in homework assignments. Some children with ADHD are so charismatic or creative that their uneven performances are excused. Some children with inattentive ADHD are so wrapped up in their own daydreaming that they slide through school "under the radar" because they never cause problems or draw particular attention to themselves. That a myriad of personal factors can lead to delayed diagnosis highlights that nobody with ADHD is "just" their ADHD; individuals deploy an array of strengths, weaknesses, and idiosyncrasies that make them who they are.

Familial factors that create barriers to diagnosing ADHD in childhood include chaos and dysfunction (often due to parental ADHD) that mask the signs that their children with ADHD are struggling. Interestingly, large numbers of parents with ADHD go undiagnosed until they bring their children in for treatment. Other families may recognize that their child with ADHD is different, but their cultures, religions, or philosophies provide alternative explanations for these behaviors, so they do not seek medical treatment for the child.

The situational factors leading to new diagnoses of adult ADHD are two-fold: those cases in which the demands on the individual with ADHD increase substantially, and those in which the amount of support and structure for the individual with ADHD decrease dramatically. Both categories emphasize that ADHD always manifests as an interaction between individuals and their environment; a workable situation can become untenable either with changes that put more stress on the individual or remove pre-existing support for the individual. Most of the adults that I see for newly diagnosed ADHD present for treatment because of life transitions. While moving to a new home, starting a new job, or beginning school can be stressful for anyone, these transitions are often particularly disorienting for people with ADHD, who usually rely heavily on environmental cues to organize their time and efforts and feelings. Most of these transitions include both increased demand—the individual needs to be demonstrating more intelligence, creativity, or productivity—and decreased structure, guidance, and social support.

I recently worked with a bright young man who was failing out of one of the most prestigious colleges in the country. He was highly distractible, repeatedly interrupting our initial session to remark upon objects on my desk or the garden outside the window. He had received top grades and test scores in high school not just because he was intelligent, but also because every afternoon his grandmother sat with him in the kitchen for three or four hours until his homework was done. She didn't provide him with any answers, speaking only rudimentary English herself, but was immeasurably helpful by making sure he studied. Without this structure to keep his learning on track, he missed lectures, failed to turn in assignments, and did not read his books. In college, for the first time he also had to manage the distractions of camaraderie, staying up late, and alcohol. Despite his superior intelligence, his ADHD plummeted him from the top of his high school class to the bottom of his college cohort. Most individuals with newly diagnosed adult ADHD had ADHD brains all along but had flourished (or barely skated through) in compatible environments; they did not need assistance from therapy or medications until their new situation put them at a big enough disadvantage that they could no longer perform adequately.

While many transitions bringing individuals into treatment for ADHD involve both increased personal demands and decreased external support or structure, I have seen a number of men and women in their sixties and seventies where the relative lack of structure of retirement created dysfunction, which led to highlighting their ADHD symptoms. Although they had manifested lifelong aspects of ADHD, the script of school or work had helped to organize their lives and provide meaning, but with the termination of this organizing framework they floundered, feeling lost and unable to create direction. (This life change could also be interpreted not just as a loss of prior support, but as the creation of a new demand—i.e., to find interesting things to do all day, every day, day after day.) Again, it was not that their ADHD became worse; rather, the mismatch between their ADHD-brain and their environment grew larger than it had ever been.

Those with ADHD can also be thwarted by changes that create too much structure. I have worked with successful salesmen with ADHD whose performance crashed when new work guidelines required that they document their work efforts in more detail or account for their time with greater precision. While the employers viewed these changes merely as increased accountability and structure, the workers with ADHD experienced the changes as new demands that were not particularly relevant to how they completed their original job tasks. Because those with ADHD are less able to organize, prioritize, and self-regulate, their performance suffers more than others in situations with either too much or too little structure.

Although Trump's ADHD was patently manifest during the campaign, it has become more problematic as president, not just because the demands of the presidency are far greater than those of running for office, but also because there is more structure (legal, political, diplomatic, societal) that he has to contend with in performing his job. Unlike running a presidential campaign, a real estate company, or a reality television show, where he was largely accountable only to himself, he not only has more work to perform as president but is also more constrained in how he can perform it. His ADHD-driven difficulties working in accord with these structures become more apparent by the day.

In Chapter 14, I will address the related topic of how changes in technology and social media restructure our whole society in ways that are more ADHD-like, and explore ways in which these changes benefit but also create more problems for those with ADHD.

Why Make Psychiatric Diagnoses?

The question of how severe do ADHD symptoms have to be to warrant a diagnosis, and why does it require a critical life transition for some individuals to manifest enough distress from ADHD to require a psychiatric evaluation, both raise the issue of why we bother to make psychiatric diagnoses at all. Psychiatrists define mental disorders, diagnose individuals, and treat patients. These roles exist as an agreement with the society we live in, and our jobs always occur in a social context. Our definitions, diagnoses, and treatments evolve over time, in accordance, one hopes, with genuine and growing knowledge about how brains work. Progressive revisions of the diagnostic manual for mental disorders have attempted to increase the validity of diagnoses, so that evaluators seeing similar clinical presentations in different times or places would come to the same diagnostic conclusions. We are striving to be more objective and scientific. Psychiatry and society are in continual dialogue about how the boundaries of mental disorders are drawn, how and when to apply our diagnoses, and the best treatment approaches.

So, why does it matter that Trump, or anyone else, has ADHD? We make diagnoses in psychiatry, as in the rest of medicine, for several reasons: to gain an understanding of the present condition, to get insight about the future, and to suggest treatments that are likely to be beneficial [29]. Let's explore those reasons more closely.

We Diagnose to Understand

None of us is born with an instruction manual regarding how our brain works, but receiving a diagnosis of ADHD, even if this occurs late in life, often provides tremendous help in explaining a person to themselves [147]. A diagnosis reminds people that others are also coping with this condition, i.e., they are not alone and do not have to invent all their own sources of solace. A diagnosis of ADHD can teach a person that their patterns of behavior are not the result of moral failings. A diagnosis of ADHD can also explicate that our actions are not simple, conscious decisions; they also reflect that brains have strong propensities to respond in certain ways to specific stimuli. Although certainly many children feel stigmatized by a diagnosis of ADHD [148], the vast majority of adults I've worked with have appreciated knowing their diagnosis, and do not view it as a derogatory designation.

Not only can a diagnosis of ADHD help someone to be more empathetic towards themselves, it can also help others arrive at less pejorative conclusions about behavior. Knowing that one is chronically late to appointments because one's ADHD causes problems with time management is both more accurate and more humane than just labeling the tardiness as laziness, apathy, disrespect, or self-sabotage. Or knowing that someone's comments or tweets are largely expressions of what that person with ADHD is feeling in the moment, rather than an intellectualized attempt to arrive at the truth, makes us less likely to label each of these utterances a lie when they are counterfactual. Depriving someone who has ADHD of the knowledge of their condition actually causes harm, because most of the alternative explanations for ADHD-driven behavior tend to be far more negative.

Trump's ADHD label provides parsimony as well as clarity; it helps us see an underlying etiology to what may seem like disparate problems. The ADHD label also provides a descriptive explanation for his behavior, rather than the more pejorative interpretations that people are likely to arrive at from looking at individual behaviors in isolation. Furthermore, these ADHD-based understandings are usually both more accurate and more objective. For example, because of his ADHD and propensity to blurt out whatever he is thinking in the moment, he makes many statements that directly contradict previous statements and that are not consistent with verifiable facts. The common response to this is to consider him a serial liar. While there may well be instances in which he makes comments that he knows to be untrue with the purpose of deceiving us, a large proportion of his self-contradictions appear to be thoughtless utterances rather than conscious deceptions.

We Diagnose to Predict

One might question whether an ADHD diagnosis helps with prediction any more than simply knowing that Trump has behaved in a brash, unreflective, and inattentive manner for decades, and is therefore likely to continue doing so. An analogy clarifies how the ADHD diagnosis aids in prediction. Septuagenarian Mr. Right has been driving on the right side of the road for more than fifty years. Seventy-year-old Mr. Write has been holding a pen in his right hand for the past six decades. Extrapolating from the longevity of the observations, we would expect both men to continue with their rightward actions into the foreseeable future. However, if we understand that Mr. Right's driving patterns are primarily shaped by the local driving ordinances, then we can predict that moving to England, or some other situational change, would lead to his driving on the left. In contrast, short of a catastrophic stroke or loss of limb, we would not expect Mr. Write to start using his left hand to write. Having insight as to why a behavioral pattern has persisted allows us to predict which conditions, if any, are likely to alter this pattern.

Knowing that Trump has ADHD does not preclude him from being polite, restrained, focused, or considerate in a given instance, but makes it extremely unlikely that he will suddenly start "acting presidential" in any consistent or sustained manner. Furthermore, his ADHD leads us to predict that he will continue to pay attention to, and become informed about, topics that are interesting to *him*, rather than attending to what others consider to be vital issues for a president. Thus we can understand why he repeatedly chooses to ignore daily security briefings [149]. Because of his ADHD-driven attention to appearances, surfaces, and imagery, he is likely to continue to be much more attentive to building walls, frequenting military parades, installing gold fixtures, and erecting tall office buildings than to studying statecraft, learning diplomacy, nurturing political alliances, or considering aspects of policy. Understanding that Trump has a brain-based condition of ADHD allows us to predict that his behaviors of interrupting others, blurting out rude comments, reiterating his perceived successes, attending to what is interesting to him rather than to what is important to the country, responding explosively to slights, and contradicting himself, will all continue.

We Diagnose to Treat

Correctly diagnosing a problem also increases the likelihood of taking measures that will effectively address the problem. Trying to treat depression, anxiety, or mania when an individual actually suffers from ADHD is unlikely to be helpful [42, 150]. In couples therapy when one or both partners have ADHD and this is not clearly identified, the relationship problems are likely to be misattributed, characterized by inappropriate blaming, and remain unresolved [25, 30]. In addition, increasing the awareness of someone with ADHD about a problem is only useful at the time they need to be conscious of it. Most people with ADHD already know that their habitual tardiness is inconsiderate, inconvenient, or disruptive—they don't need to be informed of this. Rather, they need to be reminded of these consequences in the moment when they should be departing for a trip to get to their destination on time. Telling someone in advance that they need to turn their homework in on time isn't particularly helpful, because they are already conscious of this concept. Rather, they need to hear about the importance of turning in a particular assignment at the time when they are watching cat videos, painting their fingernails, or catching up on basketball playoff games. Furthermore, they need to be helped to realize that immediate action is needed or their long-term goals will not be attainable. Without a correct diagnosis of ADHD, it is unlikely that one will receive help in the form of directing the timely flow of information needed to make good decisions.

The lack of a correct diagnosis also ensures that the person with ADHD will not have access to the right medications or therapies to treat it. I will be addressing the topic of using medications to treat Trump's ADHD in Chapter 6, but for now I want to point out the necessity of tailoring behavioral interactions to work with his ADHD-driven brain. The importance of the chief of staff looms much larger for this presidency than for any of his predecessors, because so much of what drives Trump's mental processing is not only which advisors speak to him, but when, with the most recent speaker having an exaggerated influence. Given his ADHD, Trump is particularly prone to siding with whoever has most recently grabbed his attention (gun control lobbyist, NRA, take your pick!) [151, 152]. Also, a chief of staff needs to provide an optimal amount of structure so that Trump acts neither as an unengaged leader, nor as a rebellious, loose cannon. Furthermore, anyone wanting to deliver new information to this president, regardless of how important, had best deliver it in easily digestible tidbits, particularly using a lot of "killer graphics" [153]. Because Trump so consistently makes threats that he does not carry out, reneges on agreements he has made with allies as well as opponents, and delivers ultimatums from which he subsequently backtracks, we need to regard his utterances in the ADHD framework of being simply a reflection of how he feels in the moment; unless enshrined in binding, written documentation, they should not be interpreted as actual statements of policy. Knowledge of his ADHD not only demands that we respond this way, but also helps make many of his statements less toxic, by appreciating that these are not thoughts he has deliberated over and come to a final conclusion on.

CHAPTER 3

THE FORMAL DSM-5 CRITERIA FOR ADHD (TRUMP SCORES BIGLY)

In this chapter I will walk us through the current definition of ADHD according to the fifth and current version of the American Psychiatric Association's Diagnostic and Statistical Manual of Mental Disorders (DSM-5) [2]. I will also explain how evaluating Trump based on his public record differs from the standard, clinical, in-person, psychiatric evaluation. As discussed in the previous chapter, psychiatry at present lacks simple, measurable, biologic markers that indicate whether an individual has a particular condition [154]. In order to formulate psychiatric diagnoses, we rely heavily on patients reporting their own experiences, thoughts, feelings, and motivations. We combine that information with the evaluator's observations, including an assessment of how closely the content of the patient's words agrees with or contradicts what the individual's voice and body display [155].

Psychiatric Diagnoses: Clinical Evaluations and Public Domain Assessments

The professional organizations for practitioners that treat ADHD unanimously agree that the "gold standard" diagnosis of adult ADHD consists of a personal interview by a clinician who is familiar with ADHD in adults [2, 156]. Numerous types of supplementary testing can be supportive of the diagnosis, but in my experience, they seldom add clarity or certainty to the diagnosis, or reveal alternative explanations, which is why the experts deem such testing unnecessary to make the diagnosis. The most common of these tests are psychological questionnaires that duplicate many of the questions in a seasoned clinician's evaluation. Such tests, including the Conners Scale [157], can provide standardized, quantitative ratings of the likelihood that someone with a particular score actually has ADHD. Neuropsychologists can also measure attention, short-term memory, ability to suppress responses, and other aspects of brain function, and the profile of deficits on such testing can again support, but not prove, a diagnosis of ADHD [158]. Abnormalities on EEG, PET scans, and other examinations of brain physiology can also suggest an ADHD diagnosis [159-161], but none of these approaches has yet been conclusively validated as a tool for diagnosing ADHD [160, 162]. Perversely, many of the standardized testing agencies (for the SAT, GRE, MCAT, LSAT) [163] in order to sanction accommodations for test-takers with ADHD, such as additional time or test rooms with fewer visual or auditory distractions, require scores from neuropsychological testing to "verify" a diagnosis of ADHD, despite the lack of evidence that such information actually helps to substantiate the diagnosis [164].

Because insurance companies drive our current health care system and mandate a diagnosis for any reimbursement, most clinical assessments of adults with ADHD occur after just an hour or two of clinical interviewing, in combination with a review of pertinent historical data and available input from collateral sources (usually parents, partners, family members, and teachers, but potentially including co-workers or others who have observed the individual). Because the current diagnostic criteria for ADHD require that symptoms started before age twelve [2], and that signs of it are manifest in more than one setting (not just at work or just at home) [2], and because people with ADHD often have difficulties in both assessing and recalling their own behavior [143, 144], information from collateral and collaborative sources is particularly important, even though it is frequently lacking [165]. Although our health care system usually demands a diagnosis after just a few hours of interaction with a patient, revisions of diagnoses are certainly possible after this time. Nevertheless, in the majority of assessments of individuals with adult ADHD, we lack definitive personal history data that would be helpful in making the diagnosis [165].

Our clinical evaluations gather information from two very different realms: One is the actual *content* of what the person says or does (do they say that they are frequently distracted, often lose things, can't sit still, interrupt others?), and the other is the *process* of how that person behaves and interacts during the evaluation. I have noticed, particularly as our clinical interactions are increasingly driven by checking boxes and filling out computer forms during the session, that some clinicians are so consumed with paperwork that they aren't carefully observing their patients: They don't register whether the person was tapping a foot; changing posture repeatedly; digressing frequently; left an insurance card, eyeglasses, or wallet in the waiting room or the car. Rather often, in my experience, clinicians derive a global impression of the patient based on process cues, e.g., "She seemed very ADHD-ish," without being able to enumerate the details they accumulated to paint such a picture. Also, while overviews often state that adults with ADHD rarely display hyperactivity, very often my patients with ADHD demonstrate far more shifts in posture, fidgeting, gesturing, head movements, and a need to go to the bathroom or get up and show me something in the course of a session than do my patients without ADHD. Skillful clinicians are always combining and comparing information from the content and process of an interview, and from verbal and movement domains to see how much they agree or are in conflict with each other in bolstering the case for a given diagnosis.

One way to try to increase the objectivity of psychiatric diagnoses over the last few decades has been to make them more dependent on signs (externally observable aspects of a disease) rather than on symptoms (experiences related by the patient) [166]. Currently we define ADHD almost entirely by signs, not symptoms, which is why observations alone can fulfill the diagnostic criteria, and why one can diagnose Trump's ADHD solely from inspecting extensive video footage. This emphasis on signs over symptoms doesn't mean that

ADHD is devoid of common internal experiences. Many people with ADHD describe similar sensations such as "my thoughts are constantly ping-ponging around inside my head," "my mind never rests," "I feel spacey," or "I feel driven by a motor." However, *none* of these subjective, qualitative states is necessary for the diagnosis.

My evaluation to determine that Trump has ADHD exceeds the normal diagnostic assessment in several ways, and falls short in others. I examined hours of video of Trump's behavior [167, among others], which provided much more behavioral data than is usually available from a standard office evaluation. My evaluation looked at Trump in a variety of situations and settings, which is particularly useful in that our typical clinical evaluation is limited to observing behavior in a single office setting, with only the examiner to interact with, and with behavior in other settings being limited to self-reports. Furthermore, the historical videos of Trump offer objective data spanning decades, rather than our usual situation of relying on a patient's retrospective recollection of what might have occurred at younger ages. I also had access to commentary from a far greater number of third-party observers than we usually have in any clinical evaluation. Because these observations came from political supporters as well as adversaries, were formulated without any agenda of ascertaining that Trump has ADHD, and are all remarkably consistent in providing evidence that he displays an array of signs of ADHD, we cannot dismiss this body of information as either irrelevant or biased regarding their accuracy in supporting a diagnosis of ADHD.

While the quantity and quality of publicly available behavioral data available to evaluate Trump's ADHD exceeds what we could obtain in several hours of direct psychiatric interviews, this is not true for most other individuals—although that may change with the growing ubiquity of recording systems and the increasing ease of storing and accessing vast troves of video information. I will reserve a discussion of the ethical implications of performing such an evaluation on a public figure for Chapters 10, 11, and 12.

One notable deficiency of my assessment was the impossibility of directly asking questions of Trump. In a clinical exam, even if a patient ignores or evades answering questions, how he does so can provide

Formal DSM-5 Criteria for ADHD

potentially useful information. However, as detailed below, one of the unique aspects of the current criteria for ADHD, in contrast to almost all other mental health diagnoses, is that only one of the eighteen possible characteristics involves the patient's report of an internal state: "feels restless or driven like a motor" [2]. The remaining seventeen characteristics, only five of which are needed to fulfill a diagnosis of adult ADHD, are observable behaviors. When Trump blurts out comments about "shit-hole countries" [168] or "Little Marco Rubio" [169], we don't actually know that he genuinely thinks or feels such things, but we do know that he made the comments in impulsive and socially inappropriate ways. While the inability to know what Trump is actually thinking or feeling does preclude being able to diagnose narcissistic personality disorder or most other mental health conditions, it does not impair the ability to make a valid diagnosis of ADHD.

In a clinical evaluation we could ask Trump for his impression of his own behaviors, thoughts, and feelings, whereas my assessment using past and present video footage does not allow any direct feedback from him. However, lacking this information does very little to decrease the ability to make a valid diagnosis of ADHD because of one important aspect of ADHD itself: ADHD measurably diminishes attentiveness to one's own behavior, and to one's awareness of how others are responding to one's behavior [170]. People with ADHD are often unaware of the extent to which they are inattentive or distracted, and are less aware of how their inattention, distractibility, or impulsivity affects those around them [25, 30, 82, 171]. I've had patients describe how they spend hours each week looking for keys, phones, or wallets, but then mark "never" on a self-assessment scale for how often they lose items. "I don't lose things, I just misplace them!" is a common rejoinder to my pointing out this discrepancy. A woman who lost her job because she spoke up inappropriately at company meetings reported "I don't blurt out things; those comments were all warranted!" In one study, the rate at which parents documented the existence of ADHD was *eleven times* higher than patients' ability to detect their own ADHD [172]. This does not mean that people with ADHD can't be aware of what they are missing, because they are often acutely aware, ashamed, angry, or fearful about it, but denials regarding ADHD symptoms need to be closely examined and regarded with skepticism, particularly if one can observe the individual behaving in ways that are inconsistent with their denials. Because of this, in clinical settings, we strive to find collateral sources of information when diagnosing ADHD, as well as using quantifiable measures of inattention, distractibility, or impulsivity when assessing the severity of ADHD or its response to treatment. Thus the absence of Trump's input about whether he is aware of how scattered, prone to interrupting himself or others, impulsive, and inattentive he is, does very little to diminish the accuracy of his ADHD diagnosis.

DSM-5 Criteria for ADHD

I have included in the following paragraphs the current criteria for ADHD as described in the Diagnostic and Statistical Manual - Version 5 (DSM-5) [2], and have inserted the entire definition as Appendix A. In many instances I have shortened the phrasing of the criteria in ways that are intended to keep the meaning and significance of the criterion intact. Given that many people display these behaviors occasionally, the evaluation requires that someone with ADHD acts in these ways *substantially more often or more severely* than the general population. Although the determination of what is substantial or severe remains a clinical judgment—part of why you shouldn't try this at home—in the case of Trump and others with severe ADHD, it is likely that general observers will concur with professional assessments.

DSM-5 designates three varieties of ADHD: an inattentive type, a hyperactive type, and a combined type. In adults with hyperactive ADHD, excessive physical activity is usually less extreme than the running around in circles that children with ADHD often display. Most studies, and my own experience, indicate that the combined type is the most common subtype of ADHD [173-175]. However, a few studies have found the inattentive type to be the most common, but this apparent discrepancy regarding the relative likelihood of sub-types of ADHD is likely influenced by the age and gender of the patient populations, the specific criteria used for sub-typing, and which subgroups are more likely to present for treatment [176-178].

Formal DSM-5 Criteria for ADHD

I have resisted going into extensive detail regarding particular examples for each criteria, because from anyone's life we probably could select individual anecdotes that would match the criteria described. *ADDitude*, the newsletter for the national ADHD group CHADD, has provided a wonderful collection of specific incidents from Trump's presidency that exemplify many of the ADHD criteria described in the following paragraphs [11]. However, the diagnosis of ADHD is not based on a handful of spectacular or colorful incidents, but by a *pattern of pervasively and persistently behaving* in ways that match the designated criteria. To reinforce the point that the diagnosis of ADHD is based on patterns of behavior rather than on detailed anecdotes, I have attempted to outline the repeated actions that Trump chronically displays that fulfill each diagnostic criterion.

I cannot overstate the importance of maintaining the distinction between isolated anecdotes and pervasive patterns of behavior in our era of false equivalency. Every human that I know, at least occasionally makes errors, tells untruths, or utters impulsive comments. There have been times when I have described Trump's ADHD-driven behavior, including how frequently he makes false or impulsive statements, and a supporter of his will counter with, "Obama lied about keeping your own doctor under Obamacare" or "Hillary blurted out that comment about deplorables." The fact that people keep trotting out the exact same examples regarding Obama or Clinton actually reveals how uncommon it was for these politicians to stretch the truth or speak impetuously. The public record demonstrates that in most weeks Trump makes more completely inaccurate statements than critics are likely to find in months or years of other politicians' pronouncements. In contrast to Clinton's single mention of "deplorables" out of hundreds of campaign speeches, Trump made inflammatory, derogatory slurs about immigrants a standard feature of every campaign event. We can safely say that Trump's pattern of behavior differs markedly from the societal norm, and does so in ways consistent with his having ADHD.

We require only five of the following nine inattentive characteristics for a DSM-5 diagnosis of inattentive ADHD [2], and Trump surpasses this standard by meeting the first seven: 1) doesn't attend to details and makes careless mistakes, 2) has difficulty sustaining attention, 3) often does not seem to listen when spoken to directly, 4) often does not follow through on instructions and fails to finish chores, 5) has trouble organizing tasks, 6) avoids tasks that require sustained mental effort, and 7) is easily distracted by extraneous stimuli. I don't know whether he displays the final two inattentive criteria: 8) often loses things and 9) is forgetful in daily activities. Evidence that he probably does meet the ninth characteristic is suggested by the frequency with which he contradicts statements made hours or days earlier.

1) Not only does Trump not attend to details, he often proudly boasts of this. For example, he has proclaimed repeatedly that he has no need for a daily intelligence briefing [149], and those who provide these briefings have repeatedly condensed their presentations so that they now provide short oral presentations with "killer graphics" [153]. In Trump's own words he has said, "I like bullets or I like as little as possible. I don't need, you know, 200-page reports on something that can be handled on a page [179]." Even Republican allies in Congress have reported how uninformed Trump was when lobbying for repeal of Obamacare or to revise the tax code [180, 181]. Trump makes prominent, careless mistakes every day, revealing that he has little understanding of the basics of the Constitution, governance, or the separation of powers. He famously confused provisions of national security and invasion of privacy when portions of the Patriot Act were being renewed [182].

2) Trump displays problems with sustaining attention in his debates, lectures, public interactions with national figures, and in private. Everyone from co-authors, to grieving parents who speak to him following tragedies, to aides trying to inform him about his own policies, have commented on his inability to stay on topic for more than a few moments [7, 153, 183-187].

3) Trump's ability to not listen when spoken to directly was on prominent display during the debates with his fellow Republicans and later with Clinton, and if these were isolated incidents, it could be dismissed as a debating tactic. However, in numerous interviews, in summaries given by members of

the public who have spoken with him, and in leaked emails or reports of cabinet meetings or Republican conferences, a frequent refrain is how he "isn't there" and often doesn't respond in normal conversational style to direct comments and questions [187-190].

4) Trump repeatedly has failed to complete tasks, but given that many politicians make campaign promises they do not keep, for a variety of reasons, a more meaningful examination of this criterion would be to look at his performance outside of the crush of the campaign. His emergency immigration policy (the "anti-Muslim ban") was written to be immediately implemented in order to give his government ninety days to come up with a comprehensive immigration vetting procedure [191]. No such comprehensive and clear procedure for vetting was delineated in those ninety days, and there remains no evidence that vetting procedures superior to those already in existence have been implemented since [192].

A record number of key White House positions [193] and ambassadorships [194] remained unfilled a year or more into his term. While some vacancies may be for political reasons, it is hard to fathom how leaving the ambassadorships to South Korea (filled 06/2018) and Germany (filled 04/2018) empty for a year and a half, and the positions to Turkey, Saudi Arabia (nominated 11/2018), Qatar, South Africa (nominated 9/2018), Australia (nominated 11/2018), Egypt (nominated 4/2019), Jordan (all still unfilled at the date of this writing) and others [194] empty for so long have helped his administration.

5) Trump has trouble organizing tasks. "Chaotic" is one of the most frequent descriptions, by both Republicans and Democrats, of this administration [195-197]. He has been unable to organize an effective and consistent plan or strategy for what he wanted done on health care [180], tax "reform" [198], immigration law [199, 200], revising NAFTA [201], or trade wars [196]. His positions for dealing with Syria, North Korea, gun control, Qatar, DACA [151, 202-206] and numerous other issues ricochet between extremes and

appear to be strongly influenced by whoever spoke to him most recently. His tweets about banning transgenders from the military surprised his own military advisors [207], and it then took months before he and his government actually proposed a specific policy [208]. He has not even been able to come up with a coherent framework for addressing issues that threaten his presidency. His stance on how to defend himself against a variety of substantive accusations remains very disorganized and inconsistent, including his responses to charges of Russia meddling in the election [209], his sexual liaisons and unwanted advances with numerous women [210], his entanglements of business interests and government decisions [211, 212], and the improper use of his non-profit organization [213].

6) Trump avoids tasks that require sustained mental effort. For the first months of the administration some of his defenders claimed we should not expect the president to know much about the Constitution, the independence of the judiciary, or how laws are enacted, because he was new to politics. This ignores the fact that much of this information could be gleaned from the internet by an intelligent middle schooler. Not only did he come in unprepared, he has demonstrated reluctance in learning about most policy issues, domestic or foreign, showing disdain and boredom [190, 214]. His ghostwriter for *The Art of the Deal* has documented how Trump could not be compelled to sit down and think about a given issue, even though the whole point of the book was self-aggrandizement [7].

7) Trump is easily distracted by extraneous stimuli and by his own unrelated thoughts. His propensity while giving speeches to go off track and start riffing on themes not included by his speechwriters (for a few examples, see [215-218]), is so constant that it is noteworthy when he does stay on track [219]. Even then, staying "on track" usually means that there are only a few such interruptions, not dozens. Trump's default mode of interacting with the press has been to divert into discursive claims that others—Clinton, Obama, the FBI, et al.—have behaved far worse than he has, whether or not these accusations

are germane to the question asked. Certainly, deflection is a tool in most politicians' arsenal, but Trump employs it to excess. Furthermore, in support of the diagnosis of ADHD, his deflections are usually just a shallow repetition of claims and slurs, without any documentation, corroboration, or even exposition of the themes he brings up.

We require only five of the following hyperactive/impulsive characteristics for a DSM-5 diagnosis of hyperactive ADHD [2], and Trump again surpasses this standard by clearly meeting the first six: 1) often fidgets, 2) has trouble remaining seated, 3) talks excessively, 4) blurts out answers before a question is completed, 5) has trouble waiting his turn, and 6) often interrupts and intrudes on others. Whether he 7) feels restless, 8) is unable to play quietly, and 9) is often "on the go" are harder to ascertain from the information available. However, the ninth characteristic seems supported by his physician's health report of Trump's supposed need for little sleep [220], Trump's emphasis on how energetic he perceives himself to be [221, 222], and how he belittles others for their perceived lack of energy [223].

Because he exhibits these traits of physical restlessness in virtually every public appearance, I do not believe they need more extensive substantiation. We even have quantitative data from the presidential debates, regarding how much more he spoke [224] and how frequently he interrupted others [225]; even compared to a peer group of politicians his behavior stood out as blatantly excessive.

By meeting at least thirteen and quite possibly fifteen or more of these characteristics, Trump far exceeds the number of signs required for a diagnosis of ADHD. Because he robustly manifests both hyperactive and inattentive traits, he merits a diagnosis of combined-type ADHD. Documenting this diagnosis remains separate and distinct from any judgment about the content of his opinions, or about whether he or his staff may make strategic use of these ADHD characteristics to throw others off balance, to appeal to his base, or for other personal or political reasons. Virtually every observer of the president, whether opposed to or appreciative of his views, acknowledges that he deviates from normal and usual human behavior in all of these categories.

Trump also meets the "age of onset" diagnostic criteria of symptoms being present prior to age twelve. Childhood reports indicate that Mr. Trump stood out from his peers for being inattentive, distracted, restless, and impulsive. He was sent to military school at age thirteen because his parents "thought it would be good for me because I was rambunctious" [226]. As Trump himself has stated regarding his personality, "I'm pretty much the same guy I was when I was seven years old" [227].

Trump also fulfills the diagnostic criteria that ADHD behavior must be clearly present in two or more settings. The public video evidence aligns consistently with numerous reports by those who have met with him in private, demonstrating that he manifests ADHD traits of hyperactivity and inattentiveness in multiple settings over a span of decades. He has displayed these traits in speeches before crowds, in debates with opponents, in performances on his reality TV show, in video moments when he had no awareness of being recorded, and in reports of individuals trying to have in-depth conversations with him. Again, the public record provides far more extensive documentation of ADHD-driven behavior in a multitude of settings than can ever be gleaned from an individual psychiatric office evaluation.

Our penultimate criterion for ADHD requires that symptoms interfere with, or reduce the quality of, one's social or occupational functioning. There is no question that Trump would have deeper support within his own party and have more success getting legislative measures passed and executive orders approved, were he more organized, less impulsive, and more consistent. While a huge majority of Republicans continue to support his presidency, large numbers voice concerns about his personal style and modes of interaction, almost always criticizing his ADHD-driven traits. Although Trump has met some societal measures of success in financial, entertainment, and political realms, it is apparent that his ADHD has interfered with the scope, scale, and quality of these successes. From my professional experience, as well as documented examples ([228-230]), many with ADHD have success in a variety of fields, particularly if they have other resources (financial, intelligence, family support) along the way. Ironically, Trump's ADHD may have contributed to his success in some ways (by appearing

Formal DSM-5 Criteria for ADHD

novel, disruptive, genuine), but it's clear ADHD has compromised his potential for much greater achievement.

Our final diagnostic criterion mandates that the signs and symptoms are not due to other mental health disorders or medical conditions [2]. Although aspects of Trump's ADHD-driven behavior may at times resemble mania, anxiety, dementia, borderline personality disorder, PTSD, and substance abuse disorders [42], these other conditions have critical qualities that Trump has not displayed (more on this in Chapter 4). None of these other diagnoses comes close to explaining the thirteen to fifteen signs of ADHD previously described. Trump pervasively broadcasts such an array of ADHD symptoms, and exemplifies them so classically, that we cannot ascribe this profile of problematic behaviors to any other mental health diagnosis. He robustly fulfills all DSM-5 criteria for ADHD. Of course, his having ADHD does not preclude the presence of other mental health or neurological conditions, such as narcissistic personality disorder, antisocial personality disorder, or others, but absent a clinical evaluation, such alleged other conditions are not verifiable.

Some mental health professionals, while concurring that I have demonstrated that Trump meets DSM-5 criteria for an ADHD diagnosis, maintain that there is a difference between Trump meeting the full criteria for ADHD and declaring that he has ADHD. This viewpoint implies that our current definition of ADHD misaligns with a brain-based ADHD-like disorder. Our definition may not completely capture the range of individuals who actually have ADHD, or conversely, it may falsely encompass some individuals who seem to meet the criteria but who don't actually have the condition. I believe that the extensive genetic, neuroanatomic, neurochemical, and neurophysiologic research summarized in the previous chapter refutes the even more basic objection, that no such brain disorder or disorders exists. The third section of this book addresses some related concerns, particularly those formulated by people who may accept the existence of consistent variations in human behavior that we currently label ADHD, but who are opposed to classifying people by psychiatric categories.

On a semantic level, by definition, imperfect or not, our DSM-5 guidelines actually do determine what "is" ADHD on planet Earth, in 2019. A more fundamental response—to whether fulfilling the current diagnostic criteria means that one has ADHD—relies on thousands of research articles about ADHD. This collective body of knowledge does not just support a general concept of ADHD as a brain-based condition with a strong genetic component; it substantiates that our prevailing definition of ADHD, which scientists utilized to define the groups that were actually studied, does map fairly closely to this mental health condition. Otherwise, so many consistent group differences would not have been revealed. Almost certainly, we currently employ an imperfect definition of ADHD—e.g., there appears to be an unnecessary degree of overlap among many of the signs now included, and some common aspects of ADHD, particularly emotional volatility, are not included at all.

For the past few years the National Institutes of Mental Health has been working on the Research Domain Criteria Project [231] to develop new, more scientifically based frameworks for studying the basic dimensions of mental illness and mental health. Although they have explicitly declared that this approach is not intended to replace current diagnostic systems, if it leads to new insights about what constitutes human mental health and what causes disruptions to or deviations from these processes, it will likely lead to changes in how we define mental health problems. Whether we add additional criteria, develop biologic markers to aid in diagnosis, or parse ADHD into separate disorders, all available evidence suggests that the new diagnostic definitions will pertain to a group of individuals extremely similar to the group demarcated by current descriptions of ADHD.

From the vast body of evidence in the public domain, President Trump objectively, persistently, robustly, and completely meets the diagnostic criteria for adult ADHD. From the number of ADHD signs he displays, and their severity and frequency—even if we make minor adjustments to the definition of ADHD—Trump fulfills the criteria for diagnosis. He has ADHD, and it is time to move on to understanding what this entails, evaluating the implications of this diagnosis, and coming up with strategies for helping him cope with ADHD. It is up to us to manage and mitigate the consequences of his ADHD-driven behavior, which I will address in the following chapters.

CHAPTER 4

BUT WAIT, THERE'S MORE! ADHD AND CO-MORBIDITY

Untangling ADHD from other mental health issues can be tricky for two major reasons: (1) signs of inattentiveness, forgetfulness, and hyperactivity can be present in other conditions [142], and (2) the presence of ADHD statistically and substantially increases the likelihood of having an additional mental health diagnosis [42], which is known as co-morbidity. Sometimes co-morbidities are direct consequences of having ADHD, and some cases of anxiety, depression, and substance abuse fit in those categories. In other words, a person with ADHD may develop anxiety because their ADHD-driven distractibility makes them feel overwhelmed by too much stimuli; ADHD-driven, getting-off-track behavior may cause multiple school or social failures leading to depression; or ADHD-driven impulsivity and risk-taking may lead to abuse of alcohol or heroin. However, other conditions, including some that counterintuitively seem to be the "opposite" of ADHD, such as obsessive-compulsive disorder, are also over-represented in those with ADHD [232].

A complete diagnostic evaluation of Trump, including any ADHD co-morbidities, cannot be done from afar. However, when one condition known to be present (ADHD) offers an explanation for a given symptom or sign, we usually respect the concept of diagnostic parsimony and don't add on additional diagnoses merely to explain that specific behavior. For example, during the presidential debates many observers speculated that Trump's excessive head bobbing, sniffing, and facial mannerisms were due to a cocaine habit, Parkinsonism, or a tic disorder [233]. However, given the overwhelming evidence that Trump has ADHD, and knowing that ADHD adequately and plausibly explains these head movements, we do not need to complicate the diagnostic picture by adding an additional diagnosis. Throughout this chapter, while discussing other conditions that can mimic or interact with ADHD, I will address why these other conditions are unlikely to explain the ADHD symptoms we see displayed by Trump.

Depression

Many people with depression have cognitive symptoms: difficulty concentrating and trouble making decisions are two common, possible symptoms of a depressive episode [2]. Some depressed individuals complain of a "brain fog" or general sense that their overall ability to think is muffled or impaired. While these symptoms might resemble ADHD, depression also requires a pervasive feeling of sadness, emotional numbness, or substantial irritability as core aspects of the condition [2], which are not usually part of ADHD. Irritability usually implies that someone is in a pervasively negative state, and imposes that negativity on every interaction or situation. With careful exploration, depression can often be differentiated from the emotional dysregulation present in many people with ADHD, in which feelings come up more strongly and quickly in response to stimuli, but can be positive and exuberant as well as negative, and occur as an exaggerated reaction to events rather than a prevalent mood that arises first and colors all subsequent interactions [234].

Furthermore, depression is usually an episodic condition, while in adults, ADHD is a persistent, ongoing state [2].

Depression cannot explain Trump's ADHD symptoms, because his inattentiveness, impulsivity, and emotional dysregulation have been pervasive, not episodic; his prevailing emotional tone has not been sad or numb; and he does not demonstrate other features of depression such as excessive guilt. Also, there have been no reports of changes in his sleep, appetite, or libido, which, if present, could indicate depression 2. Even though he claims to need little sleep [220], a feature that can be present in certain types of depression [2], Trump, his doctor [220], and others [235] have said that this is a chronic pattern for him, thus there have been no changes that would suggest a depressive episode.

Depression is over-represented in people with ADHD, and often seems to be a direct response to ADHD [42]. In my practice, I see many people with ADHD, who don't stay on track and thus fail to achieve the level of success in school, career, or relationships that their intelligence, creativity, and other strengths would lead them, and those around them, to expect. This apparent mismatch between expectations and performance is a recipe for feelings of failure, and of depression, particularly given that these shortfalls occur repeatedly. The under-regulated nature of emotions in many people with ADHD [234] also means that their brains experience feelings of sadness, shame, guilt, and anxiety more frequently and intensely than the general population [236]. Practicing such strong negative emotions may make it easier for the brain to eventually lapse into depressive episodes.

In addition, many people with ADHD (whether diagnosed or not) know that their inattentiveness causes them to "miss something"—e.g., overlooking steps in a list of directions, misconstruing social cues, or showing up at the wrong time for events; this sense of not being quite right, of not fitting in, of being "off"—combined with a feeling that they aren't really sure what is amiss—is another potential pathway into depression [25, 38, 77, 82]. Since ADHD affects social interactions, many with ADHD receive a plethora of messages that they are not performing tasks in quite the right way, are reading people the wrong way, have stepped on others' toes, or created negative emotional reactions in others which they did not anticipate and cannot decipher. Some ADHD experts report that this "rejection sensitivity dysphoria" is virtually ubiquitous in ADHD, and is a strong contributor to clinical depression [237-240].

Recognition of both ADHD and depression when both are present is crucial [37]. I have seen many individuals on whom psychotherapy or medications were used, often for decades, without clear resolution of pervasive negative emotional states, because the ADHD was never identified. The ADHD-based problems that contributed to their professional or personal failures kept recurring, in spite of ongoing attempts to treat the depression. Usually, when they co-occur, both ADHD and depression need to be addressed and treated [150]. However, in some individuals, focusing primarily on the ADHD will alleviate depression as well [241], again suggesting that ADHD can be the source of depression, and also reflecting that many of our ADHD medications have mood-elevating effects [135].

Distinct from the issue of ADHD and clinical depression, which requires a prevailingly negative mood state for weeks at a time [2], my patients with ADHD often report "depression" when they are experiencing intensely negative emotions and self-appraisals; such states last only minutes or hours, or at most a day or two. Numerous times I have heard such complaints of depression early in a session, only to hear sustained laughter, joy, or pride as other experiences are related within the same session. Although prolonged bouts of clinical depression can have brief interludes of positive mood, we have created semantic and diagnostic problems by commonly using the label of depression for both clinical depression and for brief periods of intense dysphoria. This does not diminish the acute misery and distress of intense, brief dysphoria, but we must differentiate dysphoria from clinical depression, although either one—or both, or neither—can be experienced by someone with ADHD.

In my clinical experience, one of the most helpful interventions for intense, brief dysphoria in a person with ADHD consists of helping the individual remember that he or she has ADHD. Remembering that ADHD tends to submerge one in whatever experience is unfolding in the moment, the individual can use this self-knowledge of ADHD to take a step back. Taking a step back and broadening one's perspective thereby provides an opportunity to remind oneself of whatever else is good, positive, and real in one's life, thus giving permission, power, and perspective to work on shifting one's focus to these positive aspects. Most often, changing the focus of the thoughts also results in changing the emotional state from negative to positive. Sometimes writing these touchstones of positivity on a card to be kept in a wallet, or maintaining positive photo reminders on a cell phone screen, can concretely and effectively remind those with ADHD of the good things in their life.

Anxiety

Cases of anxiety and ADHD overlap frequently, with co-morbidity rates as high as 50% [42]. Anxiety potently causes inattention and related cognitive problems, and can also contribute to fidgeting or restlessness which resembles ADHD [2]. When people complain to me of "memory" problems—especially when they can precisely describe objects they misplaced or tasks they neglected to do—very commonly they are actually describing anxiety that distracted them from paying attention when their brain should have been encoding pertinent information about what they'd been doing. States of extremely high anxiety usually present with such prominent worrying, second-guessing, catastrophizing, and feelings of imminent overwhelm, that individuals remain aware of their anxiety; rarely do people mistakenly blame an anxiety disorder on ADHD.

Usually the hyperactivity of anxiety can be readily differentiated from the hyperactivity of ADHD. In my clinical experience with anxiety disorders, excessive movements are usually most intense and prominent when thinking about emotionally laden topics. In ADHD, hyperactivity tends to be more pervasive, occurring over a broader range of situations, and tends to be more intense when the person is unfocused, bored, or not fully engaged in a task. However, hyperactivity can occur when someone with ADHD is intensely engaged, as in vigorous foot-tapping while working on a difficult math problem. Given that Trump has not publicly or consistently articulated many, if any, feelings of apprehension or anxiety, and given that his reported or observable hyperactivity (walking around debate halls, sleeping well below eight hours a night, constant hand gestures and facial movements) persists across time and a variety of situations, an anxiety disorder appears inadequate to explain his ADHD symptoms.

While existing anxiety disorders are rarely mistakenly blamed entirely on ADHD, the opposite occurs commonly. I frequently see people who have received treatment for anxiety, and only anxiety, for years, while their underlying ADHD remained unrecognized and unaddressed. The physical and mental sensations of anxiety usually cause more immediate, emotional, and powerful distress than do the symptoms of ADHD, which, because they often affect how one processes stimuli, can also cause anxiety. Many people with ADHD, when put in a novel situation or one teeming with visual or auditory sensations, feel flooded, overwhelmed, and panicked as their brains don't know what to attend to, and either too much or very little information penetrates their awareness [242, 243]. ADHD is the cause of, and anxiety is the reaction to, these situations.

Recently I saw a fifty-year-old man who was being treated for panic attacks triggered by shopping at the mega-grocery store or riding on crowded city buses. His anxiety had started in grade school. He was smart and performed well in the subjects that kept his attention, and he did a good job on small, brief assignments. However, the first time he was confronted with having to organize his thoughts for an essay test, he froze, unable to figure out how to start or what he wanted to say, and this triggered a panic attack. After that experience he dreaded all tests and, despite his intelligence, he was eventually shunted to vocations that required no schooling. After starting at numerous careers, he became a respected and much sought-after outdoor landscaper, which accommodated his (still undiagnosed) ADHD.

When we examined this client's individual panic attacks, it was clear that in each instance the experience of sensory overload and a sense of surprise and confusion preceded any feelings of anxiety, worry, or dread, or any perception that these situations were dangerous. As we reviewed them, he also recognized that he displayed a host of classic ADHD traits, and that his ADHD-driven sensory processing both preceded and precipitated his anxiety disorder. While years of addressing only his anxiety had brought little relief, treating his ADHD, using talk therapies and medications that did not trigger anxiety, resulted in both a reduction in ADHD symptoms and a huge decrease in the intensity and frequency of his anxiety. For those with bona fide anxiety disorders, treating the anxiety alone will not alleviate the problems if substantial underlying ADHD remains unaddressed.

Bipolar Disorder

ADHD shares more symptoms with bipolar disorder than perhaps any other condition, with the possible exception of certain drug use disorders (discussed later in this chapter) [2]. People with bipolar disorder experience alternating episodes of depression, mania, and euthymia [2]. We define euthymia as a normal, tranquil, baseline emotional state. Restless movements, excessive talking, emotional volatility, and impulsive actions comprise the central features of both ADHD and manic states. Often the colloquial concept of "mood swings" is confused with bipolarity. The term "mood swings" usually implies that someone has a rapid succession of intense moods, often over the course of a few minutes. While emotional lability (the technical term for rapid change in mood states) occurs in bipolar disorder, this lability happens in the context of a hypomanic or manic mood, which is a heightened emotional state lasting several days (hypomania) to several weeks or more (mania) [2]. People with bipolar disorder may also display "mixed states" featuring elements of both depression and mania. Neither displaying chronic emotionally lability, nor having a few abrupt mood changes within a few minutes but then remaining emotionally stable for weeks, characterizes a manic episode; in neither case does the individual manifest a prolonged interval, differentiated from that person's baseline, of sustained and elevated mood. So, if someone displays abrupt, intense, and frequent "mood swings" while depressed or generally in their baseline state, a condition other than bipolar disorder is likely behind such short-time-scale emotional perturbations. The emotional dysregulation that can be an aspect of ADHD represents one possible cause of such volatility [234]. Confusingly, the term "mood swings" can also refer to those transitions where an individual with bipolar disorder switches, for days to weeks at a time, between states of euthymia, depression, or mania. Such usage of the term more closely resembles the way researchers who study emotions use the term, where mood conveys only a prevailing emotional state, not a brief emotional reaction.

Although it is not always easy to differentiate the emotional volatility of bipolar disorder from that of ADHD, one way is to think of the former as constitutional and the latter as reactive [244, 245]. With mania, an elevated mood state arises and colors all events in its path, driving heightened responses to almost any situation. In ADHD, the specific reaction to an irritating stimulus creates a strong emotion which can persist until some other prominent stimulus triggers an alternative emotional state. In mania, the mood facilitates an intense reaction, whereas in ADHD the intense reaction facilitates a strong and abrupt emotional response. Or to get back to loosely using terms, in mania mood triggers swings and in ADHD swings trigger moods. Given that Trump has demonstrated a lifelong pattern of restlessness, impulsivity, and distractibility, with no clear intervals of normal functioning, and given that the impulsivity and hyperactivity occur regardless of his emotional state, a bipolar disorder cannot explain his ADHD symptoms.

Of course, individuals can have both ADHD and a bipolar disorder, and having either one increases the likelihood of having the other [42]. Differentiating the two is particularly difficult with individuals at the severe end of the ADHD spectrum [244]. During a brief evaluation or hospital intake, it is easy to see how someone who talks loudly, rapidly, and at length; who fidgets with their hands, taps their feet, and gets up and walks around; who talks out loud to themselves before the evaluator arrives; who is emotionally labile and makes impulsive decisions, could be mistakenly identified as displaying mania, when in fact he or she may only have ADHD. As in the case of Lucy, mentioned in Chapter 1, obtaining a detailed history to learn if the behavior is chronic (suggestive of ADHD) or episodic (suggesting mania or drug abuse) is critical. Again, an elevated emotional state persisting across numerous events over a span of time and differing from that person's baseline, rather than being a reaction to specific triggers, suggests mania rather than ADHD. Other clues to help distinguish mania from ADHD include mania's elements of silliness, bizarreness, or being slightly (or largely) out of touch with reality, as well as tendencies to focus on sex and religion [244, 246, 247]. The grandiosity of mania tends to have some of these fanciful, fantastical, and delusional elements [247], rather than the stretching-the-truth-beyond-the-demonstrable-facts type of grandiosity exhibited by Trump.

Post-Traumatic Stress Disorder

PTSD can present with fragmented attention, over-vigilance, extreme sensitivity and reactivity to environmental cues, hyperactivity, disrupted long-term planning, and emotional volatility [2], all of which can resemble ADHD. Indeed, some authors imply that most cases of ADHD actually are a variant of chronic PTSD, in which the mother's failure to be attuned to the needs of her child triggers all of the child's subsequent problems with processing information and regulating emotions [248]. The standard definition of PTSD requires a life-threatening trauma, and even stretching the definition still posits the existence of some major, damaging event [2]. If most of our cases of ADHD were actually cases of complicated PTSD, we should find such catastrophes in the lives of many individuals diagnosed with ADHD. In my clinical practice, very few individuals with ADHD report such damaging early life events; even fewer have experienced major life-threatening traumas later in life that preceded the onset of ADHD symptoms. Although failure of parents of children with ADHD to comprehend and adjust to the ways their child is different from others can add to problems of adjustment and self-acceptance later in life, I see very little to support the theories that poor parenting causes a form of PTSD that leads to ADHD. I align myself with those experts [72, page 24] who want to reduce blaming parental behaviors for causing ADHD in children. These experts also acknowledge that parenting plays a role in how children with ADHD develop; parents often need assistance in honing communication and limit-setting skills that work for their children. Further evidence against the bad-mothering-causes-ADHD theory comes from adoption studies, which consistently show that the biologic family of origin has a much larger role in the development of ADHD than does the family in which one is raised [249].

Although the interactions can be complicated, most people with PTSD don't have ADHD, and most people with ADHD don't have PTSD. PTSD seems a highly unlikely explanation for Trump's ADHD symptoms, given the lack of evidence of any reported major childhood trauma; in addition, his adult behavior is not marked by prevalent fear or by avoidance of situations tied to past traumas.

Although PTSD and ADHD have a complex relationship, ADHD has been shown to be a risk factor for PTSD [250], with the age of diagnosis for ADHD preceding the PTSD diagnosis. This suggests that ADHD, which is known to contribute to risky and impulsive behaviors, may lead to traumatic or life-threatening situations. We know that adults with ADHD are 50% more likely than non-ADHD adults to have a serious car accident, and ADHD teens are four times as likely [34, 251]. Increased risk-taking, not being properly attuned to one's environment, hyperactivity, and losing focus mid-task all seem likely to increase the possibility of getting into a dangerous situation. ADHD also increases the probability that one's experiences become disruptive or chaotic, even if not at the magnitude of being life-threatening.

Many of my patients with ADHD have been amazed to find themselves in dramatic or overwhelming situations. They often feel victimized by their own lives, and may have limited awareness that they have contributed to the chaos. One young man abruptly moved to San Francisco after the end of a relationship, and felt overwhelmed by having to simultaneously adjust to a new job, a new city, new roommates, and a new lack of partnership; he had little understanding of his part in these major life stressors having to be dealt with at the same time. Part of the rationale for treating ADHD is to help people make more reasoned decisions so that they are less overwhelmed by their own lives.

Dementia

Many types of dementia degrade the same executive functions that are strongly impaired by ADHD [3, 252]. By definition, dementias imply a decrease in functioning from baseline performance, in excess of what is expected from normal aging processes [253]. Given the lack of awareness of adult ADHD until twenty years ago, there are few studies on ADHD in advanced age [84]. Certainly one can have both dementia and ADHD [254], and early indications suggest that having ADHD correlates with an increased likelihood of developing either mild cognitive impairment (a precursor to dementia) or Lewy Body Dementia later in life [255]. However, sorting out the connections between adult ADHD and dementia are compounded by many cases of adult ADHD being missed by primary care doctors [256] and our incomplete understanding of both ADHD and dementias.

By at least some measures, Trump's use of language has degraded over time, in a pattern consistent with dementia [257]. Associates have also reported gradual deterioration in his memory, attentiveness, and language [258]. However, given that his ADHD symptoms have existed over a lifetime, dementia cannot fully account for his impoverished choices of words. An alternative explanation to the possibility that he is displaying both ADHD and dementia simultaneously is that the language decrements may be a reflection of what has worked for him—i.e., if he has been rewarded for talking in simpler, more shallow sentences ("dumbing it down" for his audience), perhaps this is a learned behavior rather than an indication of excessive deterioration of underlying brain integrity. Other weakly suggestive evidence that dementia is not the primary explanation for his behavior is his performance on the Montreal Cognitive Assessment Test, which detects cognitive impairment with 94% accuracy [259]. Trump claims to have passed this test with a perfect score [260, 261].

Traumatic Brain Injury and Other Organic Brain Problems

Physical trauma to the frontal lobes of the brain can certainly lead to problems with executive functions similar to that seen in ADHD [262]. This was extensively documented in the case of railroad worker Phineas Gage, whose left frontal lobe was destroyed by a large metal rod being blasted through his head, and who subsequently had problems with impulsivity, planning, and organizing [263]. In addition to direct damage to brain tissue, indirect damage through post-concussive syndromes also can cause ADHD-like symptoms [264]. With US hospital admissions for traumatic brain injuries increasing in the past decades, and the death rate for traumatic brain injuries actually decreasing [265] (most likely due largely to improvements in trauma surgery), the population of frontal lobe damaged individuals is steadily expanding. ADHD itself puts one at risk for trauma, including head trauma [266].

A patient with whom I have worked for two decades, who has severe ADHD and previously experienced five serious concussions, incurred his sixth head injury after jaywalking in front of a speeding limousine and being thrown forty feet. Although he retains an irascible sense of humor and considerable intelligence, he is no longer able to plan well enough to buy groceries, prepare food, or clean his apartment; his ADHD symptoms increased dramatically and abruptly with his most recent head trauma. Thus ADHD can lead to head trauma and head trauma can lead to ADHD-like symptoms, but for Trump, with no known history of brain trauma, a brain injury cannot explain his ADHD symptoms.

A few medical maladies can mimic some of the effects of ADHD, including hypoglycemia, thyroid problems, and brain tumors [267]. Usually taking a patient's careful history, with particular emphasis on the onset of the problem, helps identify whether any apparent ADHD symptoms presented as a marked departure from the individual's baseline cognitive and emotional functioning, and are thus not likely to be signs of ADHD originating in childhood. Medical conditions that might arise in childhood and persist for years or even decades almost always include some additional physical symptoms (e.g., changes in hair, skin, and temperature regulation for thyroid disease). So again, a careful history most likely will point to the correct medical diagnosis, rather than having the condition be misdiagnosed as ADHD. Only extremely rarely do medical conditions present with only ADHD symptoms. Because Trump has displayed ADHD symptoms for decades, and no public record reveals any physical symptoms suggestive of medical conditions that can resemble ADHD, we have no reason to propose a physical health origin for his ADHD-driven behavior.

Drug Use

Many illicit and prescription drugs can be sedating, which diminishes attention [268]. Chronic cannabis or opioid use can impair motivation, disrupt the organization of thoughts, and decrease the ability to make long-term plans—thus mimicking some aspects of ADHD [269, 270]. Ironically, however, it is the stimulants, the prescription forms of which are used to treat ADHD, that most often create a clinical picture resembling hyperactive ADHD. (I discuss stimulant use in ADHD in more detail in Chapter 6.) Stimulants can make people jittery, hyperactive, impulsive, distracted, and emotionally volatile [117]. It is counterintuitive that in individuals with ADHD, and at the right doses, these medications can help people to be calmer, more focused, more deliberate, and easier to interact with. However, even people with ADHD, on too high a dose, will become revved up, talk and move faster, be more distractible, and respond more abruptly and emotionally [35, 117]. Stimulants help people with ADHD not by working "opposite the way they work in normal people"; rather, they improve focus, allowing attention on one thought at a time, which leads to feeling calmer, behaving less frenetically, and creating conditions for more thoughtful responses and methodical interactions.

Many of my ADHD patients report that pharmacists demonize them and treat them as drug addicts when filling their prescriptions for Adderall or Ritalin. Some pharmacists likely experience some degree of cognitive dissonance when they repeatedly see hyperactive, impulsive, and distracted individuals with ADHD picking up orders for stimulants that can make people hyperactive, impulsive, and distracted. I have seen the same dynamic enacted repeatedly on inpatient psychiatric wards, where stimulants are often withheld from individuals with severe ADHD, out of fear that the medications will contribute to agitation, anxiety, excessive activity, and poorer compliance with rules and requests, even though the opposite is true: Such patients generally calm down and cooperate more effectively with staff when given their stimulants. (The potential for patients with ADHD to divert their stimulant medication to other patients certainly can be problematic on inpatient units.)

Trump claims he has "never had a drink" or a cigarette because of his brother Fred's struggle with alcoholism [271], and the medications listed by his long-time personal doctor did not consist of any typically abused substances [272]. Thus, drug use is unlikely to explain the panoply of his ADHD behavior. I provide a more detailed exploration of Trump and possible stimulant use in Chapter 6.

Borderline Personality Disorder

Borderline personality disorder (BPD) is often omitted from lists of conditions whose symptoms can mimic or overlap with ADHD. In part this is due to past de-emphasis on problems of emotional regulation that are common in ADHD. Another reason is that BPD is often framed in terms of intense interpersonal strife, including fears of abandonment, and subsequent self-injuring or suicidal behaviors, rather than on problems with emotional regulation [2, 273]. However, Linehan's formulation of BPD as a substantial, temperamental, under-regulation of emotion, coupled with an invalidating environment that denies, contradicts, ignores, or inappropriately punishes the individual for displays of emotional dysregulation [274], makes it clear that this recipe is present in the lives of many individuals with ADHD. Although I have worked with many individuals with borderline personality disorder who have no apparent ADHD symptoms, I have also seen several individuals with severe ADHD that seemed to explain most or all of what had been attributed to BPD, including a few whose lives were fundamentally salvaged (not savaged) by taking stimulant medication. Stimulants allowed them to regulate their emotions and process interpersonal situations in a calm, deliberative way. Although evaluating a personality disorder involves knowing the internal states and feelings of an individual [2], which is information we don't have for Trump, it seems quite unlikely that his ADHD symptoms could be solely attributed to BPD, particularly given that he is not known to have intense abandonment issues, or to have displayed suicidal or parasuicidal behaviors such as self-cutting.

Narcissistic Personality Disorder

Much of the media speculation regarding President Trump's mental health has concerned displays of grandiosity and narcissism [257]. While many of his statements and actions epitomize narcissistic thoughts and behaviors (for a few examples, see [257, 275, 276]), we need to be very careful to avoid declaring he has a personality disorder or other mental health problem in this realm. (By the way, DMS-5 does not describe "malignant narcissism," which remains an unofficially recognized diagnostic term.) One major reason for caution is that, as a result of what I believe is his ADHD, Trump has a very strong tendency to express, in speech or text, whatever is at the top of his mind, and as such these comments are not necessarily a distillation of his thoughts and his true feelings on a topic. As we noted previously, Trump routinely contradicts himself within minutes or hours or days of an utterance [199, 277-279]; while each comment may candidly reflect his sentiments of the moment, how could anyone know which utterance represents a genuine, deep-seated belief? To assess his narcissism, we would need to know his core beliefs regarding himself and others, to which we are not privy. And because of his ADHD, we can't trust any statement he may give regarding this.

Secondly, people with ADHD often come across as self-absorbed or narcissistic; researchers have documented co-morbidity between ADHD and narcissism [280]. My patient Frank (from Chapter 1) could spend twenty minutes in a session lamenting, "I was on the phone with her for an hour and I never even asked her how she was doing!" To his girlfriend, his behavior may look selfish and self-centered. Even in his own assessment it looked self-centered. However, if Frank were truly a narcissist, it is unlikely that he would spend hours worrying that he had neglected his girlfriend, whose feelings he manifestly cared about but perpetually forgot to ask her about. Berating himself at length for this demonstrated that he was not acting out of narcissism; rather, his ADHD caused him to talk about other topics when he was with her. It is crucial to distinguish between those individuals with little or no concern for others (potentially a sign of narcissism or sociopathy) and those who do genuinely care about others, but because of ADHD may not express these concerns.

Let us look further into how ADHD can resemble narcissism, or how problems in directing attention can show up as the appearance of self-centeredness. Each of us carries around our own thoughts, fears, concerns, and joys. Many people with ADHD, because of their distractibility, often jump quickly from one to another of these internal cerebrations, which keeps the content of their mind at the forefront of their own awareness. When they then enter conversation with another person, they often feel intense pressure to articulate what they are thinking at the moment, because they know that their hold on any particular thought is tenuous, and if they don't vocalize it immediately, it may slip away. Their speech then gets swept along in the flow of evanescent items, and they are unable to step outside of this flow and remember some of the niceties of social discourse. Again, that does not mean that all people with ADHD behave in a way that appears self-centered all of the time, but we know that others do frequently describe people with ADHD as self-absorbed, brusque, and inconsiderate [25, 281]. Even though Trump's behavior and comments suggest that he *is* dismissive of the needs and aspirations of large numbers of immigrants and Americans [282], we cannot be certain that he really doesn't care—i.e., ADHD alone *might* explain a large portion of his *perceived* dismissiveness.

Certainly, Trump displays an incessant, narcissistic desire to be in the limelight and to be adored for his magnificence, and he manifests this urge daily in tweets, quips, and tirades (for a few examples see [7, 17, 283]). However, many of his impulsive comments are so bizarre, inconsistent, or untrue (for examples see [216, 284-287]) that they undermine the appearance that he is a secure, decisive, reasonable, intelligent, or effective leader; hence they do not primarily serve a narcissistic function. The impulsive comments he spews demonstrating poor self-monitoring and poor self-control greatly outnumber the utterances that actually promote his interests. There may certainly be a self-gratifying component to hearing himself talk and knowing that others are listening, but narcissism cannot be the primary factor for such bloviating. If it were, then knowing that he has an audience, he would routinely craft messages that cast himself in the best light possible, whereas he demonstrably, repeatedly, and outrageously fails at this. Although reporters cited narcissism as driving his abrupt, unproductive second summit with North Korea's leader [288], a true narcissist would have planned ahead to ensure that the meeting would appear successful (if not actually *be* successful), rather than jumping in with insufficient preparation. Again, this certainly does not mean that he is not narcissistic, just that the evidence for an ADHD diagnosis remains robust and ubiquitous, and not explainable by other means;

the narcissism seems a secondary, although potentially important, factor in some situations. ADHD structures his thought process, while narcissism serves as one of many fillers.

Positive Illusory Bias (PIB) constitutes the third reason making it difficult to ascertain narcissism in individuals with ADHD. Studies indicate [289, 290] that up to 30% of boys with ADHD consistently overvalue their own abilities, and that we can distinguish PIB from mere optimism. In contrast to general optimism, PIB tends to be directed at self-assessment, not a positive view of the whole world; individuals with PIB maintain positive assessment even in the face of clear, contradictory evidence; also, PIB does not seem to improve motivation, performance, or endurance in continuing tasks. Researchers have not yet determined whether childhood PIB commonly disappears before adulthood, remains as a relatively unaltered PIB of adulthood, or predisposes individuals to develop narcissistic traits. Disentangling whether certain comments from Trump represent a narcissistic personality disorder or aspects of PIB poses significant challenges.

The facts of Trump's life make up a fourth reason that assessing his narcissism is complicated. By being born a white New Yorker to a multimillionaire father [291], from childhood he was already a member of an elite, uniquely powerful group of Americans. His further accumulation of wealth, his status as a television celebrity, and his current possession of the most powerful position on the planet, make it a judgment call as to whether specific comments are grandiose or an actual reflection of his importance or power. As all forty-four of his predecessors show, it is certainly possible to hold the position of president with more humility and grace than he has demonstrated, but that alone does not constitute a diagnosis of narcissistic personality disorder.

Misattribution

Observers frequently misattribute the motivations for behaviors of people with ADHD. Indeed the title of one of the most popular books on ADHD, Kate Kelly and Peggy Ramundo's *You Mean I'm Not Lazy, Stupid Or Crazy?* reflects how people often misinterpret behavior driven by ADHD [292]. Certainly, Trump has been called moronic, insane, juvenile, and sadistic [21-24] for actions that at least some of the time were directly attributable to his ADHD. That multiple determinants contribute to every action complicates making precise attributions of motivation. Even when powerful, prevailing forces exist, we may have difficulty identifying how large a role such forces play in each individual outcome. Global warming affects each and every storm and drought unfolding on our planet, but it is difficult to determine how important it is for shaping the weather in a given spot at a particular time [293]. However, we can say with certainty that global warming has increased the frequency of extreme weather events and will continue to do so for years [293]. Similarly, we know that ADHD makes someone more likely to be absent-minded, distracted, impulsive, or emotionally overwhelmed, but it may be hard to determine in each particular instance how large a role the ADHD plays. ADHD contributes to every utterance, act, and avoidance in Trump's life, but how much it drives a particular quip or reaction is not always clear.

The influence of ADHD on one of the most discussed incidents of the presidential campaign was missed in virtually all analyses of the event, exemplifying this misattribution of motivation. In his second debate with Clinton, television cameras showed Trump walking around the stage while Clinton spoke. He then suddenly appeared in back of her, grimaced, and backed off, only to reappear near her again moments later [294, 295]. This event was parodied in a skit on "Saturday Night Live" [296], and many commentators described how Trump intended to "intimidate" or even "stalk" his opponent, portraying the actions as planned and purposeful examples of his bullying and misogyny [297-299]. However, examining the details of Trump's behavior supports an interpretation that ADHD drove his actions.

First, Trump meandered aimlessly around the stage, rather than marching right up to Clinton and invading her personal space. (For video of a male candidate marching directly up to, and upon, Clinton with the goal of intimidation, see the 2000 tape of the New York campaign for Senate with Rick Lazio [300, 301].) Secondly, when Trump appeared right behind Clinton, he reacted initially with an expression of surprise, not anger or disgust, which is inconsistent with this being a planned act of aggression. His snarl of disapproval quickly followed his surprised reaction, and he then retreated. Yes, there are scores of examples of Trump bullying and intimidating his opponents [302-304], and numerous public displays of sexist and demeaning treatment of women [305, 306]. And while the widely ballyhooed interaction during the second debate does contain some of those elements, I regard his ADHD as underlying the whole sequence of actions, with dollops of bullying or sexism added on-the-fly to fill in the content. Regardless of his intentions, he intruded on Clinton's personal space, making it quite understandable that she felt threatened and imposed upon. However, her interpretation of the event does not tell us what was going on in Mr. Trump's head. The episode serves as a reminder to observe closely and to consider other possibilities before ascribing a motivation to a particular action, absent the actor's expressed intentions. It also highlights how ADHD-driven behavior can get people in trouble. Because ADHD-driven behaviors typically deviate from societal norms and thus clamor for explanation, if awareness of ADHD is absent from the equation, the resulting assessment is incomplete and often pejorative.

Might ADHD Influence the Content of Thoughts?

Warning! I speculate on controversial issues in the following paragraphs. I am tackling this topic—whether ADHD contributes to the content of Mr. Trump's thoughts—because it intertwines in important ways with an exploration of how ADHD influences his presidency. Some readers may find one or more of these generalizations and assumptions offensive. Feel free to skip ahead to the next chapter if you wish to avoid my conjectures.

I've stated several times that ADHD drives the process of how Mr. Trump thinks and does not dictate the content of his thoughts. While those who voted for him should be held accountable for putting into office someone with ADHD this severe, Trump is still responsible for what he says and does. When someone with ADHD blurts out what he feels in the moment, it is almost always just a subset of the thoughts and feelings he may hold about a given topic. Yet when certain themes (narcissism, sexism, xenophobia) [275, 306-308] arise repeatedly, it creates the impression that a preponderance of those internal thoughts and feelings skew in those directions. Our values, privileges, experiences, and temperaments, along with any mental health condition, including ADHD, all shape our thoughts. ADHD alone can never be the sole determinant of a thought or action. Certainly vast numbers of Americans with ADHD do not share any of the positions or approve of the actions of this president. However, many Americans with ADHD do consider Mr. Trump a kindred spirit in the content of what he says as well as his manner of expression. Clearly ADHD itself does not create particular thoughts or mandate specific biases.

While I have claimed a distinction between how ADHD affects thought processing, but does not determine the content of the ideas themselves, I am probably oversimplifying. The thoughts of many people with ADHD, including Donald Trump, appear to be more powerfully shaped by visual images than by words, and this is one way that ADHD could influence thought content. This bias towards pictorial representation in turn leads to a propensity for inductive reasoning—noticing particular examples and building overarching concepts from them, as opposed to deductive reasoning where a teacher or guide points out general concepts, and then places individual facts into this overall framework [309]. Indeed, a leitmotif of Trump's life involves rejecting experts who teach concepts and rules, and strongly favoring his own experiences and the generalizations he makes from them [149, 187, 226]. Traditional teaching methods often fail students with ADHD in part because of this reliance on inductive reasoning [310]. I am not implying that all people with ADHD think primarily pictorially, or can only handle examples rather than concepts. I know several individuals with ADHD who have lost their jobs through precipitously speaking out for coworkers, where their outspokenness stemmed from principles of fairness or injustice, rather than any particular loyalty or friendship to the individual affected.

Individuals who rely on inductive reasoning may face more difficulty changing their views than those who operate primarily through deductive reasoning, because brains face more challenges in erasing or refuting an original association that has a concrete image and story behind it, than in replacing a deductive conceptual framework with a new concept or rule. If you have an image of an evil Mexican drug dealer or Salvadoran gang member, and you reason inductively, it is hard to un-think these pictures, because any counter-examples are easily tabulated as extraneous (Of course there's a few good Mexicans!) or irrelevant (That well-behaved Salvadoran isn't like the others!). Conversely, if you think deductively, and even if you started from the erroneous generalization that all Latinos are criminals, it is easier to replace this notion with the idea that impoverished conditions, or bad parenting, or capitalist oppression, lead to criminal behavior. Or more fundamentally, that Latinos may have nothing in common beyond some elements of distant heritage. Furthermore, those starting from an inductive approach generally resist any top-down, deductive alternatives, because it doesn't make sense to them that an overarching rule can or should take precedence over their own unique experience.

Our national dialogue (or lack of dialogue) regarding gun control unfolds along a similar inductive vs. deductive framework. Those who reason inductively, from a single anecdote of an assault or robbery averted because someone possessed a gun to fight back (and the NRA skillfully and exuberantly promotes these stories), remain unlikely to be deterred in their convictions by any competing stories of trained, armed professionals who failed to prevent murder (e.g., the massacres at Pulse Night Club, Columbine High School, Marjory Stoneman Douglas High School, Santa Fe High School, the shooting of American sniper Chris Kyle). For the inductive thinker, their experience, or the stories that impressed them first, create the great truths. Demonstrating that gun ownership at both an individual and societal level clearly increases the risk of death from firearms, doesn't register as an important principle to them. Although several of the explorations of our national disagreements about immigrants or gun control conclude that the use of fear represents the most critical influence in motivating people's positions, the deductive/inductive divide seems to be at least as important a factor in shaping people's thoughts and feelings.

Because Trump's ADHD predisposes him to be pictorially driven and to reason inductively, I believe that his ADHD has had some contribution to his sexism, racism, and admiration for authoritarians. His words repeatedly reveal that when he meets a woman, he initially and strongly sees a physical woman (or wants to seize a woman) [306], and is not thinking conceptually of a person with attributes of strength, intelligence, charisma, or sociability. He has applied this approach not just to women in beauty pageants, but to heads of state, corporate leaders, and television personalities [311-313].

When Mr. Trump denigrates Latino immigrants [308], or talks about an African American supporter in his audience [215], or how he is much better for "the gays" [314], he blatantly verbalizes that he sees people as emblems of their race or their group, rather than as individual human beings. He also usually makes it clear which groups he sees as inferior to his own. When he uses the term "shit-hole countries" [168, 308] he shares his visual image of how dismissively (and with racial overtones) he views parts of the world, and that his objections rely primarily on appearances—the squalor and the filth, rather than being troubled primarily by concepts of poverty, overcrowding, corruption, or lack of opportunity that might be prevalent in those regions.

While his ADHD contributes to Trump noticing individual examples and coming to broader conclusions from them, it does not explain why the initial examples were etched in his brain the way they were. It certainly would have been possible to notice that people were of a different skin color or had different patterns of dress or speaking, and to have come up with feelings of respect, admiration, or curiosity about these differences, rather than the fear and loathing he exhibits. It seems likely, although this is speculative, that his privileged background and his allegedly racist father [291, 315] played a significant role in shaping his early impressions.

Most people, whether rich or poor, value money; likewise, many people, whether dominant or impotent, value power. But Mr. Trump's focus on the superficial trappings of power and the ostentatious glitz and gilding of wealth [7, 316, 317] reflect, in part, his ADHD-driven emphasis on visuals. In a related fashion, because his own ADHD makes him impulsive and makes it hard for him to follow others' rules and guidelines, he openly admires autocrats who create their own rules and ignore global standards and values [205]. Trump's preoccupation with the visual and the concrete contributes to his over-valuing graphic displays of military force, such as dropping bombs, and scenes of havoc and destruction [318, 319], which to him are more clear-cut expressions of power than averting a war or avoiding a confrontation. He admires those who display trappings of power and make a grandiose show of their might, rather than those, such as the Dalai Lama, who exert quiet powers of persuasion. Some of Trump's ADHD-driven failure to grasp the notion that one can project power through calmness, restraint, and preventing disasters also appears to be part of his apparent disdain for his predecessor—"no-drama Obama" [320]. I believe that ADHD has contributed to some of the least admirable thoughts and attitudes for which Trump is now known.

I am not claiming that all bigots have ADHD or that everyone with ADHD is bigoted. Indeed, I know many individuals with ADHD who have devoted their lives to social justice, resisting sexism, opposing racism, and fighting for equality, fairness, and scientific truth. I know many people with ADHD who have lost jobs or damaged relationships by fighting for such causes. In some of these instances, I believe that ADHD-driven tendencies to not let go of an idea when others have moved on, or to lock on to one truth where others see more nuanced situations, has contributed to the fervor with which these individuals have held on to their liberal ideals. And almost certainly, it was the impulsivity of ADHD that contributed to some of them blurting out their support for people or causes, and to be punished for those outbursts, when others with similar views chose to remain silent.

ADHD also plays a strong role in shaping Trump's propensity for impetuousness, superficiality, restlessness, and lack of interest in important matters of state. Whether or not he has additional mental health conditions, they cannot account for these ADHD symptoms. It is possible, but speculative, that ADHD has also had some influence in positioning him to be susceptible to racist, sexist, ostentatious, and pro-authoritarian views. However, the value system he was raised in, along with his childhood environment and specific experiences, probably had a more direct and causal role in his holding these views. It is important to remind those with ADHD who disavow what Trump stands for that such attitudes and views are separable, learned behaviors, and while perhaps influenced by ADHD, are not at all inherent in ADHD.

CHAPTER 5

FAKING ADHD? ACTING OUT OR JUST ACTING?

Imitating ADHD

I have outlined how Trump strongly and classically fulfills the current criteria for having ADHD, and I have reviewed how other mental conditions cannot explain these symptoms. Can we explain his apparent ADHD in any other way? Could Trump just be faking his ADHD symptoms? It seems extremely unlikely that he has spent years imitating someone with ADHD, particularly given the difficulty in intentionally behaving so consistently inconsistent. Successful imitation of ADHD seems particularly unlikely given that his attempts to copy people with other conditions and illnesses have been so crude and contrived [321, 322]. And why would he want to imitate someone with ADHD anyway? One might posit that this display of ADHD behavior, over several decades, represents an extensive performance art piece, but this seems implausible given that Trump has displayed little self-awareness and seldom projects a sense of humor [323]. Finally, although some aspects of ADHD can be readily faked (along the lines of the "Look, there's a squirrel!" meme), precisely imitating ADHD is quite difficult for brains that think in a more linear way.

Accurate imitation of inattentive and hyperactive components of ADHD remain difficult for at least two reasons—what I call the simultaneity rule and the timing rule. The simultaneity rule refers to the challenge of consciously displaying hyperactivity and verbal aspects of ADHD at the same time. The timing rule addresses that where we pause in the flow of speech can indicate our underlying thought processes. I propose these rules as general guidelines to help in evaluating behavior, not invariant laws that nobody can break, and I'll expound on both of them below.

Studies consistently show that the vast majority of humans do not multi-task very well [324, 325], and that rather than concurrently attending to multiple activities simultaneously, on a micro level we switch our attention back and forth between two or more behaviors. However, on an *involuntary* level the brain of someone with hyperactive ADHD readily engages in competing tasks at the same time: walking around, excessively gesturing with their hands, shifting body position, or making movements of their head, mouth, or face while talking. However, when someone without ADHD tries to imitate this behavior, both the bodily movements and the characteristics of speech must become conscious tasks. Thus, most imitators alternate between demonstrating physical aspects of hyperactivity and verbal comments that suggest inattention or impulsivity, rather than displaying ADHD movements and speech synchronously.

One curious violation of my simultaneity rule occurred in Trump's third debate with Clinton. In his previous debates with Republican candidates or with Clinton, Trump simultaneously displayed hyperactivity—excessively talking over others, walking away from the lectern, gesturing, shrugging, and making a host of lip pursing, scowling, and other facial expressions [225, 295, 298, 302]. However, in the first three quarters of an hour of the third debate, where many commentators had declaimed that he needed to "appear presidential" if he had any chance to win the election, his speech stayed on target and he provided relatively organized and focused answers to questions [326]. Many pundits duly noted this improved verbal performance at the beginning of the debate, even if it deteriorated in the second half of the debate when he went off topic more frequently, and gave rambling and tangential responses, including the famous "such a nasty woman" comment [326-328]. What nobody appeared to comment on was the striking reduction, almost a virtual absence, during those first forty-five minutes, of the relentless head bobbing and other movements he displayed in other performances. I maintain that while conscious effort (and possibly, a few hours of practice) may have enabled Trump to be more verbally focused than usual, he very likely required the aid of some chemical assistance to simultaneously restrain the numerous head and face movements that he ubiquitously exhibited during other debates and speeches. Whether coincidently or not, in the lead-up to the debate, he had made a big issue of whether Clinton was on any medication, and whether she was willing to be drug tested; oddly, he had stated he was willing to take such a test [329]. (See Chapter 6 for further exploration of the question of Trump's use of stimulant medications.)

The timing rule states that where one pauses during speech often helps in differentiating genuine ADHD from an imitation. The speech of someone with ADHD gallops forward with a topic, and then as the individual diverts their attention to a new item, language usually pivots seamlessly in this new direction. The speaker with ADHD does not usually pause until he or she is several words into the new topic, upon realizing that they have lost their audience, or lost track of their own previous thoughts on the original topic. In contrast, someone trying to mimic the distractibility of ADHD usually starts talking about one topic, and then will pause, as if their linear brain is saying "Aha, now I'm going to jump to something unrelated!" and following this pause will then divert to the second topic. A pattern of pause-then-pivot suggests an imitation of ADHD, whereas pivot-then-pause more likely indicates genuine ADHD. Even the professional actors imitating Trump routinely misplace the location of the pause in their flow of speech [330]. Trump is either the most brilliant actor of our time, a claim he might even aspire to, or his display of ADHD behavior indicates he genuinely has ADHD.

By now you may be wondering why I've gone down this path. In fact, our society struggles with the problem of fabricating cases of ADHD in ways more pervasive than whether Trump's ADHD exists as genuine or "fake news." Currently on US college campuses, and increasingly in high schools and workplaces, large numbers of people obtain and use stimulant medications [331, 332]. Although our limited

Faking ADHD?

evidence suggests that many of these individuals do so as an aid in studying or for enhancing alertness to improve performance, others abuse these drugs for their hedonic qualities [117]. Governments strictly control the prescribing of stimulant medication; successfully faking that one has ADHD potentially allows one to gain access to a supply of these medications. Websites even coach people on how to fake their ADHD symptoms and histories [333]. And medical societies provide anti-faking advice to help doctors detect those who are malingering, or faking, ADHD symptoms [334]. Psychologists have designed tests that identify those who are likely to be malingering, and these tests have good, but not perfect, track records for detecting deceivers [335-337]. Doctors, and particularly psychiatrists as the designated gatekeepers regarding who can legally obtain these medications in our society, need to maintain and improve their vigilance in evaluating patients for ADHD.

My work with Reed, an Ivy League graduate with a promising tech career and a loving boyfriend, delved into some of the intricacies of the topic of faking ADHD. Reed came to my office because of problems with impulsivity: He was using party drugs, driving too fast, and otherwise behaving in ways that he felt betrayed his own standards and values. He wondered if his drug use, or his childhood with an alcoholic father, were prompting him to behave in ways he viewed as harmful to himself. Reed was brilliant. When hyper-focused he could read and fully comprehended a complex novel by William Faulkner in a single afternoon; he had rewritten and improved the computer code for a multimillion-dollar app his company relied on. Reed only began to reveal more ADHD symptoms after several hourly sessions: He kept a backup wallet at home, complete with duplicate ID cards, because he misplaced his so frequently; he constructed an intricate alarm system that he used for monitoring his online performance and redirecting himself to work projects; and he kept a sequence of visual images in his cell phone to remind himself that he had his lunch, was properly dressed, and had his laptop with him when he left for work in the morning.

We took weeks to discuss and explore that despite his success and his extreme intelligence, he displayed a full range of ADHD symptoms that affected him negatively. We worked on several behavioral strategies addressing ADHD, which measurably (he had the spreadsheets to prove it) decreased his undesired behaviors and improved his efficiency at work. Only after we started discussing medication options (he was still losing wallets) did he divulge that as an undergraduate he had "faked" having ADHD in order to try Adderall, which had helped him in his studying for a few months. He genuinely believed at that time that he did not have ADHD and had obtained stimulants under a false pretext. Given the paucity of his original doctor's notes, it remained unclear how thorough that evaluation had been; those earlier sessions had not helped Reed to understand what having ADHD actually entails, or how to deal with it effectively. Even some of those who think that they are faking ADHD may actually have it [71].

Although in training mental health professionals we usually teach that a thorough evaluation requires a detailed history and a review of symptoms, our entire health data collection system prioritizes recording the answers to specific questions over observing how patients appear and behave. This trend is only likely to increase as the prevalence of electronic medical record systems proliferates, because these software programs focus on checking boxes, and often involve so much typing during the intake that many professionals spend little time even looking at their patient. Although we are tallying more and more data points to feed into complex algorithms, we lose many important pieces of information because we don't enter them into these new systems. I fear that aspects of "clinical wisdom" which experienced psychiatrists utilize in their decision making during evaluations and treatment planning will vanish from everyday practice in the years ahead. We need to continue to extract and make explicit some of this clinical wisdom, such as my simultaneous rule and timing rule for detecting imitations of ADHD, in order to preserve these insights.

Success and ADHD

I have demonstrated that Trump meets the full diagnostic criteria for ADHD, that neither other mental illnesses nor fakery can account for his symptoms, and that brain-based ADHD impairs performance. So how do we reconcile these facts with Trump's numerous successes over the last half century? Trump made millions of dollars in real estate (though he reportedly lost even more), starred in a popular reality television show, and won the presidency in his first race for any office. Even if you accept the claim that passive investment of the millions he inherited (or better management of his assets) would have yielded a larger present fortune [338], or if you hold reality television in low regard, or if we recall that he lost the popular vote by almost three million votes, Donald Trump has attained remarkable success by our society's standards. If he is truly impaired or disabled by ADHD, how could he achieve so much?

I have worked with successful architects, baristas, cabbies, doctors, executives, farmers, geologists, handymen, illustrators, janitors, kitchen staff, lawyers, and mail carriers (just to tackle the first half of the alphabet) who have ADHD. We have seen what that means: serious obstacles to overcome in the realm of directing and maintaining focus, or in controlling impulses, compared to those without ADHD. And overcoming those obstacles is far more difficult without that awareness that one has ADHD. I have also worked with people so impaired by their ADHD that they could not hold a job, maintain a relationship, or keep track of their finances or food. The presence of ADHD does not, in itself, inform us how strongly someone's performance in a given task will be impaired. The presence of ADHD does not provide information regarding an individual's compensatory strengths and supports (intelligence, beauty, family, money) that may help lead to success. And aspects of ADHD may actually help in certain situations [98, 146]. Trump's ADHD, by contributing to risk-taking, creativity, spontaneity, showmanship, and restless energy, may have played a role in his achievements.

ADHD does not inevitably preclude triumph because performance always results from an interaction between a particular brain and a particular environment. Success for those with ADHD requires an engaging task and an optimal amount of structural support. Too much regimentation will feel boring or restrictive, but too little structure can leave someone with ADHD floundering and directionless. Largely because he received considerable money and power from his father [339], from the beginning Trump had the luxury of pursuing activities that interested him, and of ignoring the tasks that he didn't enjoy. He was rich enough to contract out jobs that others have to perform themselves in order to succeed, ranging from having lawyers who adhere to (or skirt) tax laws and building codes, to administrative assistants who organize his schedule and activities, to wives who handle aspects of child rearing and perhaps enhance social standing. To a large extent he has been able to hire others to implement the tasks that his deficient executive functions prevent him from performing adequately himself.

The task of matching personal strengths to the demands of a job is something that Americans must take more seriously at election time. Trump campaigned, in part, on his history of being a successful businessman [340], claiming that this demonstrated he could pick the "best people" to help him run the country [341]. Although this sounded plausible on the surface, and was apparently convincing to some people, it is not at all clear, on closer inspection, that the job description of running the most powerful country on earth overlaps much with being a real estate mogul, reality television show host, or luxury product endorser. His previous experiences also do not appear to have put him in contact with people who would be competent in running government agencies. Indeed, the businesses he ran and the way he ran them, are about as pertinent to his current job demands as Sarah Palin's claim that being a mother or being able to "field dress a moose" were qualifications for being vice president [342]. One hopes she realized that her experiences as a state legislator and governor were more pertinent to that role. On the other hand, the reactionary impulse to now reject any celebrity just because Trump has proven so ill-prepared and ill-suited for the presidency, is equally inane. For example, whether you like her or not, Oprah Winfrey's record of building a media empire from nothing, spending thousands of hours on-air and off listening to people and bringing people together, spending time and money helping improve the lives of others, and delving into topics integral to public policy and people's daily lives, strikes me as more pertinent to the tasks of a presidency than was Trump's list of accomplishments.

We have certainly had several other presidents who, while in office, had diagnosable mental illnesses, particularly depression, and these men varied greatly in how much their ailments affected their ability to execute the duties of the office [343]. While ADHD clearly affects Trump in profound ways, it was initially up to the electorate, and is now up to Congress or his cabinet, to determine whether his inadequately treated ADHD makes him unqualified for office. People elected him with his ADHD on full display; I have no way of knowing whether public awareness that ADHD accounts for much of his distractibility, poor preparation, poor follow-through, impulsivity and restlessness would have changed their votes. I do think that in our modern democracies, the voters deserve access to detailed and accurate reports of candidates' current mental and physical health, along with their ongoing financial obligations and commitments.

Returning to the topic of success and ADHD, we have largely allowed Trump to define success on his own terms because during his pre-presidency career he was largely beholden only to himself, and not particularly accountable to others. As the head of a conglomeration of family-run businesses, Trump himself has been the sole arbiter of whether his company's goals were being met or not, which is quite unlike being President of the United States where the opinions of an entire nation help define "success". Trump labeled himself a "very successful businessman" [344]—in spite of losing more than $900,000,000 [345] in a single year, when the economy was doing well [346], even though it was his lawyers who spun that financial debacle into a way of avoiding paying taxes for a decade or more [347]. Furthermore, in addition to successes, he clearly has had more than his share of societally defined failures (several business bankruptcies [348], scores of lost lawsuits [349], a pair of divorces, and numerous alleged affairs [350]). All of these failures seem intimately tied to his ADHD, as they often involved bumping up against societal strictures that he was not able to navigate skillfully. At least from outward appearances, Trump's life goals have been the accumulation of great wealth and prodigious publicity; he has achieved these, and he continues to use the presidency to expand on these triumphs. However, others assess many of his "successes" much more negatively than he does. Many Trump University students feel they did not receive their promised education [351], and numerous jilted builders, construction workers, and other contractors who didn't get paid on numerous jobs [349, 352, 353] do not view these building projects as successes. Trump's pattern of big successes and big failures is quite consistent with his having ADHD.

In fact, as discussed in Chapter 2, many adults with ADHD present for treatment when a change in external structures (starting college, starting a new job) leaves them with too little guidance as to what to do. Because of weakness in their executive function of directing attention [3], they can no longer rely on repeating previous patterns of behavior, and they often feel unprepared to cope with new tasks or contexts. It is not surprising that Trump appeared more comfortable and successful in the free-wheeling campaign for office than in actually governing as president, where rigid expectations for running high-functioning domestic programs and foreign policies, and for interacting with other leaders, constrain his impulses. Although pundits cite Trump's narcissism as the source of the great contentiousness he has displayed with multiple campaign managers and chiefs of staff [354-357], his ADHD appears to play at least as important a role, since these individuals are supposed to perform executive functions for him—i.e., controlling the flow of information in and out of his office, and organizing the actions of others.

Given his ADHD, Trump's future accomplishments as president are likely to be those that he delegates to others, like filling Supreme Court and federal court vacancies with conservative activist judges, or rolling back environmental regulations. He may achieve some success in areas that interest him enough that he can stay on task and work towards a goal. However, after many months in office, vanishingly few aspects of governing actually seem to interest him. Maybe he will make breakthroughs on diplomatic fronts where his lack of knowledge, his pre-conceptions, and his willingness to break with precedent create new opportunities; but these also carry the risk of disastrous failures. ADHD will continue to shape his presidency, his life, and the country's welfare.

CHAPTER 6

A STIMULATING DISCUSSION ABOUT TREATING ADHD

Although I had not meant to treat readers to a treatise on the treatment of mental health conditions, I am including this chapter on treatment of ADHD to make it clear that we have approaches to help improve symptoms of adult ADHD. A number of medications that promote dopamine and norepinephrine neurotransmission—i.e., primarily (but not limited to) stimulants—can improve focus and concentration and reduce impulsivity and emotional volatility [135]. Medications for ADHD never completely cure the condition, reflecting our knowledge that problems with neuroanatomy and brain connectivity underlie ADHD, in addition to neurochemical aberrancies [3, 103]. However, medications can be powerfully helpful, and sometimes transformative, in the lives of people with ADHD. In addition to medications, cognitive behavioral therapy (CBT) strategies adapted for ADHD measurably improve lives [240]. We have considerable evidence that medications and CBT can each lessen the likelihood of many of the potential negative outcomes of ADHD [39, 80, 137, 240, 358].

Stimulants vs. Non-Stimulants

For decades experts on ADHD have promoted stimulant medications as the first choice for treatment, placing other medication options a very distant second [130]. I have seen stimulants work well in scores, if not hundreds of adults with ADHD. However, in many individual situations I have detected roughly equivalent improvements in ADHD symptoms when treating individuals with stimulant or non-stimulant medications. Many of the head-to-head studies in ADHD comparing the benefits of stimulants to non-stimulants demonstrate very similar results to what I see clinically; some reports that show a statistically superior result for stimulants don't demonstrate a clinically meaningful difference over non-stimulants in rates of response or degree of improvement [54]. Very consistently, both groups of medications outperform placebo treatment for ADHD, and meta-analyses combining multiple studies suggest more consistent benefits from stimulants than non-stimulants [40, 54, 241]. However, variation in factors including whether patients received optimal medication dosages, differences between patient groups being studied, and the use of different measures of ADHD treatment success, render conclusions regarding the superiority of stimulants over non-stimulants rather murky.

Another factor (alluded to earlier) that hampers our ability to know which treatments most effectively reduce ADHD symptoms continues to be our difficulties in assessing psychiatric symptoms. Although many bright individuals have diligently worked to devise scales for measuring severity of, and improvement in, ADHD [157, 232, 359], our scoring systems still fail to capture much of the magnitude of impairment in ADHD, making it difficult to precisely document real changes that occur in real-life situations with treatment. These constraints make it even more difficult to demonstrate whether stimulants actually outperform non-stimulants in the treatment of ADHD.

In my experience, patients often strongly favor stimulants over non-stimulants for treating ADHD. While this may represent genuine superiority of stimulants in addressing symptoms, I believe that we often ignore one significant confounding variable. Stimulants frequently produce some degree of euphoria, whereas our non-stimulant ADHD medications do not [117]. Even if two different treatments reduced ADHD symptoms to the same extent, we would expect more people to opt for the medications that also had an immediate effect of making them feel better. Eradicating this bias remains very difficult because making someone feel better tends to skew all of that individual's assessments more positively, regardless of whether or not they retain any conscious awareness of their improvement in mood. While I don't believe that these mood-elevating effects are inherently bad, they do contribute to the abuse potential of stimulants; when evaluating treatment decisions for patients we should always remember that the stimulants have a likelihood for enhancing mood as well as improving aspects of cognition.

Non-stimulants used to treat ADHD include the serotonin and norepinephrine reuptake inhibitors (SNRI) (Effexor / venlafaxine, Cymbalta / duloxetine, Fetzima / levomilnacipran), the norepinephrine reuptake inhibitor Strattera / atomoxetine, Wellbutrin / bupropion, a norepinephrine and dopamine reuptake inhibitor, and some of the old tricyclic antidepressants (particularly those with strong norepinephrine reuptake inhibitions, such as desipramine, and nortriptyline). Most of these agents possess antidepressant activity, and many people assume that antidepressants are simply mood elevators. However, taking away chronic unhappiness is not the same as increasing happiness. None of our traditional antidepressant medications produce an immediate uplift in mood, and they all fail to produce even gradual improvements in mood in those who are not depressed. Patients tell me that if you look hard enough, you can score antidepressants on Haight Street (one of the informal centers for the experimental use of licit and illicit substances in San Francisco), but they certainly do not register high on the list of desirable drugs to take. While stimulants boost mood, antidepressants generally do not.

Even more confusingly, we know that stimulants don't just boost mood in most people, they also possess potent antidepressant effects for those who are truly clinically depressed. We have traditionally reserved the use of stimulants to treat depression for those with cancer or another terminal physical condition, where we desired a rapid antidepressant response and considered the risks of addiction to be minimal [360]. Many researchers and clinicians believe that we should surrender the use of such terms as "antidepressant" or "anti-anxiety" medication, and instead just refer to them by their biochemical actions, because so many medications possess proven benefits for a multitude of conditions, and patients get confused by the names. I frequently hear questions like, "Why would you treat my panic attacks with an antidepressant?" that stem from such confusion in our terminology.

The well-documented antidepressant response to stimulants, often within hours of initiating treatment [360], makes much of the current infatuation with ketamine [361], in both the popular media and in the psychiatric world, rather curious. Ketamine has been employed for years as an anesthetic agent, and, at lower doses and via different delivery methods, as a street drug to induce hallucinogenic experiences. The vast majority of the recent hoopla around ketamine promotes it as the only medication to possess rapid antidepressant benefits, which is manifestly not the case. Ketamine does appear to have a distinct advantage over the stimulants in that its antidepressant benefits are not only rapid in onset but also appear to last for days in many individuals, whereas the antidepressant effects of stimulants tend to disappear as the body metabolizes the medication. Until 2019, doctors administered ketamine treatments for depression only via intravenous infusions, creating an important disadvantage compared to oral stimulants for depression. We will see whether the recently approved nasal inhalation formulation of ketamine (only authorized for use in a doctor's office) improves the accessibility or reduces the costs for treating depression.

In current research papers, web articles, books, pamphlets, and lectures about ADHD, experts consistently assert that stimulants work quickly for ADHD, while the non-stimulants take many days to weeks before they are effective [74, 362, 363]. I contend that this claimed difference in onset of action is erroneous. At a neurochemical level, I maintain that the stimulants work through their immediate action of making more norepinephrine and more dopamine available at the post-synaptic receptors [74]. Similarly, with the first dose, the neurochemical action of the non-stimulants [bupropion (Wellbutrin) [364], atomoxetine (Strattera) [74], duloxetine (Cymbalta) [365], milnacipran (Fetzima, Savella) [366]] or tricyclic antidepressants [367, 368] makes more norepinephrine or dopamine (or both) available at the post-synaptic receptors. Reasoning from this immediate biochemical action, we should expect the non-stimulants to work as quickly as do the stimulants for treating ADHD, even if the non-stimulants perform additional actions on other neurotransmitter systems or brain regions that unfold over a different time course. While a few reports do show decreased ADHD symptoms on a much faster time scale [365, 367] than non-stimulants are traditionally believed to work, this information does not appear to have penetrated the consciousness of the ADHD treatment community.

Not only does the basic science suggest that non-stimulants should work quickly to treat ADHD, but my clinical experiences agree with that prediction. Every individual with ADHD for whom a non-stimulant provided effective treatment reported that the medication started working on the very first day. I have even collected testimonials on this topic, because my observations contrast so markedly with the claims of authorities. My favorite patient testimonial begins with "I can still recall the day Cymbalta changed my life…" and goes on to describe swallowing a pill in my office, and then, two hours later, being confronted by a skateboarder rushing towards him on a busy sidewalk. Normally, because of his ADHD, my patient would have been overwhelmed by this kind of stimulus and been frozen in confusion and fear, but instead, he was able to "calmly step out of the way." For the patient, being able to rationally focus on a problematic situation and take a simple action to avoid being run over was a profoundly life-changing event. Being on Cymbalta provided him a choice of action, whereas previously he never felt that he could have such a choice. For many individuals with ADHD, non-stimulants provide viable, immediate relief of symptoms.

So why does a vast discrepancy exist between what I observe and the accepted truth about non-stimulants not working quickly for ADHD? I can identify two factors that I think contribute to this misunderstanding—what I call an antidepressant bias and a Strattera bias. As mentioned above, many of the non-stimulant options for ADHD are antidepressants or resemble them in their neurochemical actions [74, 367], and we know that antidepressants do generally take a few weeks to start helping with depression or anxiety [83]. I believe that this created the standard storyline that these drugs take a long time to have effects on the brain. However, basic lab bench biochemical studies along with the appearance of side effects from these medications, often within minutes to hours of consuming them, clearly demonstrate that these drugs have immediate neurochemical effects at brain synapses. Different effects from the same drug can have different time courses; a non-stimulant can impact ADHD immediately while also taking days or weeks to help with depression. Within seconds of inhalation, a cigarette may make you feel more alert or calm you down, or both, but any possible contribution to lung cancer will take years to emerge. There is no reason to assume that because norepinephrine or dopamine reuptake inhibitors take weeks to work for depression, they therefore must take weeks to work for ADHD.

For years atomoxetine, or Strattera, a norepinephrine reuptake inhibitor, was the only non-stimulant FDA approved for ADHD [369]. Agents that work similarly have been approved as antidepressants in other countries [370], but Strattera has not been extensively studied for depression. Because Strattera has numerous side effects, in most research protocols and in many clinical settings, we usually titrate it slowly to a therapeutic dose over the course of six to eight weeks. We should not be surprised that we do not see much benefit for ADHD when it is at sub-therapeutic doses in the first several weeks of treatment. I think the experience of waiting weeks for an ADHD response to Strattera has been misinterpreted to mean that the drug works slowly, rather than it was having minimal effects when consumed at sub-therapeutic doses.

If stimulants and non-stimulants have roughly similar benefits for ADHD symptoms and similarly rapid response rates, what distinguishes one group of drugs from the other? In my opinion, the different risks posed by side effects constitute the most significant differences between these classes of medications. Although much alarm has been raised about the side-effect burden of stimulants [371], in daily use the vast majority of patients have no adverse effects; the problem is that some of the uncommon side effects are very serious [74, 371]. Non-stimulants have the opposite profile; a considerable portion of patients will experience bothersome, but not dangerous, side effects but there is no likelihood of addiction or psychosis, and extremely little risk of serious injury [74, 117, 371]. In adults, the emergence of abrupt changes in mood and suicidal thoughts on antidepressants remains extremely rare, but both patients and doctors should continue to monitor for such potential disasters.

Curiously, even after I explain to a new patient these class differences in side effects—that stimulants have rare but potentially serious side effects, while the non-stimulants have fairly common but rarely dangerous adverse actions—a preponderance of individuals still want to start with the stimulant medications. I think part of this reaction stems from our nomenclature problems that I discussed previously—that calling a medication an "antidepressant" creates the impression that we are using it inappropriately when used to treat conditions other than depression, even when the agent has demonstrated efficacy in alleviating symptoms of those other conditions. Sticking to labeling medications by their pharmacologic and neurochemical actions may lead to fewer misperceptions. Separate from the semantic confusion, we also need to consider issues of stigma and social acceptance when interpreting patient preferences. I have treated several college students, as well as those of other ages, who had no qualms about being treated for ADHD, but were concerned about how people would perceive them if it became known they're taking antidepressants. As I discuss in Chapter 12, considerable stigma regarding ADHD continues to exist, but in some cases that diagnosis may feel less pejorative than many of our other psychiatric categories.

Stimulant Side Effects

Despite government agencies designating stimulants as controlled substances that merit strong regulations concerning prescriptions, doctors and patients usually find it easy to find optimal dosing regimens for these medications, because we see almost all of the benefits immediately. In practice we start with a very low dose and increase every few days until we see robust improvement in ADHD symptoms, or until side effects appear. The more common side effects of stimulants involve over-activation—feeling too restless, jittery, tremulous, anxious, or having trouble falling asleep, but also decreased appetite, excessive sweating, dry mouth, aggressiveness or irritability, increased heart rate or blood pressure, and gastro-intestinal effects [74]. If any of these over-activation effects show up, it is almost always a sign to back down on the dose. If the over-activation is very mild, then we may persist with a given dose for a few days with the expectation that the side effects will diminish further or disappear completely. Once we determine an effective dose, that amount of medication usually continues to be effective, although some patients require readjustments over the first several weeks or months. Also, some patients have a "honeymoon" period in which they obtain dramatic improvements in ADHD symptoms in the first weeks of treatment and never totally recapture those benefits in long-term treatment. This honeymoon may be a physiologic result of subsequent down-regulation of receptors after initial exposure to medication, or a psychological response—i.e., the first blush of taking anything that finally helps with ADHD feels overwhelmingly positive, but with time it becomes evident that the medication has not alleviated all symptoms of ADHD. In addition, if life events change to create substantially more challenging demands or greatly reduced structure and support, then some people will need a greater dose of medication to maintain optimal functioning. Dose reductions may be warranted if demands decrease or structure or other coping skills improve.

The really bad side effects of stimulant medications—addiction, amphetamine-induced psychosis, and sudden cardiac death--are each quite uncommon [371]. A few individuals with extremely rare, underlying arrhythmias have had fatal heart attacks triggered by prescription stimulants or street stimulants (cocaine, methamphetamine). Before prescribing stimulant medications, every patient must be assessed for personal histories of dangerous cardiac arrhythmias and for family members who died at young ages from cardiac arrest, in order to avoid prescribing stimulants to such individuals [372]. However, such underlying cardiac conditions are so rare that a review of large population studies consisting of over three million children in the US showed no association between stimulant treatment for ADHD and severe cardiac events [373]. Several years ago, Canada suspended the sales of Adderall for more than six months because of concern over sudden cardiac arrests and strokes [374]. However, the independent outside committee reviewing the decision could not prove that Adderall increased the risk of these very serious outcomes. The panel did recommend caution in prescribing Adderall for patients involved in strenuous exercise, with a family history of sudden cardiac death, or taking multiple stimulant medications, and also supported obtaining baseline EKGs when cardiac risks were present [375]. Implementing these guidelines and avoiding stimulant use in any high-risk individuals should further decrease these extremely rare but tragic outcomes.

The media froths with reports of the risks of addiction with stimulants. All evidence supports the claim that because of chemical differences in their structures, the street stimulants (primarily cocaine and methamphetamine, or speed) have substantially higher risks for being addicting than do the prescription stimulants [376]. The risk of becoming addicted to prescription stimulants appears to be around 2.5% [377]. Furthermore, complicating the picture, we know that untreated ADHD in childhood approximately doubles the risk of developing any substance abuse problem [378], and comprehensive studies of children treated with stimulants for ADHD indicate that this medication treatment actually lowers the risk of developing a substance abuse problem to the rates seen in individuals without ADHD [378,379]. States record the filling of controlled stimulant medication prescriptions in registries, and require doctors to check these registries, to make sure that patients do not obtain duplicate medications from multiple providers, and to further reduce the small risk of becoming addicted to these substances. Historical trends suggest an additional reason to be worried about an increasing frequency of stimulant abuse: Peaks of increased stimulant abuse cyclically follow crises of increased opioid abuse in America, and current reporting suggest that the opioid crisis has crested and stimulant abuse is already rising [380].

Amphetamine-Induced Psychosis

Amphetamine-induced psychosis alarms me more than any other adverse effect from stimulants, and consequently it is what I caution my patients most strongly about. While addiction to stimulant medications likely predisposes people to amphetamine-induced psychosis, many people who become psychotic never were addicted and many addicts never develop psychosis. Features of this condition include extreme hyperactivity, rapid speech, and little need for sleep [381].

Some authorities call this condition amphetamine-induced mania, but unlike mania, which usually involves interacting with others in an excessively happy, garrulous (and at times volatile and emotional) manner, amphetamine-induced psychosis almost always includes paranoia and serious delusional beliefs [381]. In the numerous cases I have witnessed, amphetamine-induced psychosis rarely includes the silly, joking, expansive, grandiose language and behaviors common to mania. The features of amphetamine-induced psychosis that cause me to consider it the most serious potential adverse effect of stimulants include the duration of the reaction, that many people actually seem to enjoy being in this state, the frequency with which I have observed it, and the relative lack of attention to this terrible response to medication.

Bad reactions to psychoactive substances most often involve intoxication states—altered perceptions, disturbed thoughts, and agitated behavior while the drug acts within the brain. Someone drunk on alcohol, for example, may act disinhibited, rowdy, incoherent, or even violently belligerent for a few hours, but then usually falls asleep and upon awakening may have a hangover, and may not even recall behavior from the night before, but otherwise returns to his or her baseline cognitive, psychological, and social state. In contrast, amphetamine-induced psychosis commonly lasts hours, days, or even weeks after the drug has been metabolized by the body [381, 382]. The persistence of the paranoid and other delusional thoughts indicates that stimulant substances can have long-lasting effects on brain functioning [381]. Some recent data suggests that if we follow people with methamphetamine psychosis for several years after their initial psychotic episode, as many as a quarter of them will develop a full-blown, schizophrenia-like condition of permanent psychosis, and this rate is even higher in patients who have a family history of psychotic disorders [381].

Most of the people I have seen who were hospitalized for amphetamine-induced psychosis have wanted to repeat the experience. It is pretty difficult to get into a psychiatric hospital these days, indicating that these individuals were having quite elaborate delusions and substantial problems with testing reality. In all the cases I have seen, the patients had intense paranoid feelings that people, particularly family members, were spying on them, or trying to hurt them, and were conspiring against them; they did not seem to be enjoying themselves in this state, but once out of the hospital they wanted to resume taking stimulants, many of them explicitly desiring to replicate these psychotic states. I have even had patients call me from the hospital trying to negotiate resuming stimulant medication. The desire to replicate their psychotic states is surprising, whereas with classic mania, one can easily imagine that the feelings of omnipotence, high energy, and high sociability would be fun to return to.

None of the numerous experts I have heard lecturing on treatment of ADHD conveyed much concern about amphetamine-induced psychosis, usually remarking on its rarity, often citing a prevalence of less than 1/1000, and then quickly moving on to other topics. Even if this psychosis were this rare, the potential lifelong damage warrants greater concern and attention. Paralleling the experts' apparent lack of alarm about the condition, we have conducted very few studies to pinpoint how commonly it occurs, with indications that it affects about 1/600 to 1/200 patients on stimulants [383-385]. The majority of my patients report never having been informed about this issue by past providers, although it is possible that they were not being attentive when the topic came up, or later forgot what was told to them. I also believe that seeing many cases of amphetamine-induced psychosis has sensitized me to the issue. I have treated many more adults with ADHD (several hundred) than most of my general psychiatry colleagues, but I have also observed a higher rate of occurrence of amphetamine-induced psychosis (between 1/100 and 1/10) than our epidemiological studies would predict. We should be embarrassed by the paucity of information regarding risk factors for developing this condition, given how it can destroy brains and lives. It may be uncommon, but it is not rare. We need to learn more about which aspects of stimulant use (particular substance, dosage and timing, delivery route) and patient characteristics contribute to developing amphetamine-induced psychosis.

I believe my experience very likely overrepresents the frequency of amphetamine-induced psychosis in the US population, and to avoid unnecessarily alarming any readers regarding their own perceived risk of amphetamine-induced psychosis, I will outline why I have seen disproportionately high rates. In San Francisco, general practitioners seem to be more comfortable prescribing stimulants than do doctors in much of the rest of the country. These physicians are mostly prescribing stimulants off-label for conditions such as the fatigue connected with fibromyalgia, cancer chemotherapy, or HIV+, rather than for ADHD. When treatments go well, which may be 90% or 99% of the time, I don't ever see those patients. However, when treatment results in psychosis, these doctors refer their patients out to a psychiatrist with experience prescribing stimulants, and I have been one of the possible choices. Secondly, I am identified in some insurance databases as working with ADHD, and last year alone I was contacted by three patients who had had amphetamine-induced psychosis, wanted to resume stimulants, and figured that an ADHD specialist would be more likely than a random psychiatrist to prescribe stimulants. (All three were men in their twenties, clearly had ADHD, and each had two or three hospitalizations for psychosis.) The third reason I see amphetamine-induced psychosis so often is that I work with many HIV+ gay men. We know, both from the early days of the AIDS crisis—when many patients' initial AIDS presentation was with a neurologic or psychiatric condition—and from the occurrence of HIV-related dementia, that HIV infects and potentially compromises the brain [386] and potentially renders it more vulnerable to other toxins. This patient population also abuses street stimulants, particularly methamphetamine, at higher rates than the general US populations [387]. Theoretically, both the virus and past exposure to meth could make this group more vulnerable to amphetamine-induced psychosis. All of these factors contribute to my seeing amphetamine-induced psychosis at rates substantially higher than what likely occurs in the entire population of adults treated with stimulant medications.

The only encouraging statement I can offer regarding amphetamine-induced psychosis is that most cases I have seen responded quickly to antipsychotic medication. Many patients do well after just a short course, on the order of weeks, of antipsychotic treatment. I am aware that some of my colleagues remain more permissive about reconsidering a low-dose trial after a long period of stable mental health, but even in cases of only a single episode of amphetamine-induced psychosis, I strongly recommend a lifetime ban against any further stimulant treatment, because the risk of recurrence, and of permanent damage, is so high. I also avoid prescribing stimulants initially to anyone with immediate family members who have had clear-cut psychotic disorders. Non-stimulant medications used for ADHD do not appear to have the potential to cause an amphetamine-induced psychosis-like state [371]. While a recent study suggests higher rates of psychosis with amphetamine-based products compared to methylphenidate [385], we need more studies to verify this finding. While research suggests that higher doses of stimulants and perhaps longer exposure increase the risk of developing psychosis [381]—and much of my experience leads me to concur that there is a kernel of truth in this relationship—I have also seen rare individuals obtain decades of benefit from high-dose stimulants without adverse effects. I have also seen individuals who took 5 mg of Adderall (the lowest dose available) and developed psychosis within their first week of treatment. The information we currently possess does not warrant setting arbitrary cut-offs regarding maximal doses of stimulants with the intent of precluding amphetamine-induced psychosis. Nonetheless, doctors and patients should discuss the higher risks of catastrophic outcomes possible with high-dose treatment regimens.

Non-Stimulant Treatments

Given that this is not intended to be a book about ADHD treatment, I will only reiterate that non-stimulants present no risk for psychosis, and have also been found not to have a risk for addiction [117, 388]. That said, non-life threatening but unpleasant side effects—including gastro-intestinal effects, sexual side effects, headache, excessive sweating, and dry mouth—can happen with Strattera and the antidepressants used to treat ADHD [74, 364]. The serotonin-reuptake inhibitors (SSRI) that are the most commonly used agents to treat depression have consistently been found not to be helpful in addressing core symptoms of ADHD [389].

In addition to non-stimulants that directly boost norepinephrine or dopamine, we occasionally prescribe a host of other medications to treat ADHD. In general these agents have smaller benefits or help a smaller fraction of patients than do the stimulants, although some of them have effects that are robust enough that they are either commonly prescribed "off label" or have been approved by the FDA for treating ADHD [390, 391]. These medications include the alpha agonist agents, clonidine and guanfacine, and the "non-stimulant stimulant" modafanil [54]. We also have some recent data that suggests drugs acting on serotonin-7 receptor systems may provide cognitive enhancement and modifications in impulsivity [392]. Accordingly, some patients with ADHD seem to benefit from agents like Trintellix (vortioxetine), Abilify (aripiprazole), or Rexulti (brexpiprazole), which act, in part, on serotonin-7 receptors [393-395]. Of course, all of these drugs have their own set of side effects [393, 395, 396].

Caffeine is a stimulant, and the most widely used psychoactive substance on our planet. We usually consume it at lower effective doses than our prescription stimulants. Although it is largely unregulated, when used at dosages equivalent to prescription stimulants, caffeine probably produces more tremor, more anxiety, and more cardiac toxicity [397]. For some ADHD patients it is a good idea to avoid caffeine entirely; all others should be aware that it is a stimulant which, while it directly acts through a different neurochemical system (adenosine) than ADHD medications, will interact both with stimulants and non-stimulants for ADHD to boost good effects and exacerbate side effects [398].

Non-Medication Treatments

Psychiatrist Aaron Beck developed Cognitive Behavioral Therapy (CBT) at the University of Pennsylvania in the 1960s to treat depression [399]. Mental health practitioners have expanded the use of CBT, particularly to treat a host of mood and anxiety disorders [400], and brain imaging studies show that effective CBT treatment results in changes in brain activation and neurochemistry [401]. In many ways CBT, which requires lots of repetitive homework, note-taking, and self-monitoring of thoughts and behaviors, appears to be a perfect mismatch for ADHD. However, in the last two decades research groups have developed modifications of CBT specifically to treat ADHD [240, 358]. A number of studies demonstrate meaningful benefits from CBT for patients with ADHD [402-404]. For ADHD, most CBT experts recommend the therapy in conjunction with, rather than as an alternative to, medication treatment [54]. CBT for ADHD involves teaching skills of setting up task lists, prioritizing and scheduling tasks, reducing distractions, learning to be aware of the daily internal chatter we engage in, and finding ways to counter negative and unproductive self-messages. During successful treatment with CBT, individuals with ADHD learn what types of environments and structures help them to be productive and decrease the likelihood of becoming mired in distraction.

Although people promote a plethora of other treatment approaches for ADHD, including EEG biofeedback and virtual reality games, so far, the evidence demonstrating long-term, real-world benefit for those with ADHD remains scanty. This does not mean that some of these techniques will not eventually prove helpful, only that we cannot yet make strong claims for efficacy. Similarly, while I certainly encourage my patients to maintain healthy sleep patterns, to eat balanced diets, to engage in a regular exercise regimen, and to develop a meditation practice, we have not yet compiled or extensively tested which elements of these approaches might be particularly beneficial for ADHD symptoms. Furthermore, I have not seen adults with genuine ADHD sustain substantial symptom resolution from any combination of these approaches in the absence of medications or CBT. Although many of the people I work with and treat experience greater calmness, clarity, and emotional resilience lasting hours after brief meditation sessions, many individuals with ADHD find it particularly frustrating and difficult to quiet their minds. In my experience, those with ADHD tend to be more receptive to meditation approaches that employ visual imagery, breathing, or movement/yoga rather than attempts to empty their minds of all thoughts.

One final message about treatment: Although fierce protagonists and antagonists of various approaches often stake out absolutist positions, all courses of action have consequences, no options completely eliminate ADHD symptoms, and no options are devoid of possible side effects. ADHD harms people; the "side effects" of not engaging in treatment can include failed relationships, disrupted careers, injury, and death [25, 30]. Our talk therapies, including CBT, have costs that can include substantial investments of time and money and potentially delaying initiation of more effective therapies. Although the act of taking medications to treat a condition like ADHD can lead some people to feel "broken," "defective," or "in need of fixing," psychotherapy for some individuals may inculcate these notions even more strongly because the therapy itself forces them to spend more time examining their shortcomings. Poorly administered psychotherapies can worsen despair, loneliness, and feelings of being misunderstood. I usually advocate approaching the treatment of ADHD on as many levels as possible (sleep, diet, exercise, meditation, medication, psychotherapy, optimizing work situations, and relationships), along with attempts to assess the costs and benefits of every course of action, and tailoring each option to what has been shown to work and what is acceptable to the patient.

Trump's Treatment for ADHD

Is anyone treating Trump's ADHD? Before I jump into the issue of whether he uses stimulant medications for his ADHD, I should mention that we have already seen his staff using behaviorally based treatments targeting his ADHD. One prominent example involved taking away his Twitter feed during the last weeks of the 2016 election in order to decrease the likelihood of impulsive tweets and last-minute gaffes [405]. Also, the replacement of Reince Priebus with John Kelly as chief of staff [355] seemed designed to more tightly structure the flow of information into and out of Trump's head, to reduce some of the unreflective actions resulting from his ADHD. Following the removal of General Kelly, many observers, myself included, anticipated correctly that we would see far more displays of ADHD-driven behavior by the president, because so many of the grown-ups that had performed executive functions for him had "left the room."

As I noted in Chapter 4, many of the behavioral symptoms of hyperactive ADHD resemble the effects produced by too much stimulant medication. Trump's disjointed sentences, impulsiveness, incessant restlessness, and frequent sniffing have caused many to wonder whether his unusual behaviors result from the use of stimulants. The physician and former Governor of Vermont, Howard Dean, speculated during the 2016 presidential campaign that Trump had a cocaine habit [406]. Claims by Tom Arnold and others that they frequently witnessed Trump snorting Adderall while on the set of *The Apprentice* [407], seem to bolster these speculations. Snorts of derision usually accompany mention of Trump's alleged inhalation of stimulants (cocaine, Adderall, or others), again signaling that people blame the stimulants for some of his ADHD-driven behavior. Perhaps, however, rather than riffing on his sniffing, we should be supporting his snorting, or more precisely, praising his gumption for prescription stimulant consumption.

For years, sleuths have nosed into whether Trump habitually uses stimulant medications. *Newsweek* investigated doctors who prescribed Trump diethylpropion, a weight-control medication [408]. *Gawker* reported similar claims about his use of a related medication, phentermine [409]. The FDA has not approved either of these drugs for the treatment of ADHD [410], although basic research, a few studies, and a wealth of clinical lore indicates that these stimulates can help reduce some ADHD symptoms [411]. Incidentally, due to quirks in our drug classification, government agencies restrict prescriptions for these "weight-loss" stimulants much less rigidly than prescriptions for Ritalin or Adderall [412], so they may not show up in some states' registries of prescriptions for controlled substances, thereby making their use harder to trace. Many of the rumors about Trump's use of stimulants, perhaps influenced by his chronic sniffing, swirl around allegations that he snorts the medications [407]. Crushing and then snorting of stimulants, in contrast to swallowing, allows more rapid absorption into the blood and faster entry into the brain, which heightens the euphoric effects of the drugs and increases the risk for addiction [413]. For this reason, mental health experts strongly recommend against snorting stimulant medications. Even if one has ADHD, snorting stimulants may provide markedly different results than ingesting the same stimulant medication.

Not being an investigative reporter, I had little ability to verify whether Trump was using stimulant medications. However, after the 2019 State of the Union (SOU) speech, friends forwarded Twitter links to me, commenting on how dilated Trump's pupils were during the speech, and indicating that this was a sign of his amphetamine use. Amphetamines and other stimulants certainly can cause pupillary dilation [414, 415]. When I looked at video of the SOU I was impressed by how large Trump's pupils appeared, and in contrast, were much smaller in other speeches that week. The time course of the changes in Trump's pupillary size—very large during a particular speech, then small in subsequent days and large again during another critical speech—rule out that a chronic health condition such as brain or neurologic damage has been causing these fluctuations in pupil size. Also, because his pupils remained enlarged throughout the speech, lasting more than an hour, we know that the dilation was not merely the result of over-excitation (some strong emotions, or rapt attention, can cause pupils to dilate, but this usually lasts only a few seconds) [414]. Pupillary diameter most closely tracks ambient light [415]; perhaps dimmer lighting during the SOU caused pupillary dilation compared to talks in brighter settings. This explanation proved highly unsatisfactory, because 1) others next to Trump do not have similarly dilated pupils; 2) when he moved from the podium to other positions in the Capitol, his pupils remained dilated; 3) the lighting at the SOU does not actually appear dim, nor does it appear to be particularly bright in the comparison settings; and 4) his eyelids remained hooded during the SOU, as if trying to protect his retinae from too much light; if his pupils were dilating to let in more light to enable to him to see, we would expect his eyelids to similarly open widely. If lighting, brain damage, and emotions weren't driving his pupillary dilation, what remains? A handful of medications cause pupillary dilation, foremost the stimulants (prescription or otherwise, and including decongestants), a few of our hallucinogens (LSD, marijuana), and some antimuscarinic agents, such as atropine and related drugs, which ophthalmologists use to dilate pupils in order to conduct thorough eye exams [415].

I was pretty convinced that Trump used stimulants during his SOU speech in order to treat his ADHD and be more focused, less distractible, and less impetuous. So, I conducted two small studies. In one I compared his appearance and behavior during two important speeches (SOU[416], and his Border Wall Address[417]) against a speech to the American Farm Bureau[418] delivered that same month. In the second study I compared his performance during the third presidential debate with Clinton[419] to his performance during debates one[420] and two[421]. The second study helps eliminate whatever role a teleprompter may play in some of Trump's speeches (although he is clearly capable of going off message even with a teleprompter), and also utilizes Clinton as a control subject performing under similar lighting conditions. I observed whether he was speaking in complete sentences or in language of incomplete thoughts, run-ons, and tangents. I counted how many times he made dramatic arm, hand, head, or torso gestures. And I measured, at several points, the size of his pupil relative to his iris. The results of the studies agreed so thoroughly that I have combined the results and will lump the third debate in with the "important speeches," putting the first two in the "baseline category."

In the baseline speeches, most of Trump's sentences were fragmentary and his tone strident, in contrast to uttering complete sentences and delivering them in relatively calm cadences during the important speeches. He gesticulated and moved around three times as much in the baseline speeches as in the important speeches. And while Trump's pupils occupied only 10%-20% of his irises in baseline speeches, they dilated to cover roughly 50%-60% throughout each of the important speeches. In contrast, Clinton displayed very consistent speech patterns, gesture frequency, and pupil dilation (invariant at 10%-15%) throughout all three debates. As I pointed out in Chapter 5 with my "simultaneous rule," people find it extremely challenging to be aware of and alter their patterns of speech or fidgetiness, and voluntarily controlling both at the same time, particularly for someone with ADHD. I contend that Trump's use of stimulant medications before these important speeches provides the only compelling explanation for his dilated pupils occurring in synchrony with dramatic alterations in his speech and physical movements. Furthermore, separate from the content of these speeches, the medication intervention delivered the desired effects: He appeared more calm, reasoned, reasonable, organized, and effective. Whatever stimulant he is taking, and however he is using it, helps make him act more presidential on those occasions.

I hope that the president begins to take stimulant medications more consistently, and that he consumes them in conventional ways, not snorting them because he thinks he "nose best." We should not be turning up our own noses at medications that have so much potential to help him stay on track, curb his impulses, and otherwise behave in ways more reflective, and not reflexive. I hope the awareness that his dilated pupils help indicate when he might be taking stimulant medication does not deter him from using this invaluable aid. Trump, his administration, and the whole country will benefit from ongoing recognition of, and effective treatment for, his ADHD.

Section II

(CHIEF) EXECUTIVE FUNCTION DISORDER

CHAPTER 7

BEYOND DSM-5: ADHD AS EXECUTIVE FUNCTION DISORDER

ADHD causes not just inattention and hyperactivity, but reflects a more fundamental problem with regulating and directing the flow of thoughts, behaviors, and emotions in order to function in the world [3]. While Problems Regulating and Directing the Flow of Thoughts, Behaviors and Emotions (PRDFTBE, anyone?) may be a more accurate label than ADHD, PRDFTBE lacks both succinctness and the historical usage of the terms ADD or ADHD. I have heard with increasing frequency the suggestion that "Executive Function Disorder" may be a more accurate and user-friendly label to replace ADHD, but it has yet to gain widespread acceptance.

Lesion studies, where we examine the functioning of brains with structural damage, reveal that most executive functions in humans require intact frontal lobes of the brain. My list of executive functions includes directing attention, maintaining attention, organizing and prioritizing information, managing time, using working memory, monitoring responses, suppressing immediate responses, regulating emotions, and long-term planning [4, 358]. Although we are increasingly learning about the brain circuitry underlying these tasks, our understanding remains rudimentary, and many of these tasks clearly intertwine with each other. Thus, each research group has different ways of parsing and defining the executive functions, and we lack one simple, universally accepted list of executive functions. In the following paragraphs I will attempt to show how the concept of Executive Function Disorder expands our understanding of ADHD beyond problems with attention, hyperactivity, and impulsivity.

ADHD impairs different subsets of executive functions in each individual, and the severity of impairment also differs [422], along with the compensatory strengths that each individual possesses to mitigate the effects of any particular deficit [146]. Not everyone with ADHD will display difficulties in the same way, but everyone with ADHD will show substantial problems with at least some of these executive functions.

Executive Function Disorder (EFD) demonstrates one immediate advantage over the term ADHD, because it correctly places emphasis on the impairment of the *control* of attention, rather than implying that attention itself is always defective. If ADHD globally damaged attention we would expect that individuals with ADHD would fail to be attentive in all situations, which is manifestly not the case. I am going to belabor this point, because I continue to be shocked and chagrined by the number of teachers, therapists, and patients who are convinced that someone couldn't have ADHD given the ability to focus in a favorite class, or to work for hours on an engaging project. A woman I recently evaluated worked as a recruiter and described 1) being chronically late for appointments and dates, 2) repeatedly losing her keys and her phone, 3) constantly zoning out in meetings and in phone calls with friends, and 4) routinely flitting from topic to topic in conversations until she became aware that she had lost track of whatever point she initially wanted to communicate. Yet she still proclaimed, "I can't have ADHD! I'm so attentive when I'm interviewing applicants!" If we understand that ADHD disrupts the control of attention, not attention itself, then we can more easily comprehend how her pattern of both failures and successes in the realm of attention actually describes a typical profile of someone with ADHD. Likewise, Trump's ability to stay on script and read a State of the Union speech from a teleprompter [219], or his penchant for accurately recounting some details of voting tallies from his electoral victory [423], do not refute the accuracy of his ADHD diagnosis. In ADHD, attention usually fluctuates between being under-modulated (distractible, jumping from topic to topic) or over-modulated (hyperfocused, fixated on a topic when everyone else has moved on) [2,424,425].

Executive Functions and Regulating Attention

Although they are related, directing attention, maintaining attention, and switching attention are distinct tasks [422]. To use a simple analogy: Directing attention is shining the spotlight precisely on an actress on the stage; maintaining attention is making sure the light is kept on (even during a monotonously long monologue); switching attention is moving the light back and forth between the actress and a second actor who enters the scene. Trump is notorious for problems with directing attention [184,426]. While deflection is in the arsenal of most every politician, the standard approach is to acknowledge the question and then move on to what you would rather talk about. Trump invariably starts with the deflection—he often cannot direct his brain to the question actually asked. Virtually every recounting of a one-on-one interaction with him describes the near impossibility of directing his attention, even when they are biographers or authors who are trying to get him to address a topic that he is clearly interested in: himself! [7,184] He also frequently displays problems with maintaining attention. One notable example was his inability to stick with numerous verbal and written instructions not to congratulate Vladimir Putin on his 2018 sham-election victory [427]. None of the accounts describe Trump arguing against this advice, which he would have done if he hadn't accepted it as reasonable; nonetheless, a few minutes into the conversation he lost track of the one directive he'd been given, and congratulated the leader of Russia [428]. Trump is perhaps most well-known for going off topic in his speeches [216,218]; it is considered a victory when he manages only a few deviations [219]. Trump's difficulty in switching attention was skillfully exploited by Clinton during their debates, when she brought up emotionally charged topics (the millions of dollars borrowed from his father to start his business, owing millions to Wall Street and foreign businesses, not paying any federal taxes, his verbal abuse of beauty pageant contestants) [326, 429]. He was unable to pull himself away from these topics, even though they reflected poorly on him, and he continued harping on them [326, 429]. In fact this perseveration, in which someone repeats or prolongs an action, thought, or utterance after the stimulus that prompted it has ceased, is a hallmark of ADHD [424].

Trump clearly has problems with organizing and prioritizing information. Although he repeatedly denies it, the word "chaotic" is brought up in many descriptions regarding his administration, including by those who support him politically [8, 195, 200, 430]. He most succinctly and hilariously displays this difficulty in prioritizing and organizing his thoughts with his daily tweets. Even when constrained to only 280 characters he frequently can't seem to decide what to say. During his first two years in office he often started out attacking Barack Obama or Hillary Clinton as the worst person ever, but mid-tweet would interrupt himself to claim that James Comey or Robert Mueller or some underling, aide, or ally that he was quarreling with at that moment is actually a worse example of humanity [283, 286]. Trump blatantly and less humorously displayed this difficulty organizing and prioritizing on a larger scale, when, for example, he couldn't decide to try to ignore Syria completely, or take a role in trying to impose peace, or punish their government for bad behavior [202]. His difficulty in deciding what is important, and sticking with it, is partly why his lawyers have advised him to avoid testifying under oath [431], and why his advisors don't want him to be left alone with foreign leaders [432].

Some of Trump's problems with controlling attention, and organizing and prioritizing information, contribute to his difficulties with long term planning. If all of one's bandwidth is consumed by the chaotic jumble of events occurring in one's immediate surroundings, there is little left for thinking about the future. However, as with other individuals with ADHD, even when his life is calm in the moment, Trump is unable to devote thought or attention to future events, and thus displays a strong tendency to discount them altogether. In his real estate career, he showed signs of overly focusing on the present moment, and not preparing or planning for the future; economists attest that he did not have much of a general strategy or vision, but more often focused on flashy assets that he strongly desired, and would then obsessively pursue, even if it meant overpaying for those acquisitions [7]. Insider accounts very consistently portray that not only was Trump surprised by his election victory, but that he had done virtually no planning for the possibility that he might actually win [187, 433]. Even simple planning for the contingencies of his major actions seems absent: He voiced surprise that China or other countries might want to retaliate for threatened impositions of tariffs [434], or that Russia might object to us bombing their allies [435]. Not filling ambassadorships to important countries such as Saudi Arabia, South Korea, and Germany for months on end [194], when relationships with those countries were important to "Making America Great Again," also demonstrates his deficiencies both in planning for the future and in prioritizing and organizing information.

Deficits In Working Memory

Trump's working memory deficits are at times intimately entangled with his problems managing attention, but also manifest themselves in other ways. Getting off track can arise from distractibility or from failing to remember one's own agenda, or a combination of the two. Another area in which Trump seems to exhibit increasing deficits in working memory would be the paucity of, and continued diminution of, his vocabulary, even when discounting for his neologisms (bigly, covfefe) [436]. Despite apparently having scored well on an intelligence test [260], and clearly knowing many more words than he uses, Trump fills his speech with repetitive, vague generalities and magnifiers (sad, huge, big, the best) [436] as if he can't keep specific details in mind, whether he is praising or castigating. (As discussed in Chapter 4, some of these deficits may represent more recent dementia superimposed on his ADHD.)

Executive Function and Difficulties With Self Monitoring

Many people with ADHD have difficulty with the executive function of self-monitoring, including keeping track of what their body is or is not doing. An adult who tells me that he "just forgot to eat all day" invariably turns out to be someone with ADHD, and very often not even one who is taking stimulant medications, which can certainly impair appetite. Many people with ADHD, while very sensitive to distracting noises that others make, persist in foot tapping or knuckle cracking for minutes on end without awareness that the sound might annoy others. Many people with ADHD have trouble assessing when they are getting tired, and may stay awake until they become overwhelmingly fatigued. Individuals with ADHD are also greatly overrepresented among adults who get louder and louder during emotional moments in a conversation. I have had numerous discussions in public places with adults with ADHD who displayed no awareness that they ended up shouting about some past incident that had been terribly embarrassing to them, and no awareness that the volume of their speech potentially created another such mortifying moment.

The previous example demonstrates that deficits in self-monitoring are not limited to physical aspects of the body, but also extend to aspects of how an individual presents themselves in social interactions [82]. I have moderated many couples' therapy sessions where a partner with ADHD was flabbergasted to be told that they had cut the other person off, made very insulting comments, or displayed hand or facial gestures that were strongly menacing. In contrast, when I see people without ADHD act in such ways, they are usually either extremely defensive or shameful about their behavior. Many of the comments Trump has made about having a good temperament, a good brain, or a stable mind, seem quite defensive, and he has uttered other comments about himself that come across as grandiose and intentionally inflated [286]. However, an aura of total cluelessness pervades a majority of his self-statements: Despite being a successful showman, he often lacks awareness regarding what large blocks of his behavior convey to others, because he is not registering with his own brain what he is actually doing.

Executive Functions and Impulse Control

ADHD impairs the executive functions of suppressing immediate responses, which presents as "poor impulse control" [3]. ADHD makes it more likely that one will blurt out whatever one is thinking in the moment. Trump does this on a daily basis, and pundits have written in amazement that any one of his inappropriate comments or tweets would have torpedoed the career of other politicians [437]. Trump himself has tried, often successfully, to convert this trait into a virtue, by showing how unscripted and non-PC he is, and how he "calls it like it is" [438]. However, this blurs an important distinction between candor and honesty: Just because he is saying whatever he feels in the moment does not assure that what he is saying is accurate or truthful. In fact, by numerous objective measures, he has been far less truthful than even the average American politician [439]; we could rate him an outlier among out-and-out liars. Trump's poor impulse control contributes to contradicting himself, often seconds or minutes after he has made a statement [182, 440, 441]; this has alienated friends [442, 443] and enraged opponents [303, 444], and contributes to anxiety among his allies, who worry that he will undermine his own actions by his impetuousness [433, 445].

Time Management Problems

Examples of time management problems that are rife in people with ADHD include procrastination and tardiness. Most of those with ADHD have great difficulty estimating how much time will be required for a task, although clearly CBT and other approaches can help them become more adept at such evaluations [240, 358]. One time management issue displayed by Trump is his iconic 3:00 a.m. tweeting [235] and his propensity for phone calls at inappropriate times to foreign leaders in other time zones [446]. He demonstrated procrastination problems by waiting until the last few days to try to lobby legislators on health care reform or the tax bill [181, 447, 448], even though these items were prominent on the legislative agenda for months before they came up for a vote, and both represented issues that the administration had designated as having utmost importance.

Executive Functions and Emotional Regulation

Although the formal DSM criteria for ADHD does not address emotional regulation, psychologists Russell Barkley and Thomas Brown, among many other ADHD researchers, argue forcefully that deficits in this executive function are intrinsic and important features of ADHD, and are strongly associated with hyperactive variants of ADHD [424, 449]. Emotional dysregulation is characterized by low frustration tolerance, irritability, and moods that arise quickly and intensely enough to become overwhelming [234]. Such emotional outbursts also have a tendency to be short-lived, so that if another distraction arises, it can pull not just attention, but the emotional state as well, in a new direction. My favorite example of Trump displaying poor emotional regulation was in his debate with Clinton when he started shouting over and over how his "strongest asset" was his temperament [450]. Trump generates countless new emotional outbursts weekly, and more often daily. His emotional volatility, in combination with his poor impulse control, further heightens the risk that he will overreact to a perceived insult by creating a major international confrontation—including war. Although he or his staff may use some of these emotional outbursts to strengthen a bargaining position or in an attempt to intimidate enemies [430], the vast number of these episodes display no clear strategic rationale, and thus appear to be simply manifestations of his ADHD.

Understanding that ADHD is a problem of executive functions helps explain why ADHD contributes to such a range of problems beyond just having trouble with attention. In Trump's case, knowing about ADHD reveals how pervasively and strongly this condition affects how he presents to the world, and helps explain his outbursts, utterances, actions, and absences. Without comprehension of his ADHD and what that entails, our view of him remains a confusing, self-contradictory amalgamation of hubris, candor, mendacity, decisiveness, waffling, strength, insecurity, intelligence, stupidity, creativity, banality, success, and failure. These contrasts and incompatibilities almost force people to look only at subsets of his traits and characteristics, and therefore obscure the overall picture of who he is and how his behavior threatens our country and the world. Learning about ADHD provides a pathway to predicting how he is likely to act, including his continued unpredictability, and offers a roadmap for developing strategies to cope with, and respond to, his presence. Hopefully we can take the knowledge gained in the public sphere from observing Trump's ADHD in action, and translate that information into useful approaches for working and living with other individuals with ADHD.

CHAPTER 8

PERSISTENTLY INCONSISTENT: EXECUTIVE DYSFUNCTIONS EXPLAIN ADHD SYMPTOMS

While the title Executive Function Disorder (EFD) captures how pervasively ADHD affects the flow of information into and out of an individual's brain [358, 424], most of us, most of the time, employ more colloquial language to discuss human behavior, rather than fancy neuropsychological terms. In this chapter I highlight some of the phrases that I commonly use to describe ADHD-based behavior, and then translate these idioms into their underlying executive function deficits. The folk wisdom encapsulated in these sayings perfectly targets problems that many individuals with ADHD confront in daily life. My patients have found these casual phrases about ADHD to be particularly helpful in elucidating their own patterns of action and thought. These phrases can also help clarify what patients may need to do to improve their lives, and can sometimes suggest specific pathways out of the pitfalls of ADHD.

Not Seeing the Forest for the Trees

Because of the executive function deficit in directing attention, people with ADHD often become consumed with what is right in front of them, and often lose sight of items in the periphery as well as of the bigger picture. ADHD makes it harder to contextualize and to remember that what is in one's awareness right now is always just a part of one's existence, not the whole of it. This leads to not seeing the forest for the trees—i.e., details become so salient to those with ADHD that they miss the larger picture. President Trump, having boasted that he would fix health care, immigration, and the economy, complained in his first months of office that "nobody said it would be this complicated" (or hard, or complex, depending on which topic he was referring to) [451, 452]. Of course, people had been making exactly these pronouncements [453], which he had previously ignored (largely because of his ADHD itself). Often, just reminding those with ADHD that they are in a forest can significantly help in encouraging them to broaden their perspective away from the one tree that is confounding them.

Jack of All Trades, Master of None

Many people with ADHD tend to flit from topic to topic, learning much about many things but typically not penetrating deeply into single topics. Problems with executive functions of directing attention (focus jumps too readily from one topic to another), sustaining attention (focus doesn't remain fixed on any one subject), and poor long-term planning all contribute to this phenomenon. Another phrasing of this concept was provided by the father of Frank (my patient from Chapter 1), who told him, "Don't spread yourself too thin or you'll never make anything of yourself." Although there are certainly individuals with ADHD who become fascinated enough with a subject to completely immerse themselves in it (which may signal a problem with inability to switch attention), there are many extremely bright people with ADHD who flit from project to project, or career to career, never settling on one.

Often our society deprecates this type of life trajectory, but in the modern era, where many jobs don't last a lifetime, and even entire industries may last for a shorter span than an individual's working years, more and more people do change jobs and careers. Increasingly, having performed a number of tasks moderately well (rather than being a virtuoso at one) may be considered only a different—rather than an inferior—pathway through life. Trump's careers in real estate, luxury goods, reality television, and politics certainly exemplify dabbling in many areas, and although he has achieved great prominence in some of these areas, many of his cohorts in each of these fields would not rate his performances as exemplary [454-456]; very few experts in any of these fields regard him as a top-notch real estate mogul, salesman, performer, or president.

All Surface, No Depth

The executive function problems with directing, sustaining, and switching attention contribute to an accusation lobbed at many people with ADHD, that they are "all surface, and no depth." This phrase refers in part to problems arising from the control of attention, but also highlights that many people with ADHD are particularly visually oriented. This excessive emphasis on appearances may have origins in the excessive development and abnormal connectivity of cortical areas processing visual attention, alluded to in Chapter 2 [87, 89]. If this is the case, then the excessive resonance with visual information may actually reinforce some of the attentional problems. That is, if the pictorial aspects of items or situations are particularly captivating to someone, this may encourage frequent shifting from one interesting image to another, rather than exploring in depth other aspects of the object in question. In a related vein, Trump has been quoted as saying, "The day I realized it can be smart to be shallow was for me, a deep experience" [457].

Trump displays this emphasis on surfaces and appearances with his ongoing preoccupation to build a wall on the Mexican border. A generation of politicians decried problems with border security without this becoming a prominent issue for the voting public. However, in 2017, Trump made the issue of border security resonate far more strongly, both for himself and for his supporters, despite an entire decade of actual declines in immigration across our southern borders [458]; he did this by reducing the concept of border security to a simple image of building a wall [459]. Similarly, several economists have noted Trump's reliance on what is concrete and visible when he talks about international commerce [460]: He frequently discounts the service industry when calculating trade deficits, despite it making up a large part of our economy, because if he can't see it as goods then it doesn't count, in his mind [460, 461].

Trump especially demonstrates his fixation on surface features when he describes women, attending to their superficial appearance rather than their intelligence, personality, performance, or other attributes [311]. His penchant for reducing his assessment of female beauty to a single number on a 1-10 scale [462, 463], and even rating female prime ministers, business executives, and others in a similar manner [283], succinctly captures Trump's superficiality. One completely neglected aspect of his infamous "locker room talk" in the *Access Hollywood* 2005 video highlights how bizarrely superficial his focus can be [464]. Most of the criticism of his behavior in this video focused on the sexism, violence, and vulgarity of his comments about imagining meeting a beautiful woman and wanting to "grab her by the pussy." I have heard scores of men verbalize their imagined sexual conquests, and they always talk about what sex acts they would like to perform or have performed on them. Not once have I heard anybody other than Trump utter a sexual fantasy that is both so graphic and simultaneously stops so abruptly at the surface level: All he wants is to grasp a woman's genitals. The *Access Hollywood* video strikingly revealed Trump to be a sexual predator, but moreover, because of his focus on visuals and his disinterest in penetrating the surface, exposed to me his underlying ADHD.

While many individuals with ADHD display heightened attraction to visual appearances, many also seem to contradictorily become overwhelmed by too much visual information [240]. Although all of us occasionally search for an object that is right in front of us, those with ADHD manifest this behavior much more frequently. For these individuals, exposure to too much visual information floods their processing centers, impairing their ability to discern and recognize familiar objects that they clearly had scanned. At a more extreme level, I know numerous patients with ADHD who have severe anxiety, including full-blown panic attacks, triggered by situations in which they felt so bombarded by a pandemonium of pictures that they perceived being attacked. Many of them feel completely overwhelmed by shopping at big-box grocery stores or other venues where the number and variety of items on display is simply "too much."

We can employ the knowledge that many people with ADHD are particularly attuned to pictorial information to help craft visual reminders that are far more vivid and useful to them than lists of words, or written sequences of directions. Some of my patients create chore lists by snapping photos on their phone of their sink with dirty dishes, or the car that needs to be moved to a new parking space, or their laundry hamper, because this feels relatable and manageable to them, whereas they respond to a written list of these same chores by blanking out and ignoring the whole thing. Similarly, I have worked with numerous people with ADHD who could never meditate by "emptying their mind of thoughts" but who could enter a meditated state readily through guided imagery, using pictures in their mind to calm and focus their thoughts. For those trying to engage Trump on public policy debates, it will remain easier to get him to focus on concrete images (building walls) than on more conceptual or comprehensive aspects (e.g., reasonable standards for political asylum).

Importance-Driven vs. Interest-Driven Brains

A particularly potent phrase that resonates with many individuals with ADHD is that most brains are importance-driven, whereas ADHD brains are interest-driven. This interesting vs. important dichotomy encapsulates the executive functions of directing and maintaining attention, and of prioritizing and organizing information. Almost everyone with ADHD can immediately come up with instances in which they knew there was an important task to perform (move the car to avoid a parking ticket, pay a bill, take out the garbage) but instead of doing it they engaged in a more interesting distraction (watching cat videos, checking email, arranging shampoo bottles) or a series of distractions, until they completely lost track of the important task they had intended to accomplish. Pursuing the interesting to the detriment of the important frequently and powerfully harms those with ADHD. Furthermore, these interest-not-importance-driven behaviors particularly annoy, baffle, irritate, and horrify the people around them. "Why were you doing X when you should have been doing Y?" is a common refrain among parents, teachers, partners, bosses, aides, and countries dealing with someone who has ADHD. Confirmation that Trump has an interest-driven brain is how often he uses the term "boring" to dismiss people, events, tasks, and problems that potentially have major impact on him, the country, or the world, but that he doesn't find stimulating enough to devote much time or thought to [190, 465, 466].

By replacing the important with the interesting, those with ADHD risk appearing shallow or eccentric. For example, in the presidential debates Trump knew that it was important to stay on target and "look presidential" but when some bright, shiny topic surfaced he lunged for it—e.g., with outbursts about how smart he was to not pay taxes, or to lambaste Rosie O'Donnell [283, 429]. A more horrifying example is Trump's widely reported claim that daily intelligence briefings are unnecessary because they aren't interesting enough to warrant his attention [149, 153, 187]. Other instances include focusing on personal spats (a Senator's fealty to him, NFL players' actions) [467, 468] while ignoring major ongoing issues (Puerto Ricans suffering from a hurricane or Californians suffering from wildfires) [469, 470]. While it has been suggested that at times he makes political or strategic decisions to address distracting peripheral issues primarily to connect with his base of supporters, the pervasiveness of these diversions, and how often they don't accord with his previously stated political philosophies (much less vital national concerns), shows ADHD to be the primary driving force behind his so often going off topic and wading into trivia.

Pursuing the path of interest over importance can also result in a person with ADHD being uninformed in areas that are of paramount significance. Our world is so stuffed with information that each of us remains unaware of, or unfamiliar with, whole realms of knowledge, but these lacunae do not usually encompass tasks that are vital to our daily work. Trump's ADHD accounts for why he remains profoundly ignorant of and appallingly uninterested in critical elements of the presidency, to such an extent that others frequently misinterpret his ignorance as merely demonstrating that he is stupid, an idiot, or reportedly, in the words of his former Secretary of State, a "f***ing moron" [20].

Even more dangerously, Trump seems to have no qualms about directly wading into and making pronouncements about topics of which he is utterly ignorant. His ADHD propensity for poor impulse control, along with his interest-not-importance-driven knowledge, and his (non-ADHD) hubris, all contribute to this pattern of behavior. Republican congressmen were aghast when he lobbied them about health care bills without having any awareness about what the proposed legislation contained [181]. His generals and foreign service advisors had to stage a History 101 lesson several months into his reign because he was completely unfamiliar with US nuclear capabilities and those of other countries, as well as the basics of recent world history and of diplomacy [446, 471, 472]. He has repeatedly spoken in ways that demonstrate huge gaps in his understanding of what is in the Constitution, how our judicial system works, or the basics of international commerce [190, 461, 473, 474]. While it is certainly possible that he is genuinely stupid, so far all we can know for certain is that he remains amazingly, monumentally, and dangerously uninformed. If he does possess basic intelligence, there exists at least a chance that he could learn the material, provided someone makes it interesting enough for him to even attempt it.

Motivators for "interest-driven" ADHD brains include not just strong desires and joys but also strong fears. For example, although most individuals with ADHD have issues with punctuality, almost a third of my patients with ADHD claim to not have problems with tardiness. One subset of this group consists of those who actually are habitually tardy, but who don't consider being "only five minutes" (… or ten minutes, or a half hour) as late. However, about ten percent of my ADHD patients do consistently manage to be on time, often after years of concerted efforts to achieve this. Those individuals that succeed in being punctual tend to have either a particularly strong fear of being late (e.g. shame at being perceived as disrespectful) or a particularly strong desire to be timely (e.g. pride in being seen as well prepared). For Trump, many of the fears that appear to strongly motivate him relate to his insecurity about being perceived as not smart or manly enough, resulting in over-focusing on his performance on IQ tests [475], on being "like, a smart person" [149], on his "excellent" physical health [261], or the size of his body parts [476].

Getting Off Track

Diverting attention from important to interesting topics results in people with ADHD "getting off track" very frequently. This results from executive function problems with maintaining attention, organizing and prioritizing information, long-term planning, and time management. Activities that require multiple, sequential steps are particularly challenging because they provide so many opportunities to go off track. Among other things, this results in procrastination and not completing assignments. Many with severe ADHD become so consumed by their perceived failures and how often they have gotten off track that their very focus on having been derailed becomes a distraction. Much of the treatment of ADHD is based on finding techniques or medications that help patients stay on track longer, in addition to methods for getting back on track more quickly once they have derailed.

I have a diagnostic test for ADHD based on people going off track. My office is in a two-unit building with separate entrances: a front house door visible from the street, and an office door perpendicular to the street at the end of a short driveway. Whether verbally or in writing, I always provide the same directions, stating that there is a house at the main address, and the office is at the end of the driveway with a separate address. Sometimes I know in advance that the patient is seeking help with ADHD, and at other times neither I nor the patient know in advance that ADHD is part of the clinical picture. Every client who has ever shown up at the front house door and has rung the doorbell had ADHD; patients without ADHD have never gone to the wrong entrance. Thus, the test has perfect specificity and the predictive value of a positive test has been a perfect 100%. However, the sensitivity of the test is not particularly high, as at least 60% of my clients with ADHD did arrive at the correct office door on their first visit. Again, this is not a measure of intelligence; with too much information to remember on an initial visit, many people with ADHD lose track of some of the vital facts. Clearly this diagnostic test does not serve as a screening tool for ADHD, and in any case is not applicable to most other settings.

Getting off track results in missed deadlines, incomplete projects, cancelled dates and appointments, and a sense of failure and disappointment both for the individuals with ADHD and those around them. Those with a history of repeatedly falling off track often become aware when they have gotten distracted again, which can trigger immediate feelings of being overwhelmed or discouraged; in these situations, they perceive that they can't get anything right or they have failed again. One of the most helpful interventions I make in therapy is reminding adults with ADHD that (1) while everyone gets distracted at least occasionally, because of how their brain works they are far more prone to getting off track than others—and (2) that life is more about getting back on track than fretting when one gets off track. Working to get back on results in greater accomplishment and fulfillment; staying off track leads to feelings of failure.

Trump claimed that as an experienced businessman he would govern efficiently, but because of his executive function deficits his performance has repeatedly gotten off track. He has performed subpar on numerous objective measures such as proposing and filling sub-cabinet positions, retaining cabinet officials, or presenting legislation to Congress [181, 194, 357]. His poor executive functioning has led to many projects going off track, including implementation of many of the policies that he indicated were his favored projects (travel bans, restricting transgender individuals from the military, et al.). Some of Trump's critics even applaud his inefficiency and repeated derailments, because they fear that a more organized chief executive would have dismantled many more of the programs they support than what Trump has been able to demolish so far.

Over-Promise, Under-Deliver

Over-promise, under-deliver describes another common behavior of people with ADHD, and derives from executive function deficits in emotion regulation, impulse control, planning, prioritizing, and sustaining attention. Whether in a classroom, PTA meeting, work conference, or on the campaign trail, people with ADHD are more likely to become excited by a new task or project and to jump in and volunteer to take on the work before assessing whether they have the time or skills required. Being over-committed then compounds their problems with planning, prioritizing, and focusing, because they really are trying to accomplish more than a routine amount of work. As their interest wanes and distractions arise, they squander time, become less productive, and miss deadlines.

Some with ADHD do manage productive, creative lives, but they usually have been taught or have devised structural mechanisms (calendars, reminders, low-distraction workspaces) to keep themselves on track, or they have the luxury of aides, assistants, spouses, or others to perform executive functions for them. While we don't yet know how much the Trump administration might accomplish, we already know he has over-promised and under-delivered. I predict that by 2020 we will not see a completed wall on our southern border, paid for by the Mexicans (or anyone else), or a complete halt to illegal immigration, or the creation of millions of jobs in manufacturing or coal industries, or dramatic decreases in violent crime, or an elimination of our trade deficits, or a health care plan in place of Obamacare, or a Chinese government acting subserviently to the US.

Free Time Is Your Enemy

Session after session I remind many of my ADHD patients that "free time is your enemy." Because of executive function problems with time management, organization, and planning of tasks, they squander much of their free time with meaningless tasks, or with dithering about what task to engage in at all. Often at an initial exam, after hearing about some workplace difficulties that are clearly ADHD-driven, I often suggest that weekends might be an even bigger source of distress, and consistently I hear "How did you know?" in response. Although there are certainly cases of horrible mismatches between individuals and their job requirements, most people with ADHD can manage at work, at least in part because their day is structured for them—when to show up and leave, and what tasks are reasonable to get done in a given amount of time. Often co-workers or managers help remind them of work project timelines and assist in keeping tasks on track. Furthermore, in our society, many people don't expect to be particularly fulfilled or excited by their work life, so expectations of happiness are often lower for working hours than for time away from the job.

On the weekend, however, unless a partner or family member helps make decisions, individuals with ADHD often have difficulty choosing, planning, and directing what activities will take place, often resulting in hours or days or whole weekends being frittered away. I frequently work with patients with ADHD who, lacking the structure and reminders of the workplace, will even forget to eat meals on weekends or on days they work from home. Even worse, society leads us to expect that we will fill this "free" time with enjoyable, interesting, or sustaining activities—or at least that we will complete necessary household chores. This large discrepancy between high expectations and unproductive outcomes often results in greater disappointments on weekends than on workdays.

Usually I am met with strong resistance when I propose to adults with ADHD that they actively schedule their free time. The usual responses include "I'm a spontaneous person," "I want to be free to do what I want to do," and "I don't want to be constrained." If they actually follow the advice to plan what they will do with their free time, invariably they report that they have accomplished more tasks, felt more productive, had more fun, and experienced the sense that they had more time, not less. In addition, they were actually more fully able to enjoy and relax in the hours that truly were free; they weren't in their former mode of playing a video game while simultaneously feeling that they could or should be performing dozens of other tasks that have been neglected.

I'm sure that aspects of this "free time is your enemy" issue occur during the Trump presidency; certainly, he seems to compose large numbers of his disruptive tweets at unusual hours and at times when he is not engaged in otherwise productive activities. All reports about Trump's daily and weekly routine indicate copious amounts of unscheduled time, which increases the risk of problems stemming from "free time is your enemy." Furthermore, this pattern appears unlikely to change, because he cherishes his status as the supreme boss, and doesn't like to be told what to do, and his emotional dysregulation makes it particularly unpleasant for others to confront him. If someone curtailed Trump's hours watching cable TV [477], he would have time to learn more about his duties and his world, and would likely accomplish more. Similarly, it appears appropriate, rather than just churlish, to begrudge him time on his golf courses when we don't see him balancing this free time with hours of industrious productivity at other times; it is especially galling because he slammed his predecessor's time on the links, which constituted far fewer hours [478].

I'm a Doormat

I have listened to many individuals with ADHD who use language skillfully and project an aura of intelligence and assertiveness, but who lament that they feel like "doormats." They mean that when there are confrontations, or even just interactions where someone else has a clear objective, they find that the other person frequently prevails over them—convincing them to spend their time, money, or energy in ways not in their own best interests. Executive function problems with prioritizing and organization, and sustaining attention seem particularly relevant here. If the other person stays focused on their agenda, but your brain jumps from topic to topic, or is derailed by your emotional responses, then we would expect that over the long run, the other person will prevail over you. Many of the times my patients felt taken advantage of, they were not even aware that the other person had framed the situation as some kind of confrontation. Only after the interaction ended did they realize that they had engaged in a struggle where the other person had clear goals and intentions.

Thus, many interactions result in people with ADHD feeling used, where they may have helped someone else to achieve their goals but failed to advance their own.

For individuals with ADHD who know that they are entering into a confrontation, it often helps to bring in a hard copy of their own goals, and to physically keep that in front of them, either in words or in imagery, so that if they get distracted, they can remind themselves of what they are aiming for, and use the reminder to get back on track. Some people with ADHD also need to be reminded that they can say "I need a minute to think about it" rather than agreeing to requests, especially surprise requests. Finally, many with ADHD also would benefit from learning how to retract some of their commitments by acknowledging their own impetuousness, and getting comfortable saying something like, "I didn't really think through the demands of this task when I volunteered, but on further reflection, I see that I don't have the time or resources [or whatever] to complete it."

Particularly because of their difficulties with maintaining attention, long-term planning, and prioritization, most people with ADHD negotiate ineptly. Being a skillful negotiator requires doing your homework and knowing details of your own positions and your opponents' ahead of time, being able to keep your own interests in mind at all times, keeping a long-range perspective in mind, being able to respond to unexpected approaches from your adversary, and being flexible in accepting that you might need to make some concessions to achieve your goal, as well as treating your adversary with respect and decorum. The record amply documents Trump's repeated failings in all of these realms.

Ironically, Trump remains extremely proud of his professed prowess at "the art of the deal," [479] even as his executive function deficits make him spectacularly unsuited for the complex task of being president. Generally speaking, in the past Trump has employed an ADHD-based strategy for his deal making: choosing a narrow goal based more on interest than importance (problems with attention direction, impulsivity); hyper-focusing on this one goal (problems with shifting and maintaining attention); employing bullying and angry outbursts (emotional dysregulation) to convey strength or determination; and finally distractions (poor impulse control, emotional dysregulation) to keep opponents off balance. Occasionally he also uses ADHD traits of creativity and novelty-seeking to make connections or breakthroughs that have eluded more conventional thinkers. Even his perseveration in viewing deal-making as a zero sum game, with one clear winner and one loser [479], is emblematic of an executive function problem (troubles with shifting focus). Trump's record in deal-making—whether overpaying for Trump Plaza [480], or failing to convince senators to vote down Obamacare [181], or bestowing military hardware on countries that flatter him without apparent consideration of strategic consequences [481], or other diplomatic shortfalls [446]—display failures in negotiation and diplomacy that should not be surprising in light of the severity of his ADHD. Whether the advantages (creativity, unconventionality) outweigh the deficits (interest-driven not importance-driven, distractibility, ignorance, impulsivity) accruing from his ADHD in his negotiations with the North Koreans, Chinese, Russians, Saudis, Mexicans, Canadians, Europeans, and others, will be revealed over the coming years.

Understanding that problems in executive functions underlie ADHD helps reveal why the real-world difficulties manifested by people with ADHD extend into many more aspects of daily living than the symptoms outlined in the DSM definition would suggest. The concept of executive function deficits also helps explain why somebody with ADHD can perform so unevenly in different situations, and also why the expression of ADHD varies so much among individuals. It is particularly unsettling that despite Trump's problems with attention, impulse control, planning, time management, and emotional regulation, we have chosen as chief executive someone with an executive function disorder.

CHAPTER 9

NOTHING SUCCEEDS LIKE EXCESS—POSITIVE ASPECTS OF ADHD

Many authors highlight that ADHD may be associated with positive traits, with psychiatrist Ed Hallowell being one of the most prominent promulgators of this view [482, 483]. Increased risk-taking and increased creativity jump to the top of the list of positive traits associated with ADHD [482]. Before exploring positive aspects of ADHD in more depth, I will clarify a common misconception about natural selection and genetic traits.

We create evolutionary fables to explain why certain physical or psychological traits prevail, or are at least retained, within populations; these stories always remain speculative. The principle of natural selection proposes that rare mutations become more widespread in a population when they contribute to differential reproductive success. For humans, that means that rare variants of a gene will become more prevalent in future generations when, on average, they contribute to having more children who will grow up to have more children, who, carried out over time, will have more children to pass along the trait. Evolutionary biologists don't consider natural selection to be a force that rewards "desirable" attributes or punishes "detrimental" characteristics except to the extent that these traits lead to greater relative reproductive success. Thus, for example, we have brains capable of much greater computational power than our hominid ancestors, because those brains allowed us to raise more children to an age where they could have their own children. Although there may be myriad advantages we accrue or attributes we admire about possessing such brains, these would all be evolutionary side effects, according to natural selection.

Given the strong genetic contribution to ADHD [106], and that people on the ADHD spectrum constitute roughly 5%-10% of the human race [55, 60, 114], one would conclude that natural selection worked to preserve the genetic variants giving rise to ADHD. Since ADHD actually increases the risk of early mortality [34, 63], the ADHD-contributing genetic variants must have had a particularly potent effect on reproductive success of the survivors in order for ADHD to be as common as it is now. In modern populations, ADHD is associated with having sex at younger ages [63], with an increased number of partners [63], and less regard for reproductive consequences [484]. To natural selection, the evolutionary "intent" of ADHD genes is to increase successful procreative behavior; all the other traits we associate with ADHD, good or bad, constitute just incidental byproducts of this promotion of propagation.

Regardless of the biologic reasons for the persistence of ADHD, in modern society it appears to convey certain positive attributes. Creativity and risk-taking have already been mentioned, and from my professional experience, ADHD is also associated with candor, enthusiasm, and irrepressibility. As with the negative traits and problems that travel with ADHD, not everyone with ADHD will express any of these positive traits to the same extent, and for each individual, manifestation of particular positive traits will vary depending on the context and with time. Since I attribute ADHD to deficiencies in executive functions, I must now address the conundrum of how positive (socially valued) traits could arise from deficiencies in executive functioning.

Creativity

Researchers define creativity as making novel, productive linkages between objects or concepts. Both impulsivity and difficulties regulating attention prompt people with ADHD to make such new connections. Some have speculated that the underlying aberrations of neuroconnectivity—less pruning away of diffuse connections throughout the brain in those with ADHD—may structurally and functionally underlie a greater aptitude for creativity. One study, using validated tasks that measure creativity, found on average that those with ADHD scored higher than non-ADHD participants [98]. Many great artists and inventors have retrospectively been credited with having had ADHD [51, 228, 485]. Trump certainly displayed creativity in making the leap from real estate to reality television to presidential politics; previously these would have been considered implausible transitions. Whether he will be able to unleash his creativity to derive workable new solutions to old problems on either domestic or international fronts remains to be seen.

Risk-Taking

Executive function deficits in planning, and response inhibition, as well as a drive for novelty and excessive stimulation, all appear to contribute to the greater frequency of risk-taking in individuals with ADHD [486]. While risk-taking inherently carries a chance of failure, it also introduces the possibility for successes not previously attainable, for potentially larger payoffs than more timid behavior elicits. In addition to such benefits to the fortunate risk-taker, groups of individuals benefit by entering the new frontiers that risk-takers have opened up. Some people have even speculated that countries like the US may be overrepresented today with people with ADHD because progenitors willing to take large risks were prevalent among the populations of voluntary immigrants [487]. Certainly, a propensity to take risks has also propelled Trump's career into ventures for which he was not particularly well prepared. The available evidence clearly supports that spontaneous decisions drove Trump's career trajectory rather than years of calculation and planning. Time will tell whether his risk-taking ventures to strip away environmental protections [488-490], add massively to the national debt [491], reduce access to health care [492], disrupt international trade [493], or navigate peacemaking in the Middle East [494] and North Korea [495] provide benefits to our country.

Candor

Because poor impulse control leads people to speak before they can censor themselves, many people with ADHD are known for their candor—they often speak what they feel, without sugarcoating or crafting their words to make them palatable to others. Many ADHD self-report scales ask about blurting out comments [2, 157], and several times I have heard people with ADHD respond with "I don't blurt out comments, I just tell the truth!" as if the two were mutually incompatible. When Trump's supporters give him high marks for being "authentic" [496, 497] they appear to be applauding his candor. Mr. Trump often says that he "goes with his gut," preferring his unformulated hunches to what the experts might espouse on a given issue [283, 479, 498, 499]. His emphasis on trusting his gut helps to clarify that his candor pertains more to his concern with boldly expressing his feelings than valuing whether his comments are truthful or consistent with known facts. Since the beginning of politics, the public often has mistrusted those politicians who appear too careful in crafting their phrases to appeal to their audiences, with the implication being that those who select their words ultra-cautiously do so primarily to obscure the speaker's true intentions and convictions. It is not surprising that voters found it both refreshing and welcome to hear unvarnished feelings from someone running for office.

Confusingly, this candor provides less information than it appears to. Most of us, most of the time, on most topics, actually have a multitude of feelings, thoughts, anecdotes, and misgivings: Ambivalence rules! Merely conveying which sentiment is uppermost at a given moment does not particularly reveal much about whether one has any overall internal consensus or conviction about a matter. So when Trump degrades women in one sentence and minutes later tells us how much he respects them [500], these two statements are contradictory, but do not reveal whether one, or neither, or both statements are actually true; he is just delivering two different feelings on a topic at two different moments. Having paradoxical feelings about a subject does not intrinsically make someone a liar, but it fails to convey whether the person has a prevailing attitude or sentiment regarding that subject.

Successful lying requires the ability to plan, to maintain attention, and to inhibit immediate responses—skills that people with ADHD tend to perform poorly. Indeed, many testimonials and textbooks contain the generalization that people with ADHD are much more likely to be truth-tellers than liars [501, 502]. How can we reconcile Trump's ADHD with the dozens of reports that document what a profligate liar he is, consistently uttering untruths more frequently than the general population or even than other politicians [439, 503]? I would reserve "lies" for statements that are intentionally deceitful in order to obscure the truth. When Trump says that he is a "very stable genius" [283, 504], that "there is no chaos" in his administration [283, 505], or that he has "accomplished more than almost any administration in the history of our country" [506], it sounds intentionally deceitful to many people. However, when he has been pressed on such subjects, he usually defensively retorts that he does not value the criteria that others use to assess him; from his perspective, those statements feel accurate *to him*. Even if we established that the overwhelming society consensus deems certain behavior unstable, certain situations chaotic, or certain goals unattained, that would not necessarily make Trump a liar; rather, it would indicate that his perceptions lie far outside of these societal standards. While indisputably we possess recordings of instances when Trump has been intentionally deceitful regarding specific facts or events, and he is lying at these times [507], the vast majority of his utterances we have been calling lies don't meet the standard definition of lying.

Nuanced differences also exist between my definition of lying as an intentional, deceptive, misrepresentation of the facts and some of the legal definition of lying. When Bill Clinton argued about "what your definition of is is," and whether fellatio was part of "having sex," he was intentionally using language to exploit different interpretations of common words. He chose his words in an attempt to avoid perjuring himself by simultaneously construing the words to mean something other than what he knew his questioners were intending them to convey. My assessment, and that of most Americans, was that he was lying, but whether he did it cleverly enough to evade breaking the law remains less clear-cut. Trump is unlikely to be very skillful at this type of deception, because his ADHD renders him inept with the finer distinctions of language. His use of speech to convey his feelings rather than to encapsulate any actual facts is a big part of why Trump's lawyers have valiantly resisted letting him speak under oath before investigators [431]. Their other major concern, of course, is that he may have actually done things that they want him to hide, and they fear he would not be very adept at hiding.

Enthusiasm - Eternal Freshman Syndrome

Many (but by no means all) adults with ADHD manifest an ongoing enthusiasm with which they delve into and talk about their interests. Combined with a tendency to seek out novelty, candor in talking about their interests, and exuberance in expressing emotions, including positive emotions, this creates what I call the "Eternal Freshman Syndrome." Their speech conveys their enthusiastic experience that everything feels so new and so exciting and so previously unknown! As one of my patients recently stated, "My husband says I'm always interesting—in a good way." Observers often feel intrigued and invigorated by interactions with those with ADHD because of how they bring these elements of novelty and passion to the conversation. Executive function deficiencies of decreased response inhibition, under-regulation of emotion, and impaired direction and maintenance of attention, all undergird this chronic enthusiasm.

This enthusiasm, in combination with ADHD-driven tendencies to respond spontaneously, and to have difficulty in perceiving the bigger picture, also contributes to behavior that defies traditional norms, but often in ways that feel delightful and amusing to observers. Part of the charm of such fictional characters as Pippi Longstocking, Anne of Green Gables, and Dennis the Menace (and part of what delights some of Trump's followers) continues to be this self-delight, high energy, amusement, and amazement with their own iconoclastic behaviors. Much of Trump's appeal as an entertainer and politician resides in these aspects of ADHD: He often comes across as fresh, energetic, surprising, and unconventional.

Irrepressible / Resilience

The final trait I often see associated with adult ADHD is a specific kind of irrepressibility and resilience [508, 509]. Many individuals with adult ADHD just "keep on keeping on" regardless of what has befallen them. This doesn't mean they don't feel the pain of disappointment; rather, their emotional volatility allows them to move on more quickly when a new emotion arises to clear the slate. Their restricted ability to maintain focus also plays a role, as does the drive to seek out new and fresh experiences, with the consequence that they often don't dwell on (and sometimes don't learn from) their past mistakes. Interestingly, this resilience and seeming ability to avoid being scarred by major events that fell short can also co-occur in the same individual who perseverates on a few specific traumas. Thus, in general, as they march through life, oblivious to most failures, they may repeatedly revisit certain anguishing moments from the past. Overall, Trump appears undaunted by four or five bankruptcies, two divorces, thousands of lawsuits, and countless misstatements and verbal gaffes [182, 283, 348, 349, 507]; in spite of all, he just moves on merrily with his life without much apparent regret or reflection. To his credit, Trump has been able to proceed following numerous breeches with allies [443, 510, 511], or to promoting other products when his university failed, his airline crashed, and his magazine folded [455].

Arguably, ADHD helps build resilience simply by provoking so many derailments in life. Those with ADHD experience vastly more opportunities for practicing getting back on track than most individuals without ADHD experience in a lifetime.

In summary, ADHD permeates all aspects of one's life, because it so profoundly alters how each individual with ADHD attends to and responds to information. We currently recognize it as a mental health condition because in our current, industrialized societies it leads to predictable and fairly consistent problems in completing tasks and interacting with others, resulting in dysfunction and distress.

However, these same ADHD traits and predispositions can lead to advantages and benefits in certain situations, as discussed in this chapter. Trump's personality wonderfully exemplifies this because so many of his strengths *and* weaknesses derive intimately from his ADHD.

SECTION III

THE CHANGING WHIRLED OF ADHD: ETHICS AND POLITICS OF DIAGNOSING ADHD

CHAPTER 10

THROWING COLD WATER ON THE GOLDWATER RULE

In the previous sections I described how conceptualizing ADHD as an executive function disorder helps explain many of the behavioral manifestations of ADHD, and how Trump's ADHD diagnosis explains a broad and pervasive range of his behavior. This final section highlights the rationale for diagnosing ADHD in individuals who have the condition, with particular emphasis on Trump. In Chapter 10 I explore some of the ethical issues regarding diagnosing public figures with ADHD. Chapter 11 examines the potential harm arising from diagnosing or not diagnosing ADHD. And then we delve into aspects of stigmatization of ADHD in Chapter 12. Technologic advances are churning and spinning our culture so quickly and chaotically that the planet I describe in Chapter 13 might best be called ADHD Whirled. In Chapter 14 I explore the feedback loops making our society more ADHD-like, so perhaps ADHD Whorled more precisely describes how we are altering our existence.

Outlining Ethical Principles

From the time Trump declared his candidacy for the presidency, mental health experts and society at large have debated the appropriateness of talking about his mental health. Much of this discussion has focused on claims of violation of confidentiality (as a reason not to speak up) and of potential harm to the country (as reason to be talking) [512]. These topics highlight the ethical principles of autonomy (patients have the right to make decisions about their health care, including not revealing information to others), beneficence (doing good for the patient or society), and non-maleficence (minimizing harm to the patient or to society). The ethical principle of veracity—that we speak truthfully and accurately—lurks silently in the background of this conversation, a particular irony in the Age of Trump. We need to address veracity because it undergirds the proscriptions against talking about Trump's mental health.

The practice of medicine always requires balancing the potential harm of not diagnosing and treating a condition against the potential harm of identifying and treating it. "Do no harm" remains a guiding principle of psychiatry just as much as for the other branches of medicine [136]. We make diagnoses to identify what aberrant biologically based processes are occurring, to predict the course of these processes in the absence of interventions, and to shape our interventions to minimize, mitigate, or reverse these toxic processes. "Do no harm" should not be misconstrued to mean avoiding any potential harm, because all medical interventions, including diagnoses, can or may cause damage: All surgery involves cutting into living tissue; all medications pose some risk of side effects; even inoculations cause some local trauma and pain. Any potential harm from diagnosing Trump's ADHD must be weighed against the estimated damage of not making the diagnosis. In the following two chapters I flesh out why I believe that diagnosing Trump's ADHD likely produces very little harm either to him or society, whereas we are already suffering significant damage from remaining ignorant of, and not properly addressing, his condition.

The Goldwater Rule

Organized psychiatry maintains that psychiatrists should not comment on the mental health of public officials without an in-person evaluation and the individual's consent, a decree known as the Goldwater Rule. The American Psychiatric Association (APA) created this ethical edict after a public humiliation of psychiatry in 1964 [513]. In that presidential election year, *Fact* magazine published an opinion poll, along with individual commentary, selected from more than a thousand psychiatrists, who offered marked criticisms of Arizona Senator Barry Goldwater's fitness for the presidency. Many of the published comments included harsh personal and political judgments about the senator, cloaked in psychoanalytic and psychiatric terminology. Goldwater sued *Fact*'s editor and won a sizable judgment for libel, a decision that stood even after appeals all the way to the US Supreme Court. Interestingly, Goldwater himself claimed to have been more traumatized by the slurs on his masculinity, and the implication that he was homosexual, than by accusations that he was a "megalomaniac" or a "paranoid schizophrenic." This experience may actually have helped push him along a path of greater tolerance, as decades later he became one of the first prominent Republicans to make any positive public proclamations about gay rights and gay marriage.

The APA appended the Goldwater Rule to its Principles of Medical Ethics in 1973 with the concluding proclamation that "it is unethical for a psychiatrist to offer a professional opinion unless he or she has conducted an examination and has been granted proper authorization for such a statement" [514]. The ethical concerns embodied in the Goldwater Rule appear to be threefold: 1) that such a diagnosis might be inaccurate (violating veracity) and hence cause harm to both the public figure and the psychiatric profession; 2) that such a diagnosis might be accurate but inappropriate (violating confidentiality), which again might cause harm to the figure and the profession; and 3) that such a diagnosis might be accurate but could be stigmatizing, potentially harming the figure, others with the condition, and the profession. I agree with the spirit of the Goldwater Rule, that psychiatrists and other mental health professionals should maintain awareness of veracity, beneficence, and non-maleficence when discussing mental health topics in public, but I view the rule as an imperfect and outdated embodiment of these values.

A desire to avoid further professional embarrassment, in addition to the high-minded goal of protecting our patients, motivated those who wrote the Goldwater Rule. The public statements about

Senator Goldwater made psychiatrists sound judgmental, petty, silly, inconsistent, and unscientific. Our lack of veracity probably created a bigger negative impression in the public's eye than our lack of probity [515]. Because psychiatrists created the Goldwater Rule, at least in part to protect the credibility of the guild of psychiatry, I consider it a form of "guild tripping"—an attempt to coerce silence in order to safeguard the professional reputation of psychiatry. In the remainder of this chapter I will address veracity, confidentiality, and the roles of psychiatrists in society to explain why I feel that we can publicly and ethically discuss Trump's ADHD.

Veracity

Ethical commentary depends on veracity; all false statements about the mental health of public figures are inherently unethical. The Goldwater Rule addresses veracity by implying that nothing less than an in-person interview constitutes a thorough evaluation. However, a large body of research demonstrates the fallibility of the in-person interview for psychiatric diagnosis [516]. An evaluation of a few hours provides insufficient basis for rendering judgments about whether an individual displays *pervasive patterns* of behavior. Furthermore, interviewing a famous, important, or powerful person exerts its own set of coercive forces that may impair the likelihood of obtaining an accurate diagnosis. Researchers have also obtained evidence that the immediacy and time constraints of an in-person evaluation create biases in favor of more dramatic and florid diagnoses, while more subtle problems may be overlooked. Although the official refrain is that the in-person interview remains the gold standard for diagnosis, this claim rests on assertions not particularly supported by empirical research.

In the real world, experts frequently disagree about psychiatric diagnoses, even after conducting open-ended, in-person evaluations. Although we consider carefully scripted questionnaires to more accurately guide us to diagnoses, disagreements about what condition an individual manifests occur even when clinical researchers follow such templates. In numerous court cases, experts who have interviewed defendants arrive at diametrically opposed assessments regarding culpability, motivations, and even basic diagnoses. In my own practice I routinely see adults who unequivocally meet the full definition for ADHD, yet were previously only identified and treated for depression, anxiety, or substance abuse problems. Clearly the in-person interview does not unerringly lead to diagnostic truth.

Psychiatry has attempted to reduce subjectivity in diagnosis through successive revisions of the Diagnostic and Statistical Manual (DSM), by increasingly basing diagnoses on observable behaviors rather than on feelings, motives, or putative psychodynamic progenitors of a condition. As I described in Chapter 3, our current definition of ADHD epitomizes this trend by relying entirely on observable behaviors. Although others have pointed out that we use behaviors to define many of our psychiatric conditions [517], the criteria for ADHD consist of simple behavioral symptoms (e.g. interrupting others, being inattentive, fidgeting), *devoid of any imputation about the driving motivation* for the acts. In contrast, the behavioral symptoms used to define personality disorders, and all other mental illnesses, explicitly require knowledge of what motivates the individual to act in those particular ways. So, for example, personality disorders defined, in part, by patterns of behavior demonstrating "disregard for the rights of others," "a need for admiration," or "attention-seeking" require not only that we have witnessed a particular set of repetitive actions, but that we also know the individual's subjective reasons for behaving in these ways. For an evaluator to obtain knowledge of motivation requires direct information from the patient; otherwise the examiner must make assumptions regarding why the individual repeatedly acted in such a manner. For most non-ADHD mental conditions, we should refrain from making such assumptions about motivation unless we perform an in-person evaluation or have other means to extensively corroborate what inspired the behavior.

In the modern era, we have created vast video libraries of the behaviors of many public personalities, in a variety of settings over a span of time, along with collateral information from numerous sources. The volume of relevant, behavioral data in public databases dwarfs what we can possibly obtain from our own interviews of patients.

Using this public database, we can assert with certainty that Trump's behavior thoroughly and precisely meets the criteria listed in DSM-5 for a diagnosis of ADHD, dispelling ethical concerns that we are violating veracity. Whether we shall alter the definition of ADHD in the future does not change the conclusion that he fulfills the current diagnostic requirements. While good practice dictates that all of our diagnoses are provisional, and modifiable by new information, pragmatically we often must take actions based on our working diagnoses. We craft psychotherapeutic interventions, prescribe medications, and draft billing statements using our best formulations of a problem at that time. Although I made my ADHD diagnosis of Trump in 2016, the data accumulating on a daily basis has only strengthened the case for his ADHD.

By making my diagnostic considerations transparent with the publication of this book, I hope to provide a roadmap so that others can evaluate for themselves whether my claims appear accurate. When we eventually modify the Goldwater Rule, I recommend that we include requirements for transparency regarding which diagnostic criteria we employ, and what behavioral or other data we utilize to fulfill those diagnostic criteria, so that others can ascertain the accuracy of our statements. Although I have heard psychiatrists lament that by publicizing Trump's ADHD diagnosis, because it is based on publicly available material and publicly described criteria, the public will begin to fear that psychiatrists routinely make diagnoses without in-person evaluations or without adhering to rigorous criteria. However, I know of no evidence that suggests the public will fail to distinguish diagnosing a public official from copious amounts of relevant data from how we evaluate private individuals who are invariably strangers to us before we see them in our office or hospital room.

The field of psychiatry has worked hard to improve the objectivity of our diagnoses, which are measurably much less subjective than the DSM-2 criteria used during the Nixon era, when the Goldwater Rule was written. Clearly, we must continue to improve on these efforts, and we will likely advance this endeavor with a confluence of genetic, neuroscientific, and psychological approaches.

Confidentiality

I am not violating Trump's confidentiality by discussing his ADHD, because he has never been my patient, and my diagnosis does not rely on access to any private or secret information. This book is not a con(fidentiality) job. Trump provided no information in confidence, revealed no secrets, and demanded no non-disclosure agreement from me while I was preparing this book. Could my evaluation undermine some more nebulous spirit of confidentiality? After all, a patient's ability to trust that their therapist or doctor will not reveal the content of their sessions remains a cornerstone of our work; without this guarantee of confidentiality patients would not willingly disclose their private thoughts and feelings. Again, it appears unlikely that the general public will genuinely confuse the sanctity of their private therapy sessions with public proclamations made about public figures from publicly available information.

In actuality, we often break confidentiality with our patient's consent—for example, to collaborate with other professionals in treatment, to obtain accommodations for our patients in work or school settings, or for billing and reimbursement purposes. Even writing a prescription imposes a betrayal of confidentiality, because we have invited a pharmacist, and often an insurance company, into our private conversation. Part of the essence of psychiatric work involves understanding the context in which people make decisions and frame their actions and thoughts; without understanding the context we often make wrong conclusions about an individual's action. Context explains why our patients routinely consent to these routine betrayals of confidentiality, because we are sharing limited information and this sharing is conducted to help the patient obtain appropriate treatment or services. If I am wrong about this public's understanding about patient confidentiality, then some of my ADHD patients, being among those least likely to hold their tongues, will let me know.

Furthermore, we violate patient confidentiality in some situations without, or even in opposition to, a patient's consent. We are obliged to break confidentiality when patients reveal concrete, plausible, and imminent plans to kill themselves or others and refuse to follow treatment plans that would prevent such tragedies [518]. In that context, our society considers the ethical need to protect lives more important than the ethical need to protect the patient's privacy. We also violate confidentiality when courts mandate evaluations of criminal behavior, and demand evaluations and diagnoses as part of the legal process for determining culpability and punishment [518]. In those cases, our society and legal system deem that the concepts of truth and justice supersede the patient's privacy rights. The standard ethical practice in such situations requires having other professionals evaluate the defendant for the legal process than those who treat the patient clinically, and making sure these other professionals clearly identify their separate role to the defendant/patient. These uncommon, but routine, exceptions have not impinged on the public's overall confidence concerning patient protections.

I have heard some argue that these exceptions to patient confidentiality are ethical only because specific laws mandate them. However, such laws merely enact the underlying ethical balance between individual rights and collective rights in society. The presence of the law itself does not create an ethical imperative. Similar conflicting ethical demands exist in situations where we do not yet have laws or legal mandates. For example, legislators at the state and federal levels have proposed laws requiring that candidates for president have a full physical and mental evaluation and release all relevant findings [519], and mandating the release of tax returns for a predetermined number of years [520]. To claim that we have no ethical rationale for requiring these disclosures, just because such laws have not yet been passed, conflates what is ethically appropriate and what is legal. Our laws usually follow from, rather than create, ethical principles. We do not require a law stating the acceptability of talking about Trump's ADHD for this activity to be an ethical endeavor.

Some contend that even if I rely entirely on information in the public domain, I violate Mr. Trump's autonomy by proclaiming a psychiatric diagnosis without his permission. In a democracy where freedom of speech remains one of our bedrock values, when we maintain transparency regarding how we arrived at such a conclusion, and where the information we use is readily available to everyone, I fail to see how

Trump's privacy is violated by a revelation regarding his ADHD, whether he welcomes it or not. Does such a declaration substantially differ from the observation that he combs his hair elaborately to obscure that he is balding? Should we remain silent if the emperor wears no clothes?

Those who desire to hold immense power over their fellow citizens in a democracy surrender some of their privacy rights for the sake of the public's ability to make informed consent about their leaders. Thus, we place higher obligations on elected public officials to reveal aspects of their health and finances than we request from other celebrities, such as movie stars or sports heroes. Given that ADHD strongly affects how one might make decisions, and act on or explain those decisions, the presence of ADHD reveals important information to the voting public. Furthermore, undiagnosed, untreated, or unrecognized ADHD in a public official compounds the problems for society caused by the ADHD itself, including misconstruing the reasons for problematic decisions and utterances. The potential magnitude of societal damage inflicted by a president's unacknowledged ADHD vastly outweighs any concerns about violation of privacy; indeed, we have an ethical *obligation* to talk about Trump's ADHD. (An exploration of those societal damages ensues in the next chapter.)

Changing norms regarding privacy also reframe the context of concerns about confidentiality and autonomy. Decades ago, the press considered it proper to conceal the marital infidelities of presidents. The public no longer accepts such reticence. Governments, corporations, and individuals possess vast powers in our modern culture to track and monitor our computer histories, current locations, email and phone conversations—dramatically altering the line between what we consider private and public. Even if ethical principles remain constant, we must learn to reformulate our rules for ethical behavior so that they apply to the societies we live in; enshrining edicts like the Goldwater Rule from a half century ago makes little sense when that world has ceased to exist.

The Role of Psychiatrists in Ethical Society

Some mental health professionals have proclaimed that the opinions of psychiatrists should be irrelevant to political elections or to governing [521, 522]. I respectfully disagree; even the APA ethical code (Sections 1, 2, 3, and 7) urges psychiatrists to speak up in order to protect patients and society from harmful public policies [523]. In a democracy, in order to make informed voting decisions, citizens require knowledge about conditions that may impair a candidate's judgment or decision making. Because psychiatrists possess expertise in identifying and understanding mental illness, then they, along with other sufficiently trained mental health practitioners, should be leading the discussion regarding the mental health of public leaders. It is unethical, on the grounds of veracity and non-maleficence, to abdicate our obligation to society and relegate such conversations to those with less training or knowledge. Do we forbid climate scientists from publicly discussing global warming and leave that task to TV weathermen, untrained pundits, or anyone who has been caught in a storm?

When a president demonstrates *clear evidence* of having a mental health condition, I believe that psychiatrists should be at the forefront of the public assessment and discourse. Furthermore, we should be as specific and detailed as we can regarding the information we have, rather than halting at bland generalizations. We should describe what data we are using to make conclusions and provide any valid alternate interpretations of the data. We should clearly demarcate what we know and what is speculation. As detailed in this book, Trump meets the full criteria for ADHD, and that information, derived from public sources, is now, and should always be, available to the public. How the public makes use of this information is for each individual to determine, but psychiatrists, being among the individuals who have examined these issues in most depth and rigor, should be contributing to the dialogue. We must be diligent in providing the most accurate information available, and leave it to the citizenry to use that information wisely.

Summary

The Goldwater Rule was formulated a half century ago when all psychiatric diagnoses were conjectures, all mental illnesses were deeply stigmatized, and notions of privacy differed radically from today. In the process of achieving substantively greater psychiatric diagnostic veracity than we had back then, we have altered the entire framework for determining beneficence and non-maleficence in making psychiatric diagnoses. Our changing psychiatric knowledge and privacy standards have thrown cold water on the Goldwater Rule. We must upgrade the Rule to reflect how ethics apply in our modern world.

In the early days of the AIDS epidemic, ACT-UP groups promoted the slogan "Silence Equals Death." In our own era, an impulsive action by the president could easily trigger conventional combat or even a nuclear war. Rationality and ethics demand an honest and accurate evaluation presented in open discussion about the origins of Trump's impulsivity. If we do not revise the restrictions imposed by the outdated Goldwater Rule, we may well be colluding in a situation where our professional Silence Equals Death.

CHAPTER 11

FOCUSING ON DAMAGE CONTROL WHEN CONTROL OF FOCUS IS DAMAGED

The Harm Reduction Model

Harm reduction has risen in popularity over the last decade as an alternative to the 12-step, Alcoholics Anonymous stance requiring total abstinence when treating substance abuse [524]. Harm reduction maintains that abstinence may not be a possible or desirable goal for everyone with a substance abuse problem. (But to correct a common misunderstanding, harm reduction does not preclude abstinence.) Instead of "just saying no," harm reduction relies on identifying the most damaging problems arising from a given behavior and finding ways to modify the behavior to mitigate that destruction. In this chapter I will outline the harm that I believe is caused by Trump's ADHD, again striving to differentiate that harm from the trauma inflicted by and attributable to his policies. Then I will address possible strategies for lessening that damage and offer strategies for coping with the damaging effects.

The harm done by ADHD is not restricted to those wielding great power. ADHD inflicts damage on the lives of anyone afflicted with it, and on those around them. The general forces of disruption and uncertainty unleashed by ADHD constitute the major sources of damage. Although I use Trump as an example, because his prominence and importance magnify the problems that ADHD can cause for others, many of these illustrations can be readily translated into the hardship and suffering delivered to family members, co-workers, classmates, and friends of those with ADHD.

Harm Caused by ADHD-Driven Behavior

Trump's ADHD-driven actions of blurting out insulting comments, abruptly dismissing appointees as if they were candidates on his reality show, and taking petty actions to vent his grievances, directly harm individuals. His ADHD causes indirect harm in countless ways: by fostering chaos, increasing anxiety, decreasing trust, and diminishing power. Because his ADHD leads him to act in ways that are unpredictable, poorly conceived, and inconsistently executed, Trump creates chaos and volatility. These in turn increase the risk for disasters, slow down or block the completion of goals, and encourage extremism and violence. Trump's ADHD creates anxiety in others through both his unpredictability and ineffectualness. Trump's ADHD, by contributing to behaviors and statements that are self-contradictory [525-528]—not tied to transcendent philosophies, and lacking awareness or understanding of historical precedent [528, 529]—violates trust and decreases his own credibility as well as that of our country and our social and political institutions. And finally, because his ADHD-driven behavior has eroded trust [357, 510, 530], alienated allies [442, 443, 531], and derailed his own endeavors [532], he has diminished his own power, as well as the power of the US and the stability and strength of our democratic institutions. Ironically, the man who campaigned to "Make America Great Again" has diminished America in a multitude of ways, many tied directly to his ADHD. While I provide an accounting of damages caused by Trump's ADHD in greater detail below, the list is not exhaustive, as many more examples exist than could be contained in these pages.

Trump's insults, slurs, and other verbal attacks hurt people directly. His attacks have tended to be more personal [533], directed at people's physical attributes [311, 321, 534, 535], more emotional, and more petty than those usually uttered by public figures, most especially by the President of the United States. The ADHD-fueled rancor of these onslaughts increases the likelihood that recipients experience them more deeply than the criticisms hurled during a more customary political brawl. Most people in public and private arguments avoid such invective, in part because they realize that sooner or later, they may have to cooperate with their adversaries. While Trump's ad hominem attacks on the campaign trail may have been designed to diminish or demolish his opponents, the pervasiveness with which he continues to insult not only opponents, but also his domestic and international allies [287], suggests that there is a large ADHD component to this behavior. His inability to curtail these impulses alienates those whose support he needs, including members of his own cabinet [536], Republican allies in Congress [467, 537, 538], and leaders of friendly countries [507, 531].

Both the nature and the targets of his verbal attacks appear to be driven by his personal whims rather than by calculated strategies. Many of his insults are based on personal appearance or physical traits rather than on a need to counter the ideas espoused by those whom he targets [169, 539, 540]. Most presidents have saved their public opprobrium for foreign enemies of the US, like Adolf Hitler, Muammar Gaddafi, or Osama bin Laden. Trump, because of his ADHD, lacks the self-restraint to not lash out at US citizens, including grieving family members of fallen solders [534], sports heroes [541], rescue workers he deems cowardly [542], or journalists who report facts he doesn't like [283, 543, 544]. Given that a large number of those he slurs are people of color [545, 546], it is not surprising that a majority of Americans view him as racist [547]. Again, while this might have some value in appealing to white supremacists, it does not appear to be behavior that is thought-out or driven by a well-constructed strategy. Even presidents known to voice racist commentary in private (Nixon's anti-Semitic and anti-black comments captured on tape [548]) took care to not make racist statements in public. Trump's ADHD-driven insults harm not just individuals, but also the concept that America is a welcoming and inclusive country.

Trump's ADHD also seems to contribute to the abrupt, capricious, and inconsiderate way in which he fires appointees. Again, similar to his insults, there are occasional strategic reasons for why he might want to be seen as punishing or demeaning individuals, but this behavior is so pervasive and so undermining of his own authority that it seems largely ADHD-driven rather than strategic. When firings are leaked to the press or revealed by tweet rather than by addressing his subordinates directly [357], he seems unaware of how inconsiderate and callous he appears; it is hard to discern a strategic value in epitomizing being crass, impulsive, or cruel. This is particularly so given that many of those being dismissed are people he had chosen for their positions; his firing them—and demeaning them in the process—belies having chosen only "the best people" for his administration [341]. It seems far more plausible that much of his hiring and firing, and the harm it is causing, is driven by his ADHD rather than by rational reflection.

Trump's ADHD contributes to the substantial personal, personnel, and political chaos that he creates. The evidence that tumult and disarray comprise his operating system, rather than being a conscious strategy to put others off guard, is demonstrated by how often this approach harms *him*—his stated goals derailed, former favorites fired or demoted, opportunities lost, his reputation eroded, and his occasional successes insufficiently appreciated [195]. That doesn't mean that he and those around him don't use the chaos at times to divert attention from topics they don't want to have examined, or to put opponents off balance [549]. If he operated for a single week without some significant self-inflicted chaos, disaster, or turmoil then we might conclude he intentionally creates such disarray, but no week in his administration has unfolded without examples of self-inflicted, destructive drama. Just because he can navigate the chaos, extricate himself, and move on is not sufficient to claim, as some pundits do, that all this is a well-conceived game plan [430].

Creating chaos increases the risk of cataclysmic events. The Bulletin of the Atomic Scientists moved their doomsday clock closer to midnight in part because of Trump's "unpredictability" and "controversial tweets and statements," indicating their belief that his hair-trigger belligerence increases the likelihood of nuclear war [550]. When many national security experts, including prominent Republicans, proclaimed that he did not have the temperament to be commander-in-chief [551], they were speaking directly to how his ADHD contributes to chaos and potential catastrophes. The risk of nuclear war with North Korea [206, 318], armed conflict with Iran [319], or catapulting ongoing conflicts into large-scale war in the Middle East [202] have all increased markedly under Trump's reign. He has prompted ill-advised trade battles with China [434] and our European or North American allies [493] with his ADHD-driven comments, along with knee-jerk policies that respond to immediate circumstances and reflect ignorance or lack of awareness about the more comprehensive and long-term consequences of his actions. The country and world may certainly sidestep or eventually undo some of the disasters that his ADHD triggers, but only time will tell.

Trump's ADHD-driven chaos also causes harm by fomenting inefficiency. The speed and extent of turnovers in his cabinet have set historical records [357]. His administration has had unprecedented levels of vacancies at sub-cabinet positions [552]. Both of these measures directly reflect his ADHD-driven management style. Furthermore, ADHD plays a role in Trump not having a clear idea of what many of his cabinet members are supposed to do [553]; presumably he didn't understand the roles, the topics didn't interest him, and so he didn't attend to this. His impulsive style ("I go with my gut") [283, 499] has led him to choose people whose expertise does not match their duties [554-556], who were personally incompatible with him or other members of his team [357, 557], or who carried criminal or scandalous baggage into their role [558]. Although some of the vacancies may be "strategic" in that they are philosophically driven to diminish the impact of, say, the State Department or the EPA, it is clear that in other areas (ambassadors to Turkey, South Korea, or Saudi Arabia [559, 560]) vacancies have hampered this administration's ability to advance its own agenda [560]. ADHD-driven chaos has slowed response time to dealing with issues he himself has deemed important, including fixing infrastructure [561, 562], revising health care [181, 452], and addressing the opioid crisis [563, 564]. As we have said, when people with ADHD get off track and don't complete tasks, it causes harm.

By impetuously proposing actions without consulting relevant, key individuals, or giving limited notice to the departments within his own administration (travel bans [565], barring transgenders from the military [207], agreeing to meet with the North Korean dictator [566]), Trump has repeatedly undermined his own team, decreased the speed with which policies can be enacted (because no prep work was done first), and appeared capricious, weak, or corruptible (e.g., initially he "bravely stood up to the NRA"; the next day, after meeting with them, he abandoned the majority of gun control ideas he had endorsed the day before [151]). Often, he moves so precipitously that his allies are unprepared to act in support [567-569]. Given that his party controlled both chambers of Congress for his first two years as president, many pundits concurred that the biggest obstacle to achieving his administration's own goals was the administration's bungling [570-572]. I contend that this bungling represents his ADHD in action.

W. Robert Connor, in *The American Scholar*, formulated an important distinction between populists (like Bernie Sanders) and demagogues (like Trump) [573]. While both ride out under the banner of being "for the people" and supporting the "common man," the populists propose specific polices aligned with specific philosophies regarding what will serve to improve the lot of the populace. The populist can be defeated if either the ideas or the laws that get enacted don't appeal to or don't help the people. The demagogue, on the other hand, depends on chaos, spectacle, and crude attacks on opponents to create his appeal, is much harder to attack (because there is no fixed belief system for him to defend), and is prone to slide into autocracy and dictatorship. Although there is nothing preventing someone with ADHD from being a populist, the traits of a demagogue that professor Connor highlighted have a remarkable overlap with the ADHD-driven personality of our current president.

While some of his defenders hold out the possibility that by breaking hidebound traditions, Trump may create an opening for peace in North Korea or the Middle East [430], or resolve other previously intransigent problems like immigration [574] or health care [575], two plus years into his term Trump has achieved little. If he does garner some success, we should roundly applaud him. A substantial stumbling block so far in attaining these bold and innovative goals has been Trump's ADHD, which has driven him to make pronouncements that are profoundly ignorant because they relied on his impulses and were "too boring" for him to bother to consult experts or follow scripts [187, 433, 576, 577]. Nixon's trip to China [578, 579] or Reagan's challenge to Gorbachev to tear down the Berlin Wall [580] were not impromptu events; they were based on a lot of leg work and consideration of the nuances of the underlying problems. Global challenges persist because they are complicated and contain conflicting and often incompatible goals, not because all world leaders and diplomats are uninformed or mendacious. Even if the impetuous Trumpian path to Korean denuclearization (or other goals) ultimately succeeds, he has subjected us to the far greater possibility of nuclear annihilation or other disaster than would have been risked by a more carefully thought-out and diplomatically negotiated route.

Trump's ADHD causes anxiety both through the chaos he creates and the inefficiency and derailments his actions introduce. Surveys during his presidency have shown that both Democrats *and Republicans* have been more anxious and stressed about the future of our nation [581, 582]. While some of this may be policy driven, much of the anxiety presumably arises from how Trump's ADHD increases unpredictability and uncertainty—e.g., whether proposals will actually be acted on, whether we will stumble into cataclysmic disaster, and whether crises that arise will not be handled calmly or competently. Anxiety has increased even among his political supporters [583] because they realize that many of Trump's proposals and intentions will never become policies or laws because he will sabotage them with his comments, or he will be distracted before completing the steps necessary to enact them. The hyperactivity and poor impulse control arising from Trump's ADHD also contribute to anxiety in America by leading him to insert his words and visage into almost every news cycle, in ways that profoundly deviate from decorum, truth, and historical precedent. These noxious intrusions are so constant, that at least in the minds of many of my patients, they have created the expectation that there will be a new provocation at any moment, causing people to be perpetually on edge, or to withdraw from watching the news at all. Again, all of these ADHD-driven contributions to America's angst appear to be separate from any anxiety caused by Trump's actual policies and positions.

Because popular attitudes and problems shift over time, most politicians have to express some ability and willingness to change or evolve over their careers. However, because of his ADHD, Trump makes so many impetuous, self-contradictory, and untrue comments that he has diminished trust and credibility in his presidency, and in the country. His capriciousness makes it hard to believe anything he says because it is likely to change within days, if not hours. Furthermore, seeing that he is so strongly influenced by whoever last spoke to him makes him appear malleable, since he displays little apparent allegiance to any underlying principles that drive his decisions. Trust is further eroded by his lack of follow-through—creating marked discrepancies between what he proclaims and what gets enacted. His betrayal of promises during health care and immigration negotiations makes Democratic leaders less trusting and less willing to venture any political capital in further negotiations [584-586]. His abandonment of the role of honest broker has substantially decreased the likelihood of any Middle East peace deal through his alienation of the Palestinians [587]. Trump's inconsistency, and the frequency with which he has completely abandoned ultimatums, makes it particularly farcical to block pieces of federal legislation unless the president professes willingness to sign a particular bill, because he has repeatedly endorsed laws he previously vowed to oppose. Because his ADHD creates the perception that he is untrustworthy, Trump has alienated partners and has frightened and discouraged potential allies at home and abroad.

Through ADHD-driven actions, Trump has created chaos, decreased effectiveness, diminished trust, and thereby weakened his own presidency, and America. The strongest nation on the planet is seen as less coherent, less reliable, more corruptible, and more hypocritical than it was before he took office [588-590]. By embarrassing the country and its allies, repeatedly encouraging tyrants, and disengaging from whole realms of international engagement, Trump has essentially ceded power to our theoretical enemies (world economic trade to the Chinese [591, 592]; control over Syria to the Turks, Russians, and Iranians [593, 594]; and possibly access to our electoral systems to the Russians).

Reducing Harm Caused by ADHD

Given that his ADHD causes the problems I have been enumerating (and again, there are certainly other problematic aspects of this presidency that are not originating from his ADHD), what can we do? Making either him or those around him more aware of his ADHD may encourage him to seek treatment for his condition. However unlikely that may be, we know that the environment and context are important variables in shaping how an ADHD brain works [483]; we should work to promote the presence within his administration of "adults in the room" who will exercise some executive functions for him. We should applaud those in his own party (Senators Romney, Paul, Collins) who occasionally point out how his ADHD-driven behavior harms himself and the country, and we should encourage other Republican leaders to do the same. We can also speak out against those who encourage and support Trump's most intemperate outbursts. We can continue to vote for officials at all levels of government who stand up to, rather than acquiesce to, his behavior. We can start treating some of his comments, given their disconnect from reality, more like the utterances of a figurehead—regarding him like a ceremonial president rather than a prime minister with actual power. However, the utility of this latter approach is limited since he does possess real power.

Finally, we should be finding ways to make his job interesting to him, since Trump's brain is not importance-driven. He has been more interested in tearing up treaties and smashing programs created by his predecessor than in creating his own solutions to most of these issues [595-597]. An interesting exception that proves the point has been his avidity to reach a deal with the North Koreans, particularly when the prospect of an international prize was dangled in front of him by the wily South Korean leader [598]. We have also repeatedly witnessed how Saudi, Egyptian, and Russian leaders, with their appeal to Trump's emotions and love of pageantry, more successfully capture his attention and generate policy change than the rational-engagement approach of respected leaders of our allies in Europe, Asia, Australia, and Canada [599-601]. Trump is a president who can be steered, but it will be by rewarding him with praise and glitzy honors, not by trying to convince him to do what helps the welfare of Americans, or the world, or the environment.

Coping Strategies for the Current Era

Individuals face significant limitations in directly changing Trump's ADHD-driven behavior or preventing harmful outcomes, necessitating an emphasis on strategies for coping with the damage. As a start, I recommend reading more of your news rather than watching it. When we read, we place more emphasis on facts and rational aspects and somewhat less on the storyline and emotional responses. Also, reading makes it easier to interrupt the flow of information, to completely stop it, or to control the pace of our exposure to news, than does watching it on a screen. By controlling the flow of information into your mind you not only reduce contact with noxious elements, but you also reinforce the idea that you are able to take actions that shape at least part of your own environment—and having a sense of control improves mental health [602].

Secondly, unless you work for the media, restrict attending to the news to just once a day. For a century, daily newspapers kept us adequately abreast of events. In the current era, we have constant updating of the "news"; while much of it may be new, very little of it is newsworthy. Often the media repeat the same information over and over. On evolving stories, do we really derive value from hearing fourteen updates on the seesawing preliminary vote count of an election, or the growing body count in a bridge or building collapse, or a mass shooting? You can just wait for the final result, or at least the daily tally, to give you the relevant information. While the preliminary details are real (we hope) data, they usually don't contain meaningful information. The catastrophically important news that you have to act on immediately (your house is on fire, missiles are headed toward your city) will probably find you through other sources (your senses, phone calls, or texts) rather than through constant news updates.

Thirdly, remember that particularly with this president, often the news isn't news: He proclaims great accomplishments when usually these are mere pronouncements of what he would like (in that moment) to see happen (in some indefinite future) [603, 604]. He talks about his feelings and opinions as if they were actual occurrences. Many of his proclamations of jobs created, or of new policies regarding religious freedom or immigration restrictions, or Mexico paying for a wall on the border, have not been actual facts or accomplishments [604-610]. Also, he changes his mind so frequently, it may be best to wait to see if he is really for or against raising the age for buying guns [611], or supporting or opposing citizenship for Dreamers [204], until he signs a bill or executive order. That doesn't mean everything can or should be ignored in the discussion phase, but remember that there will almost always be plenty of time for input, whether you support or oppose a position, before anything really happens.

Fourthly, keep in mind that even though the president's decisions can have a huge impact (e.g., nuclear war), the vast majority of even his most heinous polices are unlikely to impact the most important aspects of your daily life: You will still be the one deciding whom you love and how you spend the majority of the hours of life. Even in those horrible instances where his actions result in lives being uprooted and families torn apart, he is not changing whom you feel connected to.

Fifthly, remember that Rome wasn't destroyed in a day. Most major changes to health care policy, tax laws, or the dismantling of organizations and protections take time. In San Francisco I remind people that it took almost two decades after an earthquake damaged the Bay Bridge to dismantle it and build a new one, even *with* concerted efforts by local and state citizens and office holders [612]. Many of Trump's proposed policy changes will evoke a multitude of individual bureaucrats, grassroots organizations filing legal motions, and state and local governments passing countermanding or compensatory measures to mitigate the damage potentially wrought by his actions. The time for change to take place allows counterstrategies to evolve.

Sixthly, because of his ADHD, time is not on Trump's side. He will continue to over-promise and under-deliver, and he will continue to insult and undermine his supporters, and to focus on what interests him rather than helping the country—all of which will slowly, but cumulatively result in dwindling support. Also, because of his ADHD, for his opponents he is a political gift that keeps on giving. Unlike a more restrained politician, Trump will keep energizing his enemies and reminding voters with his gaffes, crudeness, misinformation, and contempt; he lacks the restraint to keep his flaws hidden. His

ADHD-driven actions have already set in motion multiple possible trajectories for his downfall.

Finally, don't forget that this too, shall pass. People with ADHD don't stay on track. Because of his ADHD, Trump is considerably less likely than other recent presidents to complete his term. Your life, America, and the planet, will likely outlast, at least in some form, this presidency, even if he completes a full four-year term. As I tell my patients, I am a psychiatrist, not a psychic, so I have no secret knowledge about what the future will bring, but I do know that having ADHD increases the likelihood of certain eventualities. As I explain in the following paragraphs, ADHD increases the likelihood that Trump will either quit, be removed from office, or die in office before his term is up, although it certainly does not guarantee any of these outcomes.

People with ADHD get off track, because they are so prone to distraction and boredom. When the presidency doesn't interest him any longer, Trump may walk away from it. Although he proclaims that he is not a quitter, this is a man who has had two divorces [350], several bankruptcies [348], and numerous promotional entities that have gone bust, and he has walked away each time [455]. He has demonstrated a pattern of giving up and moving on while declaring himself a winner. If one thinks that people don't abandon positions of power, recall that Sarah Palin (another politician who at least appears to share substantial ADHD traits) walked away from the governorship of Alaska, just because [613]. Whether it is Positive Illusory Bias (Chapter 4) or narcissism, Trump's over-valuation of himself will actually help him follow his ADHD-driven impulses to leave office if he becomes bored or overwhelmed. Before his inauguration, I put in writing the prediction that Trump would start telling himself that in just a few months in office he had already accomplished more than any other president in US history (made easier for him to believe because of his inattention to history). In September 2018 he started routinely making this claim [614], and by March 2019, had convinced a majority of Republicans to believe his statement [615]. Remember, this is a guy who proclaimed that losing $900 million makes him a smart businessman [345]. Believing that he has already surpassed everyone else in history actually makes it much easier for him to leave the presidency before the end of his term.

Trump's ADHD is also a large factor increasing the likelihood of his impeachment. His capricious decision-making, his not learning about the intricacies of situations he was messing with, his ignoring what others consider important (including the laws of the land), have made it quite likely that he has already committed impeachable offenses [616, 617]. And even though Republicans retained control of the Senate in the 2018 midterm elections, Trump's ADHD-driven behavior has substantially diminished the number of members of his own party who respect him, feel a personal loyalty to him, or who will continue to support him if they conclude that they risk their own political future by backing him.

ADHD could directly play a role in Trump being removed from office by evoking the 25th Amendment. Section 4 of that amendment creates a procedure for the vice president and a majority of the cabinet to declare that the president is "unable to discharge the powers and duties of his office," and remove him from office [618]. Trump demonstrably meets qualifications for a mental health condition (ADHD) that clearly impedes his ability to be an effective leader.

The electorate showed insufficient concern about Trump's display of symptoms and impairment from ADHD during the election campaign. We should respect the election result regardless of whether it would have been altered had we known that ADHD was an important factor driving his actions. However, it is possible that with ongoing age and/or job-related stress, the mismatch between his capacities and the demands of the role will be large enough that the vice president and cabinet officials are forced to act on the prerogatives of the 25th Amendment. One potential stressor could be defending himself against impeachment—we saw the toll that took on Nixon's mental health. It is possible that one motivation for Trump constantly reshuffling his cabinet, and blatant demands for fealty, is an attempt to minimize the risk of coalitions that might invoke the 25th Amendment. Interestingly, that amendment does not require that a specific diagnosis be made to support the charge of incapacitation.

ADHD also increases the likelihood that Trump could die in office. We know that ADHD increases mortality rates, largely from accidents [34, 619]. Specifically in Trump's case, ADHD seems to have influenced lifestyle choices (propensity for eating fast food [620], disinclination for exercise [261], intemperate sleep patterns [220]) that all impact health and mortality. Furthermore, despite being purportedly in better health than any previous president [621], he was the oldest president to be elected [621], in part due to the atypical, ADHD-driven career path he took to the office.

Perhaps most speculatively and most ghoulishly, I believe that Trump's ADHD-driven invective, provocations, and demeaning of others increases his risk for assassination. Although all politicians have their detractors and opponents, Trump's ADHD leads him to make comments that appear so provocative, insulting, and dismissive that he inflames passions to a greater degree than most, if not all, of his predecessors. In contrast to "no-drama Obama"—opposition to whom mostly came in spite of his overt statements of unity, connection, understanding, and healing—Trump's intemperate speech actively *promotes* division, rancor, and animosity. The number of presidential assassinations is small enough to make extrapolations of relative risk based on presidential characteristics highly unreliable. (Perhaps our blandest president of the last half century, Gerald Ford, narrowly avoided two serious attempts on his life. [622]) Nevertheless, Trump's repeated invocations to violence by his supporters during the campaign [623], his ongoing provocations against opponents [287], and the proliferation of guns in the United States [624], seems to increase his risk of premature death.

Trump's ADHD has harmed his own efficacy as president. His inability to restrain himself from making contradictory, untrue, and hurtful statements has diminished the prestige, credibility, and power of the country. His lack of emotional control and impetuousness and his petty vindictiveness have greatly increased the risk of war and catastrophe, particularly with North Korea and the Middle East. His unpredictability has made Americans deeply anxious. His inconsistency, along with the emotional fervor and personal focus of his responses, reduces our faith that he will be able to handle a real crisis should one arise. His ADHD-driven trait of strongly reacting to whatever is going on in front of him, routinely creates crises out of very trivial matters, which inherently undermines the tranquility of the general public. That pattern of behavior undermines the worldview that some issues or values are more important than others, that some constant, guiding principles structure our world and keep it safe, and that there are strong, principled leaders to protect us when necessary. Once again, I am pointing out the damage arising solely from Trump's ADHD, not from his policies or other mental health issues. The lack of awareness and treatment of Trump's ADHD is profoundly, negatively affecting the country and world's mental health.

CHAPTER 12

IS THE ADHD LABEL LIABLE TO LIBEL SOMEONE? STIGMA AND ADHD

Stigma and ADHD

Many children and adults continue to be bullied, insulted, and made to feel different and inferior because of their ADHD-driven behaviors, indicating that in addition to any dysfunction directly caused by ADHD, individuals also must contend with the negative impacts of stigmatization [148]. Stigmatization of children with ADHD can be particularly deleterious when it contributes to the creation of negative self-views [625], with potentially lifelong impact—e.g., increasing the risk for depression and anxiety [626], substance abuse [627], and compensatory narcissism [628] later in life. Frederickson's "broaden-and-build theory" of positive emotions even posits that forces that engender a preponderance of negative emotions can quicken response times and encourage responses designed to provide immediate relief [629], i.e., the stigmatization of ADHD may lead to additional ADHD-like behavior. Fostering greater understanding about ADHD should lead to less stigmatization, and thus better long-term mental health for members of our society with ADHD. Another reason for discussing ADHD-related stigma is to refute the claim by organized psychiatry that talking about Trump's mental health could itself be stigmatizing [630]. Often these comments are made without differentiating whether they fear that Trump would be stigmatized or whether publicizing his ADHD might stigmatize others with the condition. I address both possibilities in this chapter.

Groups of people can be stigmatized because of real or perceived religious (Jewish, Muslim), ethnic (Roma, Rohingya), racial (Black), mental health (schizophrenic, ADHD) or sexual identity (gay, transgender), but in all cases stigmatization involves assigning individuals to groups that are deemed different, alien, and inferior to mainstream society. Stigmatization involves dividing humanity into "us" vs. "them" and denigrating "them" for deviating from social norms. Very frequently the dominant group promotes the notion that these deviations indicate moral failings (e.g. people with ADHD are lazy, stupid, or crazy, to paraphrase one of the more popular books about ADHD [292]). Stigmatization entails societally sanctioned hatred of members of "minority" groups. Although minority groups often comprise a small subset of the total population, in some societies with a small but powerful elite, members of "minority" groups may constitute an absolute majority in the society: It is power, not numbers, that determines "minority" status.

The term micro-aggressions has become popular in the last decade to describe how majority group members subject members of stigmatized groups, perhaps dozens or hundreds of times a day, to belittling, derogatory, or injurious comments and gestures [631]. Often the attitudes conveyed are so embedded in the dominant members of the society, or in the "lower caste" members themselves, that they are expressed without much conscious awareness. One ADHD expert estimates that by the time they reach age twelve, children with ADHD may hear 20,000 more negative comments than those without ADHD [632]. Even if one has a supportive family, it is hard to escape such attacks in schools, the workplace, or social settings. Unfortunately, the term micro-aggressions draws attention to the "micro" which emphasizes the pettiness and small scale of many such attacks, and thus tacitly conveys that anyone actually suffering injury must be a "snowflake" who needs special coddling. For that reason, I prefer the term "ubi-agros" for ubiquitous aggressions, because it emphasizes the potential and prevalence of pervasive damage from the accumulation of such messages. Whether ubi-agros lead to a sense of failure or deficiency in a given individual, or to a compensatory over-insistence on one's own superiority, or to some healthier outcome, all members of stigmatized groups must contend with them.

Dealing with Differences

We are all different, we are all imperfect, and learning how we each can be valued for our individuality and recognized for our commonality is a major task for every individual and every society. All children have some sense of being misunderstood and that their specialness is not being appreciated—hence, the appeal of characters like Harry Potter, many of our comic book heroes, and fairy tales such as Cinderella. However, in those children who do appear or act differently, whether in subtle or overt ways compared to the mainstream, this feeling of alienation often intensifies and grows; they can sense their own differentness, making it harder for them to refute the daily barrage of ubi-agros. In my psychotherapy work I often detect similar tendencies of heightened sensitivity to rejection, feeling that one is "damaged goods," and overshadowing shame in my gay patients and those with ADHD. I believe that these feelings arise because the brains and behaviors of these individuals do differ from the majority of their peers, and that observers perceive some aspects of this differentness (e.g. for the ADHD child, missing social cues, blurting out comments; for the gay boy, avoidance of rough-and-tumble play), leading to the child's own awareness of his or her differentness, even when the underlying source of being different may not be consciously articulated or even identified. Furthermore, even when parents and family members completely accept the ways that child is different, the child almost always receives direct or indirect messages from neighbors, classmates, and other adults in their environment that they are not only different, but in some way bad or wrong. We need to keep promoting, through both religious and secular humanist approaches, self-acceptance by individuals and tolerance by society, because, except for the seven or eight perfect people on this planet, we are all in some sense "damaged goods."

What *Is* a Psychiatric Disease?

I have been describing ADHD as a brain condition, rather than labeling it as a disease. Technically, the inclusion of ADHD in the DSM currently makes it a disease state. However, there is a trend, both in society at large and in the mental health field in particular, in understanding that some of the conditions we have labeled disorders often just indicate differences from the mainstream, rather than deficiencies or defects. This trend is increasing, paradoxically parallel to our growing knowledge that biologically based brain differences seem to underlie many of these conditions. Just because your brain or body is different does not inherently make you sick. To take it to a farcical extreme, men and women show group differences along many biologic measurements, but that does not make maleness a "diseased state" of femaleness, or vice versa. Conditions that exist along a spectrum of severity, such as ADHD [120], highlight the difficulty in determining where, if anywhere, a line separates "diseased" from "normal" or even between having a condition and not having a condition.

When my father was in grade school, the public school teachers (no archetypical old nuns there) would rap the back of his hand with a ruler when he tried to hold a pencil in his left hand for writing. Today we don't scorn left-handed people as lazy, sloppy, mentally defective or possessed by the devil. When I was born, I was mentally ill; the American Psychiatric Association cured me at age eleven by initiating the process to remove homosexuality from the list of diagnosable mental illnesses [633]. The number of individuals who still consider homosexuality to be "evil" or a "disease" continues to shrink, and currently the majority of Americans believe homosexuality should be accepted by our society [634]. Psychiatric diagnoses are always made in a social context, and if the views of psychiatrists are too discrepant from the society they exist in, psychiatry cannot function in any meaningful way. That does not mean that psychiatry should slavishly follow all the prejudices and superstitions of a society. Scientific knowledge about how the body, including the brain, functions is the foundation for all medical practice, including psychiatry. Psychiatry's job is to improve the mental health of individuals—not only with direct interventions to help people function better, but also by changing society through education, lobbying and legal action, in those instances where public policy contributes to dysfunction.

Creating a coherent and accurate nosology (the system of classifying diseases or conditions) for psychiatry challenges us in part because of difficulties in developing objective measures for mental health traits, in determining normative ranges for those traits, and in identifying and quantitating ways in which individuals differ from group norms. However, it is monumentally more complicated and controversial to determine whether these deviations from the norm actually produce the dysfunction and distress required of a disease state. Often problems correlated with a minority group status result from stigmatization or discrimination of members of that group, rather than from the condition itself.

In some circles, the historically higher rates of smoking, substance abuse, depression, anxiety, and suicide in the gay community have been viewed as evidence that these are "sick" individuals [635, 636]. However, having supportive environments, such as gay-straight alliance clubs, lowers the rate of these problematic behaviors [637, 638]; overall, the elevated rates of such problems continue to decline, in parallel with homosexuality gaining acceptance in society [634, 639]. This demonstrates that these negative outcomes were not intrinsic to homosexuality, but part of how gays have historically responded to an abusive, homophobic society. Stigma creates inequalities in group health, harming the fitness of devalued communities [640]. In contrast, with ADHD, some of the harmful associations (car accidents, failing classes) become less common when the condition itself is treated [80, 251], and thus appear to be intrinsically linked to the condition itself, not to the stigmatization. It remains to be seen how much of the burden of ADHD will be reduced by treating the condition, and how much will be reduced by lowering stigmatization associated with it. This again emphasizes the need to accurately identify ADHD when it is present, and to make available the treatment modalities that lead to a reduction in problems associated with the condition.

Other mental health examples of the trend to de-pathologize extend to our currently defined diseases of autism and schizophrenia. There is a substantial movement among individuals on the autism spectrum to self-identify as "neurodivergent" rather than diseased [641]. Some professionals working with people with schizophrenia see their primary job not as eradicating hallucinations and delusional thoughts, but in helping to provide a context for the individuals to make sense of their symptoms for themselves, and to live autonomously in the world [642]. In their view, the "primitive" societies that ascribe potent and magical qualities to schizophrenic behaviors, and accept that their society needs such members in order to connect with something that is holy, special, divine, or otherwise unknowable, are actually more advanced than our own. Our streets, prisons, and morgues are full of individuals for whom we clearly have failed to find functional roles because of their anomalous abilities and ways of experiencing the world; those conditions include severe ADHD as well as schizophrenia and substance abuse [33, 34, 79, 643, 644]. On many levels our society appears diseased or ill for failing to accept and embrace individuals with ADHD, whose differences from the norm do not diminish their individual humanity and do not cause major harm to the public. If our societal views continue to evolve in this de-pathologizing direction, it is possible that someday the whole spectrum of ADHD may be considered a condition, not a disease, but at the present time, when it causes distress and diminishes functioning, we still define it as a mental illness.

My patients and colleagues worry that if we evolve to a point where ADHD becomes a condition rather than a disease, then insurance companies, and possibly the medical community, may deem it not worthy of treatment. However, several medical specialties have historically taken conditions, rather than specific disease states, as their whole field (pediatrics for childhood, obstetrics for pregnancy, geriatrics for aging). There will continue to be value in identifying specific conditions, and in finding approaches to help alleviate any associated distress or dysfunction, whether the problems associated with the condition are primarily caused by that condition, by the response of society to the condition, or both. Even if we eradicate the stigma about ADHD, those who have it will still benefit from medication or psychotherapy approaches that help them organize time, reduce distractibility, and inhibit some of their immediate responses.

Stigmatization, Hate, and Disgust

Stigmatization at its most extreme form moves beyond ubi-agros into the territory of "hate crimes": discriminatory and aggressive behavior or violence targeting individuals belonging to stigmatized groups [645]. However, "hate" is a term that confuses because it is so imprecise; we use it to describe any strong negative emotion. I hate being hit in the face. I hate lima beans. I hate corporations that pollute the environment. I hate funerals. I hate going bald. We use hate to designate the various emotions embodied in each of these statements. To hate being hit indicates fear. To hate lima beans indicates disgust. To hate injustice indicates anger. To hate suffering and death indicates sadness. And hating appearance suggests an underlying shame. This multiplicity of meanings for the word "hate" causes confusion when we label certain acts "hate crimes." Many murders, assaults, and other vicious crimes involve strong negative emotions, but most of them are not hate crimes. In short, I hate the word "hate" because of its imprecision.

Curiously enough, it's hating lima beans that comes closest to the meaning of *hate* in hate crimes or stigmatization. Disgust, meaning "bad taste," is one of the basic emotions, and appears to have its origins in sorting out whether objects in our environment were palatable or good enough to incorporate into our own bodies, to distinguish food from non-food [646]. It was a potentially lethal question for our ancient ancestors to determine whether a recently found carcass was a bountiful meal of powerful proteins or a poisonous potpourri of bacterial toxins. Properly employed disgust could save your life. The facial expressions accompanying disgust, a thrusting downward and outward of the tongue, and a crinkling of the nose, were designed to eject toxic foreign substances from the mouth and banish foul odors from the nose [646].

Human brains over the millennia appear to have expanded the triggers that elicit disgust, to include not just bad food, but bad people whom we reject as alien and try to thrust out of our society. This appears to be why, across centuries, dominant groups depict despised groups as "animalistic" and enumerate alleged, sordid details about how unsanitary the excretory and reproductive behaviors of these people are [647, 648]. Words related to malodorousness, decay, sliminess, foulness, and greasiness have been associated with Jews, gays, women, minority groups, and lower-class people through hundreds of years of Western writing [648-650] and actions.

We should probably re-label hate crimes as either "disgust crimes" or "dehumanization crimes"—which are horrible not only because they involve strong negative emotions, but because they arise from the basic emotion of disgust and thereby assert that some people are subhuman and thus somehow deserving of abuse, abasement, and expulsion from the human race. While demagogues often employ fear and anger to justify or rationalize antipathy towards members of minority groups, disgust remains the central emotion designating these people as different from and inferior to the group in power.

Many young children develop disgust for certain foods, particularly those with bitter or other strong tastes. Research shows that most such food disgusts can be overcome simply by multiple exposures and a positive framing of the food item [651]. Given that stigmatization is disgust-based, it follows that we can counter stigmatization by repeated exposures to, and embracing of, members of stigmatized groups— bringing them into our bodies, our societies. Decades of studies show that the most effective way to reduce stigma is for individuals to reveal aspects of their stigmatized identity to their acquaintances and the public at large, to put a human face on formerly despised categories [652, 653]. We have been able to measure the reduction of homophobia in society brought about by increasing numbers of gay people coming out of the closet [654]. Having more people with ADHD share their experiences will decrease stigma, and foster understanding of this condition; psychiatry should play a leading or at least a supportive role in this conversation with society. Research also shows that destigmatization is a process [655], a conversation unfolding over months and years, because people need the elements of exposure, a positive or at least neutral context, and time to change their views.

Trump and Stigma

The argument that revealing Trump's ADHD could be stigmatizing to him seems rather curious when contrasted with the assumption underlying the alternative—that his condition is so unspeakable that we cannot or should not reveal it. How can we applaud each newscaster, novelist, or ballplayer who reveals a history of depression, bulimia, panic disorder, OCD, or other mental health issue, and yet claim it increases stigma to identify a mental health condition in the president? The revelation that Trump has ADHD actually reduces his stigmatization; it is an improvement over current characterizations of his behavior as being "a serial liar" [656], "completely unhinged" [657], "unstable" [658], or "an insane bigot" [659]. Learning that ADHD explains his impetuous tweets, lack of attention to detail, vacuity of verbal expression, rambling sentences, and emotional outbursts when slighted, harms his reputation or his sense of self far less than the other assumptions used to explain these behaviors. It seems highly unlikely that a man who has had so many derogatory labels thrown at him would be traumatized by understanding that he has ADHD.

Trump's ADHD also helps protect him from being traumatized by an ADHD diagnosis because his ADHD is a central factor in his tendency to focus on what appeals to him and ignore what doesn't interest him. A man who interprets losing the popular vote by almost three millions votes as a "massive landslide victory" is unlikely to be troubled by an ADHD diagnosis [660]. It is doubtful that an ADHD diagnosis would lower Trump's self-estimation or deter his supporters.

If we needn't worry about ADHD stigmatizing Trump, do we need to worry about Trump's condition stigmatizing ADHD? This possibility offers the strongest argument against the existence of this book, because the revelation of Trump's ADHD at least has the potential to diminish or embarrass others with ADHD, particularly those who do not share Trump's politics or do not voice narcissistic, sexist, or racist comments. Certainly some of these people may initially feel tarnished by the comparison. However, that same statement can and has been made by individuals from other categories that Trump represents—e.g., those who feel ashamed to be an American, or male, or a true conservative if the president is the embodiment of that label. People work through this stigma by acknowledging the essence of what they have in common, and by not taking collective responsibility for that person's other attributes or beliefs unless those characteristics fit them as well.

Analogously, many members of the gay community were dismayed that the serial killers John Wayne Gacy [661] or Jeffrey Dahmer [662] were identified as homosexuals [663, 664]. Although some homophobic extremists appear to have held these men up as exemplars of what it means to be gay [665], reasonable individuals can discern that their murderous impulses were not a manifestation of their homosexuality, even if their sexual identity directed their choice of victims. Furthermore, these killers' difficulties in having healthy human interactions, which may have shaped their criminal behavior, is much more plausibly attributed to growing up in a homophobic society than to believing that homosexuality intrinsically leads to murderous behavior. Currently we are seeing a similar invocation to hate Hispanic immigrants because some members of the notorious MS-13 gang have committed heinous crimes [666-668]. We can simultaneously condemn these individual actions while embracing the knowledge that immigrants overall have lower rates of murder and other criminal behavior than native-born Americans [669]. Bad actions by individuals do not need to tarnish all members of the groups to which they belong. Similarly, Trump's bad policy decisions are largely driven by characteristics of who he is as an individual; they do not represent a group liability for all of those with ADHD.

Knowing that someone with ADHD can still be president of the most powerful country on earth helps reduce stigma about ADHD, whether Trump acknowledges the condition himself or is outed by others. Much has been written about the ethics of outing individuals, when being gay was a potential career breaker or could lead to losing one's home or life [670]. Having ADHD has not been stigmatized to such an extent in our society, so the potential downside to outing Trump or anyone else for having ADHD is much lower, and as argued in these pages, the potential benefits, both for himself and society, clearly outweigh remaining silent about his observable behaviors. Were Trump to embrace his ADHD, it might help decrease the stigma about this condition; it being a public matter, whether he acknowledges it or not, still helps increase awareness and diminish negative misconceptions.

I have worked with dozens of adults with ADHD, many of whom are not fans of Trump. Many of them initially recoiled at the thought of sharing significant traits with the president. However, for the most part they have expressed support for publicizing that Trump has ADHD, because his very public example would help demonstrate to others that their own behaviors were not just "laziness," "impulsivity," or "bad decisions"; they reflect an underlying brain condition that presents challenges in certain contexts and situations. Exposure to, greater understanding of, and conversations about adult ADHD, including Trump's, decrease, rather than increase, stigmatization.

Chapter 13

BIG DATA TO THE RESCUE? TECHNOLOGY ALTERS ADHD ASSESSMENT AND TREATMENT

Advances in technology are changing all aspects of our society, including how we practice medicine, how we practice psychiatry, and how we will be diagnosing and treating ADHD in the years to come [671-673]. We bring technology into psychiatry for the same reasons that psychiatry exists: to deepen our understanding of biologic and psychologic processes of the brain (thus enabling enhanced detection of conditions), to enhance our understanding of the natural progression of these processes (who will get better, who will get worse, and what conditions might promote either outcome), and to develop more powerful interventions to ameliorate conditions and identify which individuals are most likely to benefit from a particular treatment. Advances in technology may allow individuals and society to relish and share what is good and helpful about ADHD, and to minimize the distress and dysfunction that it can cause.

Improved Understanding and Detection of ADHD through Technology

As we deepen our understanding of how the brains of those with ADHD differ from those without, we will create new diagnostic criteria for identifying ADHD. More fundamentally, we will change how we conceptualize and define ADHD. Almost certainly, what we currently label ADHD will be viewed as a collection of separate conditions affecting executive functions. We do not yet wield Star Trek tricorders where a simple scan with our device brings up a diagnosis, but we are trending in that direction. Rather than clinging to traditions, valuable though they once were, our goal should be to improve our accuracy in identifying ADHD and our power in ameliorating it and other mental health conditions. As a society, we also need to start thinking about some of the consequences that our increased understanding of the brain will bring—for those with ADHD, other conditions, or no conditions at all.

One example of how new technology (next-generation gene sequencing) has led to new understanding and new treatment comes from the field of oncology [674]. In the last decade, cancer research and treatment have gone through an encouraging metamorphosis. For decades oncologists organized cancers by their organ of origin. The more recent and useful classification system combines new information pertaining to genetic mutations in tumor cells that lead to rampant and aberrant growth, along with traditional information about the organ of origin [675]. Knowing the lineage and biochemical mechanisms that promote cancerous growth has allowed us to find more precise and effective approaches to treating cancer. Although the brain is more complicated than cellular reproduction, the hope exists that by understanding on a neural or network-level which processes are disrupted in mental conditions, we will be able to better classify these conditions, and treat them more effectively. Identifying subsets of ADHD should lead to more specific, individualized, and helpful approaches to treatment.

We marvel when Sherlock Holmes or Dr. Gregory House examines an individual, extracts a few esoteric clues, and arrives at insights and diagnoses without conducting an exhaustive interview or evaluation. In many ways their approach differs little from our own approach when seeing a man talking loudly and disjointedly on a subway platform—could he have ADHD? mania? schizophrenia? be intoxicated? or just be distracted and talking on a cell phone with a poor connection? We make observations, generate a list of potential diagnoses, try to eliminate all options until one remains, and seek additional information to confirm it. Much of the diagnostic power of a Holmes or a House lies in having an immediately accessible and comprehensive body of information about health conditions, in order to identify those few isolated and seemingly disconnected observations that are truly critical and revelatory. Computers are rapidly improving the speed and accuracy in performing such tasks, and will soon, consistently, outperform our best human diagnosticians.

Currently, detecting whether a person has ADHD is a personal and private matter. If you suspect you have it (or if your parent or guardian suspects you do), you must choose to go to a professional to be evaluated. This requires both awareness of the condition (or at least of the existence of some problem), and willingness to be evaluated. Many who suspect they or their child might have ADHD choose to avoid being evaluated due to fear of diagnosis or treatment, or out of belief systems and values that don't attach particular importance to diagnosis or treatment [32, 94, 115]. In a plausible future, ADHD might be diagnosed in public places by video systems detecting eye movements or other facial behaviors, whether you want to be evaluated or not. Already facial recognition scans are being used as part of anti-terrorism safeguards at the entrances to Madison Square Garden and other public arenas [676, 677].

If you use a computer to research information, connect with friends, or make purchases, large corporations and the government likely already know you better than you know yourself [678, 679]. Their datasets reveal who you interact with, what you like reading and watching, and what you have purchased. Their algorithms can accurately predict your probable future purchases and who you are likely to vote for. Our computers, phones, watches, wired clothing—the whole Internet of Things—glean information not just from the content of what we look at, but from *how* we browse through websites (how long you linger on an item, how many tangents you go off on) and how we navigate the entire world [679, 680]. These systems will gather vastly more accurate, numerous, and relevant information regarding who consistently behaves in ADHD-like ways in their daily lives than we can collect presently via in-person interviews and collateral information. My current assessment of Trump's ADHD reaches beyond current standards by basing a diagnosis on public information, and without his consent, but in the near future the ability to assess each of us for ADHD, or other conditions, will be prevalent from data that will be routinely collected. What rules will we impose to ensure that diagnoses based on such information will be conducted responsibly? How will we deal with the eventuality of being able to diagnose an individual with ADHD without their awareness of their condition or that others have identified them as having the condition?

We already screen and reject pilots for substance use and for ADHD [681, 682], and we disqualify vehicle drivers who use certain illicit substances [683-685]. Will we someday disqualify those who have ADHD but may be unaware of it? Should we be testing elected officials for substance abuse or mental health conditions? If preserving the safety and security of citizens is the rationale for testing the person who drives your bus or pilots your plane, isn't the presidency at least as important for public well-being?

Every method of detecting who has, or who will develop, ADHD carries ethical implications. We can already identify markers in several genes that increase the likelihood of developing ADHD [105, 111]. How should that influence those who are carriers of the genes regarding trying to conceive, or to carry a pregnancy to term? If ADHD and its severity can be definitively identified by a future intrusive brain scan, could schools or prospective employers require applicants to be scanned as a condition of entry? What if your employer is the whole nation and you are running for president? If we can obtain diagnoses without a person's awareness or cooperation, in what situations will it be appropriate to do so, and how will we prevent it from happening in those situations where we deem it inappropriate? So far, the growth of our technologic capabilities appears to be outpacing our public conversation of either the ethical or pragmatic implications of these advances.

Modern technologies provide two major pathways for amplifying our knowledge about ADHD and other brain conditions. One approach uses equipment to view aspects of brain structure or brain activity that we could not previously access. These tools let us see in greater temporal and spatial resolution how our brains are organized and how they function [686]. The other general research approach is to use the massive data-crunching power of computers to sift through vast arrays of data to extract correlations and create algorithms about human behavior from information that was previously undecipherable [687-689]. Although I have differentiated between these two ways that technology expands our knowledge of the brain into technology and big-data realms, many of the technological approaches (e.g., functional MRI) rely on, and only became possible with, ready access to the ability to perform immense numbers of calculations on a gargantuan amount of basic data points. Both sets of tools are likely to help us identify and understand the origins of ADHD within the brain, leading to better diagnosis and treatment.

Better Brain Imaging/Interacting through Technology

Neuro-imaging technologies that enable us to map brain structures and patterns of regional brain activation include the use of infrared (DOI), visual light, x-rays (CAT), gamma-rays (SPECT), radioactive isotopes (PET), magnetic fields (MRI, fMRI), electrical activity, and ultrasound [3, 162, 686, 690, 691]. Although the precision of these tools has been increasing, their resolution is still orders of magnitude larger than detecting the activity of a single neuron, so at best we are measuring large aggregations of neurons along with supporting, or glial cells [686]. With many of these technologies, we measure metabolic activity of collections of brain cells as a proxy for actual nerve cell firing [692]. Finally, neuro-imaging methods most commonly look at correlations rather than proving causality [693]: We know brain cells activate with certain tasks or in certain states, but don't always know if this is a result of the task, a cause of the task, or a coincidence. Despite these

Technology and ADHD Assessment and Treatment

logistical limitations, we are making progress in understanding how brains create thoughts, feelings, and behavior.

One approach using brain waves to study ADHD caused a flurry of publicity a few years ago. In 2013 the FDA approved NEBA, a medical device that extracts information from electroencephalograms (EEGs) to help clinicians more accurately diagnose ADHD in children [694]. Some viewed NEBA, which measures the ratio of the power of brainwaves in the beta and theta ranges, as a medical breakthrough, moving us to a new era where ADHD could be diagnosed by an objective, physiologic measurement [695]. The FDA was careful to point out that NEBA was not a standalone diagnostic tool, but rather it provided additional information that in conjunction with clinical evaluations and other forms of testing could be helpful in identifying which individuals have ADHD [694]. The imprimatur of the federal government encouraged some entrepreneurs to push NEBA as a way to diagnose ADHD and to promote ADHD treatments involving neuro-feedback systems that trained patients to increase their theta/beta ratios or manipulate other aspects of their EEG [696-699]. However, a collection of subsequent studies and analyses suggests that NEBA is not yet particularly beneficial in diagnosing patients with ADHD. These approaches have been less helpful than desired because they are not yet accurate enough to correctly diagnose a patient with ADHD [700], since the theta/beta ratio in control groups has been found to be similar to that of groups of individuals with ADHD [701, 702]; in addition, training with neuro-feedback systems has not yet demonstrated greater efficacy than sham neuro-feedback or in changing real-world aspects of ADHD, as measured by the Conners scale [703]. Whether or not some variation of these diagnostic and treatment approaches someday proves accurate and useful, their popularity has demonstrated both interest in, and a market for, more objective ways to diagnose ADHD and non-medication approaches to treat it.

For more than a decade, some clinics have promoted the use of SPECT scans, which employ radioactive markers to assess localized changes in brain metabolism and hence brain activity, in the evaluation of ADHD [704]. SPECT scans have been presented as a more scientific and objective way to diagnose subtypes of ADHD, and provide treatment recommendations specific for those subtypes [705]. Although these claims may contain elements of truth, they have yet to be replicated by other research groups, and it is not clear how well the reported variations in regional brain metabolism adequately differentiate those with ADHD from those with other conditions, or with no conditions at all [706].

One study using MRI to examine childhood ADHD not only found differences in the brains of children with ADHD compared to controls, but also found differences between those children who outgrew most of their ADHD symptoms by adulthood, compared to those who still robustly met ADHD criteria as young adults [104]. Similarly, Shaw's research group found that a specific genetic marker present in the dopamine receptor subtype 4 gene was associated with a subset of children with ADHD who went on to outgrow their ADHD by late adolescence [707]. If we can replicate these studies and verify the findings it would provide important information for individuals about the likely progression of their ADHD. For many families this information would strongly influence deciding on treatment options for their children with ADHD.

As functional brain imaging approaches advance, in the future we should be able, for each individual with ADHD, to find out which subsets of executive functions demonstrate inefficiencies or impairments. Moving further in the direction of individualized medicine, we should also be able to discover what types of environmental situations are most likely to elicit problems for these individuals. This might lead to highly individualized prescriptions for medication or for psychotherapeutic, behavioral, or physical brain activation approaches. Perhaps more invasively, this information may lead to predictions, and depending on our societies, pressure or even mandates to take or shun certain jobs, live in or avoid certain areas, and associate with or eschew certain partners.

In addition to directly looking at the size and shape of brain structures, or the metabolic activity of clusters of cells in the brain, other technological advances allow us to examine a variety of other output from the brain in trying to detect ADHD or other mental health conditions. For example, spectral analyses of sound recordings can pick out differences in pitch and speech patterns that correspond with differences in mood states, with greater sensitivity than most people discern just through listening [708]. Video cameras and software analysis can reliably detect micro-expressions of emotions that occur more rapidly than most untrained humans perceive [709-712]. Researchers and entrepreneurs have been investigating and capitalizing on approaches that measure involuntary, tiny, anticipatory eye movements during a computer test (test of variables of attention, T.O.V.A.®), which provides data on attention and the ability to suppress responses [713, 714]. Evidence suggests that individuals with ADHD have eye movements that distinguish them from control groups, and furthermore, that treatment with methylphenidate (Ritalin) normalizes these eye movements in people with ADHD so that they more closely resemble the control group [713]. This technology was recently cleared by the FDA to aid in the assessment of, and evaluating the treatment for, ADHD [715]. Within a few years, information from EEG ratios, SPECT scans, eye movement detection, or some other technology will likely lead to tests for ADHD that are more objective and possibly more accurate than our current clinical evaluations.

As of this writing (spring 2019), noninvasive electrical stimulation of the trigeminal nerve emerged as the latest technological advance in ADHD treatment [716]. A small patch that straps to the forehead delivers low voltage pulses to the trigeminal nerve, which relays the signal to brain stem centers, then to the midbrain, and on to the frontal cortex, where it appears to increase brain cell activation. Not only did children improve on real-world measures of ADHD symptoms, but they also had changes in EEG that have been correlated with better performances on executive function tests. While only several dozen children have been studied so far, the results are encouraging enough to suggest that we may have devised another method to alter brain performance, and improve functioning, in individuals with ADHD. Technology is providing more tools not just to map and learn about the brain, but to directly impact it at the level of neural networks.

Benefits of Number Crunching

In contrast to the technology-based approaches that bring us new information about brain structures, brain connectivity, or brain activation during certain tasks, number crunching looks at piles of data and tries to extract the lessons buried within. By allowing us to parse much larger troves of information than we could analyze with our limited computing power or brain functions in the past, these approaches give us access to previously inaccessible information buried in the reams of data. It is likely that some of these data-extraction methods tap into the same insights that are expressed/revealed/uncovered by what we call clinical experience or wisdom.

Telemedicine, or the use of video systems to conduct mental health evaluation and treatment remotely, is already one way that technology is expanding how we practice psychiatry [717]. Particularly in areas with limited access to mental health professionals, both ongoing video sessions and initial video evaluations are becoming increasingly common [718]. In contrast to the clandestine or covert gathering of information by governments and corporations discussed a few paragraphs earlier, telemedicine implies at least some direct consent and awareness that the system is collecting and recording relevant health information; however, ethical issues arise regarding the extent of information collected and the ways that clinicians or researchers use that information. As techniques advance, telemedicine will increasingly be able to provide information on tiny movements of the eyes, head, and body, which are too small or fast for most humans to register. Its capabilities to monitor the flow of speech, to detect gaps that might show inattention or digressions suggesting distractibility, will continue to grow. These systems will observe and process vastly more information relevant to diagnosing ADHD or other mental health conditions compared to what any person can accomplish. Being able to diagnose Trump's ADHD from available video represents a minuscule expansion in our ability to accurately assess ADHD, compared to the fundamental transformation in our capabilities that technology offers.

Video and audio-crunching algorithms already are able to mimic a therapist and allow some patients to open up and disclose more to an avatar therapist than to a "real human" [710, 719], with the ability to not only listen but also track fidgeting, eye glances, micro-facial movements, and whole body shifts, and to calculate whether these behaviors occur at times of heightened tension, as measured by speech content, changes in tone, and facial expressions. Furthermore, these systems can then reply with appropriate comments [709, 710]. Currently, the scientists developing this technology caution that these approaches are not yet a substitute for a human therapist, and are not ready to be relied on for making diagnoses [709]. In the not too distant future, we are extremely likely to witness these algorithms and computer deductions making conclusions and interpretations never reached by humans.

One of the older, well-publicized uses of such a data-mining approach in clinical neuroscience was employed in the Nun Study. Autobiographical essays that novitiates wrote in their twenties and thirties were later scored for linguistic ability, and those whose writing displayed high levels of language complexity when young were less likely than their lower-linguistic ability peers to develop dementia decades later [720]. A derivative study, also of women (and men) in religious orders, found that conscientiousness seemed to offer some protective effect against the onset of dementia [721]. A slew of more recent approaches have used natural language processing (NLP) programs (not to be confused with Neuro-Linguistic Programming, aka "NLP") to scour vast collections of medical records and hospital discharge notes (much simpler now that many of them are computerized) to ascertain who is at increased risk for being re-admitted to a hospital in the following month [722] or to die from suicide or accidental death in the years following a psychiatric admission [723]. Some of these studies use hypothesis testing, identifying variables beforehand that may be connected to future outcomes, whereas others more broadly assess as much information as is available, and look at whatever correlations arise. Knowing which of our ADHD patients display increased risk for stimulant abuse, stimulant induced psychosis, suicide, or accidents could aid in determining who might benefit from approaches that help make such outcomes less likely.

New Errors in the New Era and Psychological Barriers to Adopting New Approaches

Technological advances bring consequences. New technologies may reduce errors that were inherent in the old system, but they also bring about new errors of their own. Even if a new diagnostic system proves to be more precise or accurate than current standards, we will still have to decide how much better the new system is before we abandon our old classifications and diagnostic criteria. We expect the powers of computing to render new technologies more precise and accurate than their predecessors—but will they prove to be so, with ADHD?

Often, while eliminating or reducing old errors, we introduce new ones. Initial problems implementing the first wave of electronic prescribing illustrate this point. Researchers were somewhat surprised to find that the rate of errors with electronic prescriptions resembled that with the old handwritten prescriptions—both were roughly 10% [724, 725]. But the type of errors differed substantially: Electronic systems had less confusion with drug names that looked similar in sloppy handwriting, but new problems emerged from apparent inadvertent clicking on the wrong box for the dosage or formulation of a medication [724, 725]. User interfaces had to be redesigned and practitioners to be better trained in order to improve the accuracy of electronic prescribing [726].

The variables a system is designed to examine and the databases employed both constrain the utility of algorithm-based approaches. We have the infamous example of the Google facial recognition program that had difficulties differentiating African-Americans from African great apes, and Microsoft's and IBM's problems differentiating the gender of non-white individuals from photos, presumably because the original datasets relied so heavily on white, male faces [727]. If we omit important information from the databases, it remains unavailable for later analyses. Maybe (not that I think this is too likely) in the Nun Study the color of ink that the young women selected to write their diaries provides a better predictor of dementia outcomes decades later, but if that material was never entered into the database, the algorithm can't extract it.

Even when new technologies bring advancements to psychiatry, resistance to change will arise for several reasons. Clinicians may cling to their old systems of assessing who has ADHD even if we develop more accurate tests for it. Some of this represents an unwillingness to cede control. Some doctors and therapists believe that their judgment or experience surpasses all others and will not want to let go of their tried-and-true approaches.

Another source for resistance to new approaches derives from our attentional processes. Humans are considerably better at detecting the introduction of something novel rather than at registering the absence of something old [728]. People are much more likely to notice if you suddenly start wearing eyeglasses than if you chronically wore them and suddenly stopped. We will be more aware of new problems that are created or caused by novel systems and less aware of the problems that have disappeared because we have averted or avoided them. And if we don't attend to the improvements and the problems solved, then we tend to not appreciate them. Our tendency to focus on new problems and ignore what we have resolved creates a barrier to adopting new approaches.

Numerous studies also indicate that humans are biased toward attending to the negative more strongly than the positive [729, 730]. Evolutionary psychology proposes that this negative bias developed because ignoring negative information often has more severe or lethal consequences than ignoring positive information. Knowing (and avoiding) where the cave bear lives saved more lives than knowing where one tasty root grew. And the day you broke your leg is much more memorable than all of the days you avoided breaking it; we generally consider avoidance of calamity as simply part of the background noise of life. This negative/positive attentional bias strengthens resistance to adopting new technologies because we are likely to register the problems more strongly than the benefits.

Furthermore, new technologies can disrupt our old attitudes regarding how to apportion blame when there are system failures, which can slow down implementation of new technologies. Our current flurry of concern over self-driving cars illustrates this point. By several measures (number of traffic violations, number of minor accidents, number of fatal accidents per miles driven) some of the new technologies are safer than humans driving cars [731-733]. However, each calamity caused by the autonomous vehicles gets blamed on the self-driving technology itself, whereas existing car crashes get blamed on drunk driving, bad road conditions, inclement weather, et al. We act like none of these factors presents a threat to us because they are already part of the fabric of our lives (and deaths). Even if self-driving technology reduces US car fatalities tenfold, to around 3,500 a year [734], or ten a day, each of those remaining deaths will still be a tragedy, and will garner media attention regarding the dangers of the new technology, ignoring the thousands of lives saved. It remains unclear how much safer the new technology needs to be before a majority of the population will accept it.

With autonomous cars (if we deem safety as the most important variable), we at least have an objective measure to assess what is an improvement, but with diagnosis of ADHD by new technologies, measuring improvement is more difficult. What if we move into a realm where the new standard actually surpasses the old? How do we assess a yardstick that is better than the gold standard? There will be at least some people in that future who will be diagnosed with ADHD who wouldn't have received the diagnosis under current standards. What metrics will we use to decide whether the current or the future standard for diagnosis is "better" for individuals or for our society? And if our diagnoses change, what subsequent changes ensue regarding treatment, personal acceptance and awareness, or societal attitudes?

Further Implications of Technological Advances

Beyond advancing our understanding of ADHD and other brain conditions, and changing how we detect and diagnose them, technological advances alter us as individuals and as a society. While the next and final chapter focuses on how changes in technology and society form feedback loops making our society more ADHD-like, I will complete this chapter with further musings on some of the social and ethical implications of how our technology changes us.

A few paragraphs back I addressed how much information our wired world has learned about us, but these systems are already shaping us as well. Not only does your computer know your purchasing and voting patterns and predilections, internet systems already send information to increase the likelihood of you taking specific actions. Not only do online ads overtly manipulate our behavior, the algorithms bombard us with additional information that is intentionally selected and skewed to influence our behavior. The options that come to the top of our internet searches are influenced by what we have searched for in the past [735]. We are being influenced and shaped with very little conscious awareness of the biases that are being fed to us, and we have less volitional choice than we think [736]. We are being manipulated in a multitude of ways without knowing we are being manipulated [737]. And even when these manipulations are pointed out, the human response that I commonly see and experience myself, is to believe that while others are being duped or influenced, "I'm not as susceptible to these forces." (See, I knew you'd say that!)

How much free will do we have if others are shaping our decisions for us? What is the meaning of voting in a democracy if we have been so pervasively manipulated that we are substantially following the directions of others rather than making "independent" decisions? While elections have long been designed to persuade voters, and while many of the most effective rhetorical appeals have targeted emotional factors rather than rational thinking, the sophistication and sheer volume of modern approaches substantially shifts the balance of power toward those delivering the information (or intentional misinformation, or probably most often partial and skewed information) and away from the voters who are ostensibly the decision makers.

One particular irony of the 2016 presidential elections follows the "others may be duped, but I'm more aware" mantra. Although many individuals spent considerable effort and thought, and thoroughly canvassed their own values in deciding for whom to vote, it is hard to refute that on a collective level, the groups most substantially swayed/influenced/coerced by waves of propaganda were actually the voters who viewed themselves as the most non-conformist, untrusting of elites, and opposed to the system—the extremes of both the pro-Trump movement and Bernie-ites [738]. Are we already approaching a time when we have become so programmed by the information we are fed that it is pointless to have elections at all?

Our advances in technology are increasingly blurring what is personal and what is social. The diagnosis and treatment of ADHD is already both a social and a personal issue [31, 116]. Many children are steered towards an evaluation of ADHD because of their classroom performance, particularly whether they disrupt the teacher or other students [130]. Parents may receive veiled or direct threats that children with ADHD will be removed from a school if they don't agree to treatment [36, 72]. If some schools are already making such demands, what if governments mandated testing or treatment for ADHD? Already in China people are being given "social compliance" scores depending on how well they conform to behaviors that are considered to promote the social good [739]. Should people with ADHD receive special accommodations for their scores? Is how we value people based more on their performance or their potential? Should societies decide whether to maximize safety and security if it is at the expense of individual expression, creativity, and freedom?

Separate from screening our entire population, should people running for public office or being appointed to vital decision-making and leadership roles be vetted for ADHD or other mental health conditions? Isn't the mental health of our leaders more relevant to their behavior and performance than most aspects of physical health? Over the history of our country, we have been moving towards demanding greater transparency for the pubic, and reducing the right to privacy concerning the health and personal lives of our public officials [740-742]. Isn't Donald Trump's ADHD at least as relevant to his presidency as FDR's polio [743] or JFK's Addison's disease [744]? I don't personally feel that any of these conditions should prevent somebody from having a position of power, but I do think that the public can't make a reasoned decision regarding a leader without such information. And we should keep in mind that although psychiatrists' diagnoses remain imperfect, we can make psychiatric diagnoses with considerably more precision and accuracy than we could fifty years ago.

If, in the future, we know more about the brains of our presidential prospects, how do we determine what makes the "best" leader? The one who keeps us most safe? most prosperous? happiest? most sustainable as a society or species? And how do we measure safety: Is it about averting disasters or reducing the risks of mortality? Is it more important to improve opportunity for all, or to generally improve living conditions for the majority? Are different traits more desirable in some political or historical eras than others? Can we ever be sure of what type of era we are in at the moment? Given that there is no apparent unanimity among historians about what makes a great president, I doubt that we will reach a consensus, and to some extent that is the point of a democracy—for us to make decisions based on what we feel and think and know at the time that we vote.

In summary, how we diagnose ADHD is changing, and while today it may be heresy to some if we diagnose Trump with ADHD without a clinical evaluation, in a very few years our current standards will have certainly changed. At the very least, we will have a variety of new ways to acquire more accurate information. While the clinical interview is likely to continue as a source of important information and insight for the foreseeable future, other sources of information will grow in importance for diagnosing and treating individuals with ADHD and other mental health conditions. My hope is that the empathy and humanity imbued in the clinical evaluation is not lost as we become more precise, scientific, and quantifiable in our approaches to helping people with the distress and dysfunction in their lives.

Chapter 14

IS ADHD CONTAGIOUS? CULTURAL APPROPRIATION OF THE ADHD COMMUNITY

ADHD Feedback Loops

Working to reduce the stigma associated with ADHD is reasonable, desirable, and attainable. Should we venture even further as a society, beyond changing attitudes, to building structures and supporting practices that would make our world more ADHD-friendly? One answer would be to acknowledge that we are already in the midst of a vast cultural appropriation of the ADHD community. In my personal and professional view, the incursion of the internet and other information technologies into our daily lives, and the struggle to process this vast input, encourages all of our brains to function more like those of individuals with ADHD, and multiple lines of research support this contention. We are already borrowing and adopting an ADHD-like mode of experiencing life without asking permission from the ADHD community, or thinking through the consequences of our appropriation. We have immersed ourselves in the midst of a large-scale experiment, to which none of us gave informed consent, potentially making society, and each of our individual brains, more like a brain with ADHD.

ceptive to these modes of thought, and the more likely we are to respond in a similar manner ourselves.

For most traits, including those related to ADHD, genes generally don't dictate which exact point on a spectrum we fall on, but rather what range or sector of that spectrum we will operate within. Our environment and experiences modulate where within that genetically prescribed range we function at a given moment [85]. How we collectively use our brains shapes our society. The principle of neural plasticity indicates that how we use our brains also reshapes our brains, by strengthening the connections we use and exercise, and atrophying those pathways we no longer activate regularly [749]. Because of the malleability of our brains, our experiences and practices can push us to one end or the other of our inherited range of potential behaviors. The environments we grow up in and the behaviors that are reinforced contribute to who we are and what we are becoming, both as individuals and as a society. As we practice being more distracted, less patient, more immediately responsive, more driven by images than words, et al., we shape our brains and our cultures accordingly.

When I discuss the ADHD-ification of our society, I am employing it as a metaphor, just as societies can be seen as friendly, or anxious, or belligerent. Clearly this does not imply that everyone in the group displays these characteristics, or that anyone displays them all the time. However, I am arguing that on an individual level, cultural forces create and promote specific behavioral patterns, and even change brains, with the result that over time more individuals meet full diagnostic criteria for ADHD. Some may mistakenly claim that if our current culture generates new cases of ADHD this demonstrates the fallacy in claiming that ADHD is a brain-based condition. However, we know that other biologically based diseases become more common through cultural changes. When more people smoke, or we allow industrial smokestacks to spew into urban communities, the prevalence of asthma, COPD, and lung cancer all increase—which does not refute that these are "real" conditions. We also know that in war zones, more people exhibit a full range of PTSD symptoms than in realms with less violent conflict. Decades of research, and tens of thousands of studies, indicate that ADHD is a biologically based brain condition influenced by

Some of our societal changes seem likely to help those navigate the world more successfully. Our cell phone electronic devices act as surrogate brains that maintain ou track our to-do lists, and provide access to tremendou. information. Much of this information is available pictoriall images, and videos, rather than the encyclopedias of written inf that served as the reservoirs of information for past generation. several patients with ADHD who are daunted by a list of errands, but who can manage with a series of pictures (a bath be cleaned, shirts to go to the cleaners, a dentist's appointment to help them navigate a catalog of chores. By providing conven reminders during the day, phones and watches can cut down on number of appointments missed and can help break larger tasks in manageable pieces. In our world, many tasks can be outsourced t others (maybe not the dentist visit), so individuals with ADHD are left with fewer time-consuming tasks to manage than in past generations. Although inundation with too many reminders makes it easy to override or ignore these alarms and cues, in some cases technology furnishes the structure and organization that those with ADHD find difficult to provide for themselves.

The ADHD-ification of our society appears likely to intensify for a multitude of reasons. The very ease of being connected through modern communication systems to more people with ADHD may alter our own behaviors. The application of network theory to psychology provides a method to quantify how behaviors might be transmitted through a society; one's susceptibility to certain mental illnesses and other conditions relates to the number and strength of the connections to others with that condition or who have pertinent prevailing factors [745]. Studies demonstrate that having more depressed people in your community reinforces the likelihood that you will develop depression, and the same is true for becoming overweight, or for developing PTSD [745-747]. Could the same be true of ADHD characteristics? Is ADHD a contagious mental health condition [748]? It seems likely that the more we interact with people who behave impatiently, who flit from topic to topic, who are tardy, who are driven by images, and who don't plan ahead, the more our brains become environmental factors. We should expect "ADHD-ogenic" environments to provide conditions that produce more individuals who fully manifest the condition, and to cause many in the "normal" range to move closer to the ADHD end of their potential behavioral repertoire. Given the world we live in, we should expect to see the prevalence of ADHD continue to increase, and since younger brains show more neuroplasticity and are more likely to be fully immersed in this modern cultural milieu, increases in ADHD should be most prominent among the young.

Numerous feedback loops, based on network theory and neuroplasticity [750], combine to modify human behavior. One well-studied feedback loop involves depression and alcohol intake. Greater alcoholic intake damages the brain, making it more prone to depression [751,752], while depression itself promotes excessive drinking [753]. In the worst-case scenario more drinking leads to more depression leads to more drinking, potentially resulting in death by suicide, cirrhosis, or accident. In our modern societies, numerous such feedback loops reinforce the severity of ADHD symptoms in individuals and the prevalence of ADHD-like behavior among the populace. These ADHD-promoting feedback loops include those that involve diet, sleep, exercise, internet use, and both personal and public communication, each of which I examine in the following sections.

When I describe these feedback loops to patients, they often react with a fascinated horror, as if I am describing an inescapable, perpetually reinforcing system in which they will be trapped forever. I remind them that while feedback loops do tend to reinforce and strengthen themselves, the very nature of such circuits means that *anywhere* you cleave the circle, you interrupt the pattern of self-reinforcement. Feedback loops always provide multiple potential sites for disruption. At the conclusion of each description of an ADHD-feedback loop in the following pages, I will offer suggestions for how one might break that ADHD-reinforcing feedback circuit.

The ADHD-Food Loop

Dietary deficiencies or sensitivities may contribute to ADHD, while ADHD itself may encourage poorer eating habits, thus completing a feedback loop. Decades of studies suggest that some Western diets high in processed foods, and perhaps most particularly food dyes, may increase the risk or severity of ADHD in children [754-756]. Children with low levels of omega-3 fatty acids are more likely to display ADHD symptoms [757], and supplementation with omega-3s may improve ADHD symptoms [757]. Similarly, multiple studies have detected a correlation in children between ADHD and low levels of vitamin D [759]. Supplementing the diets of children with ADHD with micronutrients appears to improve ADHD symptoms [756]. Infants with low levels of omega-3 fatty acids in their body at birth are more likely to develop ADHD [758], as are children with low levels of vitamin D [759]. Thus, there are several indications that poor nutrition may contribute to the development of ADHD or exacerbate symptoms of ADHD in individuals with the condition. On a societal level, we consume vastly more sugar, along with more chemical additives (including inadvertent additives like pesticides; prenatal pesticide exposure has been associated with development of ADHD) than people did a generation or two ago. We also eat far more meals outside of the home (more potential distractions), take less time to eat, and more often eat while engaging in other activities (watching television, using mobile electronic devices). It seems likely that the further we deviate from having wholesome and natural diets and from feasting in relaxed and non-distracting environments, the more we risk problems with concentration, distractibility, hyperactivity, or other ADHD-like behaviors.

Evidence also suggests that having ADHD increases the likelihood of eating an unhealthy diet [755, 760], perhaps by contributing to impulsive food choices. Not that any one product deserves singling out, but we might label this self-reinforcing ADHD-diet cycle the "Fruit Loops loop." Numerous studies find a higher rate of obesity among those with ADHD [761, 762]. Extensive literature supports that distracted eating results in making poorer dietary choices and consuming increased calories [763-766].

ADHD not only contributes to the problem of distracted eating and poor food choices, but also contributes to distracted non-eating. Whenever a patient recounts to me the events of their day and mentions that one evening they suddenly realized that they "hadn't eaten all day," I always hear this as a possible indicator of ADHD. In my clinical experience, and that of other practitioners, many individuals with ADHD are less attuned to signals from their body: They miss meals until they are really, really hungry, or don't go to sleep until they are very, very tired. Although the stimulant medications used to treat ADHD possess appetite-suppressing properties, many individuals with ADHD miss hunger cues even when they are not taking medications. Skipping daytime meals has two adverse effects: People tend to overeat when they have been deprived of food [767] and calories consumed in the evening hours are metabolized more slowly, causing greater weight gain than from eating an equivalent number of calories during the daytime [768]. Overeating, nighttime eating, and less thoughtful food choices likely all contribute to the higher rates of obesity among those with ADHD.

Several studies and a meta-analysis of this research fail to validate the popular view that high-sugar intake *immediately and directly* promotes hyperactivity [755]. The over-exuberance exhibited by a child with ADHD at a birthday party probably has more to do with the intensity and amount of social stimuli than with how much cake or ice cream has been consumed. However, Robert Lustig, a pediatric endocrinologist and a crusader for lowering the amount of sugar in our diet, has proposed a mechanism by which sugar may have more global effects on generating ADHD-like behavior than by merely promoting hyperactivity [769]. He maintains that sugar is an addictive substance and that sugar consumption rewires the brain in favor of immediate-reward-dopamine-pleasure systems at the expense of serotonin-driven-contentment systems. Thus sugar consumption may promote responding instantaneously and seeking immediate gratification while simultaneously weakening long-term planning and evaluation of long-term benefits, thereby increasing the likelihood for developing ADHD-like behavior [770].

Many of the practices useful for breaking the eating-ADHD feedback loop include common recommendations that dietitians make to most Americans: Eat a varied diet, decrease the intake of processed foods, have regular mealtimes, and for some, supplement with micronutrients or fatty acids. In addition, be more mindful when eating: Don't try to multi-task; rather, focus on the food at hand, and remove distracting devices including reading material or other items not germane to enjoying a meal. Keep snack items out of sight in cupboards, so that you have to make a conscious decision to obtain them, rather than grazing from countertops. Eat sitting down, not while standing in front of the refrigerator or walking around the kitchen. For people with ADHD, it can be particularly useful to schedule mealtimes on their daily planner and use reminder systems to indicate when it is time to eat. When those with ADHD decline to eat at mealtime because they "aren't hungry," remind them that we are no longer hunter-gatherers on the brink of survival, and in modern times we eat to *prevent* hunger, not in *response* to hunger. Doing a better job of fueling our brains goes a long way toward helping our brains take better care of us and making fewer "fuelish" mistakes.

The ADHD-Sleep Loop

Poor sleep contributes to attention problems, while ADHD can lead to insufficient quality sleep; together these constitute the ADHD-sleep feedback loop [771]. Disruption of a single night's sleep leads to troubles with distractibility and poor concentration the following day, while long-term sleep deprivation exacerbates these effects, resulting in greater deficiencies in attention, more errors in calculating, further slowing of reaction times, and increased errors of judgment [772, 773]. As a byproduct of being alive and awake and thinking, our brain cells produce metabolic debris; our brains cart away this cellular sludge during sleep [774]. Accumulations of cellular waste are neurotoxic and correlate with the development of Alzheimer's dementia; accumulations of this type of debris can be found even after just one day of sleep deprivation [775]. Thus, sleep that is not long or deep enough worsens ADHD symptoms in individuals, and at a societal level contributes to more ADHD-like behavior overall.

While sleep deprivation harms all humans, people with ADHD may be particularly sensitive. As mentioned in Chapter 2, the severity of symptoms in most people with ADHD varies significantly day to day, and most individuals I have worked with find that a poor night's sleep is the best predictor for functioning less than optimally the next day. Severe and persistent sleep problems, like obstructive sleep apnea, can create a clinical picture that resembles ADHD, with problems in an array of executive functions [776]. Furthermore, studies have demonstrated resolution of the ADHD-like problems in children when their sleep apnea was corrected surgically or with medical devices [777-780]. Thus, at least some of the detrimental effects on the brain of insufficient sleep are reversible.

Although public service announcements have been telling Americans for years to get roughly eight hours of sleep each night, and extensive research suggests that this amount of sleep is optimal for most adult brains [781], more than 75% of adults age twenty-five to fifty-five sleep less than eight hours on workday nights [782]. For adolescents and teens, recommended sleep needs are even higher at nine or more hours, with 87% of high-schoolers getting inadequate sleep [783]. The trend among youth and adults in America of obtaining less and less sleep has persisted for years [784, 785]. Many individuals even adopt a macho pride in boasting of how little sleep they had the night before. Would we brag about trying to work while drunk, or driving while sitting on one hand, or trying other tasks while functionally impaired?

The public proclamations of our sleep experts have underemphasized that our brains require not just eight hours of sleep each night, but the *same* eight hours. Mathew Walker's informative and delightful book, *Why We Sleep,* presents a rare exception to this trend [773]. If one regularly sleeps from midnight to eight a.m., then trying to sleep from four a.m. to noon does not provide the same rest or recuperation [773, 786] despite being the same length. Desynchronization of our circadian (twenty-four hour) clocks can sabotage our executive functions to a similar extent as sleep deprivation [787]. Interestingly, preliminary studies of utilizing morning exposure to the bright lights used to treat seasonal depression have shown improvement in cognitive functions and symptoms in people with ADHD [788, 789]. Who knew that in addition to his other accomplishments, Ben Franklin was a chronobiologist ahead of his time when he codified the "early to bed, early to rise" maxim?

Completing this feedback loop, we also know that ADHD correlates with and contributes to disturbances of sleep. A strikingly large majority of individuals with ADHD are night owls who habitually stay up late, and subjectively feel that they function best in the late evening or at night [790-794]; strong genetic factors influence this trait [791, 795]. In addition, the stimulants that are widely used to treat ADHD often make it more difficult to fall asleep or stay asleep. (Interestingly, I and other clinicians work with a subset of individuals with ADHD for whom taking a small dose of stimulants at bedtime actually aids in falling asleep. For these individuals, having numerous thoughts ricocheting through their head makes drifting off difficult, but the stimulant reduces this mental chaos and allows them to corral their remaining thoughts, thus slipping into sleep more easily.) Poor sleep worsens ADHD symptoms and creates ADHD-like behavior in the rest of us, while ADHD, and our increasingly ADHD-like culture, contributes to sleep deprivation and disruption.

Ensuring regular and sufficient sleep remains one of the most important and challenging tasks for many adults with ADHD. Setting an alarm for going to sleep provides a clear, external signal to stop engaging in daytime activities and begin preparing for bed. If the time-for-sleep alarm does not suffice, I recommend timers on room lights to darken the space, or apps that will lock individuals out of their social media or shut down their electronic devices at bedtime. Developing bedtime rituals also reinforces circadian rhythms and provides a clear demarcation from frenetic daytime life to peaceful sleep time.

However, since many individuals with ADHD have night-owl tendencies as well as a drive to act spontaneously and to resist authority, I often find it necessary to add several cognitive therapy approaches to the behavioral recommendations. I inform individuals that respecting a regular bedtime is a biological mandate, not just a social construct. Life evolved on this planet for four or five billion years in environments with powerful day vs. night differences in temperature, sound, and electromagnetic radiation (most clearly experienced by humans in the visible light part of the spectrum). Plants, animals, unicellular bacteria—we all have circadian clocks to regulate our biologic functions.

We can either work with Mother Nature and follow a consistent schedule for sleep, or battle against her, and against our own brains, by ignoring a regular bedtime. Many individuals with ADHD are less resistant to following a biological demand for regular bedtime than to succumbing to what they feel are arbitrary or authoritarian social rules about lights out.

To those night owls who really do function best at night, I remind them that every day of their life (except maybe their last one) will contain an evening and night—they don't have to try to cram everything in *tonight*. Staying up late doesn't create a twenty-fifth or twenty-sixth hour to the day; this isn't a zero-sum game. And for every extra hour one stays up late today, one steals several hours' worth of productivity from the next day, because of the inefficiency of our sleep-deprived or circadian-rhythm-shifted brains. On a societal level we should continue recommending eight hours of sleep and emphasize that getting the same eight hours is important, even on weekends. If you don't feel ready to adopt these recommendations for proper and healthy repose, then just sleep on it—you may change your mind!

The ADHD-Exercise Loop: One More Rep!

Numerous studies [796], along with comments from scores of patients, indicate that exercise can help improve attention and other executive functions in those with ADHD. Thus the evidence that Americans overall are engaging in less physical activity, and that the proliferation of screen-time leisure activities makes people more sedentary [797], suggests that our current societal trends are contributing to an increase in ADHD symptoms in affected individuals and making ADHD symptoms more prevalent in the general population. The second half of this feedback loop, that ADHD contributes to exercising less, remains largely anecdotal. I have met hundreds of individuals with ADHD who say that they like running, lifting weights, or other physical activity but find it hard to sustain a routine. They get intensely involved for a few weeks or months, and then lose interest and derail their activity, becoming markedly less active for months at a time. Thus, a lack of exercise is believed to contribute to ADHD, and ADHD may contribute to achieving lower levels of physical fitness.

The greater prevalence of being overweight or obese among those with ADHD supports the claim that, as a group, those with ADHD are not exercising enough (at least relative to their dietary intake). Furthermore, being overweight exacerbates the exercise-ADHD feedback loop. Being overweight makes it more difficult to move around, and makes one more prone to overheating with movement, both of which increase the barriers to exercising. One might anticipate that the hyperactivity of ADHD would contribute to having lower body mass indices, since even non-exercise activities such as fidgeting burn measurable calories and could facilitate weight loss [798]. We know that stimulant medications can reduce excessive motor activity in those with ADHD [54], which may be one pathway by which those treated with these agents may actually burn fewer calories, and thus gain weight.

Being physically active is one of the best lifestyle choices one can make to preserve cognitive functioning and prevent dementia [799]. Having a healthy body provides support for a healthy brain. Being sedentary may be as bad for one's health as smoking, diabetes, or heart disease [800]. General recommendations for maintaining an exercise regimen apply to those with ADHD as well: Choose activities that you enjoy doing and have a regular schedule for performing them. For many people making exercise a social as well as a physical activity makes it harder to get off track, so work out with a friend, or in a class or group. Setting goals, either related to improving performance or maintaining a number of workouts each month, helps many to continue when they might otherwise waver. Many find fitness watches and activity monitors particularly helpful for maintaining motivation and monitoring progress. Periodically remind yourself what you enjoy about any particular physical activity. Enjoyment motivates more strongly than telling yourself that you should, or need to, or ought to perform a given exercise. If you do interrupt your schedule, getting back on track matters more than lamenting getting derailed. A good mental exercise for everyone is to work out your objections to working out!

The ADHD-Cyber Loop: Video Killed the Radio Star (and Whom Else?)

What I call the cyber loop consists of hours of uninterrupted computer usage that weakens some executive functions, especially given that those with ADHD are more prone to immerse themselves in such activities for prolonged periods of time. By analogy, on a societal level, as we increasingly devote hours to such uninterrupted staring at cyber screens, we may also be pushing our collective brains in ADHD-like directions. Some of the evidence supporting the first half of the ADHD-cyber loop comes from studies of individuals with video game addictions [801, 802], and there are reports of gamers playing so extensively and with such neglect of bodily functions that the behavior led to their deaths [803]. Recent work has also demonstrated correlations between the amount of time children spend in front of screens, and the incidence of inattention problems [804, 805].

Up to 80% of children in some societies develop myopia (near-sightedness) following historically abrupt and extensive increases in close-up studying and computer use [806], demonstrating the impact of behavior on at least the visual-processing part of the central nervous system. We also know that being bent over a smart phone screen can damage the body, as indicated by substantial increases in neck injuries among young people [807]. It seems likely that some of the executive function problems found in video game "addicts" result not just from the specifics of game playing but also occur in those fixated for hours without breaks on their computers, tablets, or smart phones. In the following discussion of the ADHD-cyber feedback loop I describe how excessive screen time may contribute to ADHD-like problems, reserving an exploration of related feedback loops pertaining to personal and public communication for later. While the cyber loop focuses primarily on the process of interacting with computer screens, and the communication loops focus primarily on the content of what we are viewing, the process and content of our lives online clearly overlap and reinforce each other.

Brief blasts of screen imagery that toggle into tangential topics increasingly propel us to attend to what is interesting rather than what is important, and coerce us to respond to the immediate while ignoring the long-term. The visually driven process of reading requires looking at symbols, converting these stimuli into words, and then building images, characters, plots, and whole worlds from these collections of letters. The process is slower and inherently more reliant on thinking than the visual processing required for watching cyber images. Imagery pulls up emotional connections more quickly, and often more powerfully, than do written words, contributing to more reactive, less reflective, responses. This onslaught of visual information pushes our brains to behave in more ADHD-like ways.

Those with ADHD are overrepresented among people with addictive use of video games and social media [801, 802]. In ADHD, the weakened control over directing attention increases the tendency to hyper-focus and ignore external cues from off-task activities [425]; hyper-focusing appears to me to be a major contributor to internet addiction. Anecdotal evidence highlights the dangerous outcomes of hyper-focusing in cyberspace—e.g., individuals so intent on playing Pokémon Go that they were robbed or harmed [808], or people so absorbed in taking selfies who become oblivious to cliffs, trains, or other risks, and die as a result [809]. Ironically, these types of screen fixations encourage physical activity, in contrast to most forms of excessive computer use that promote sedentary behaviors, as presented earlier in the ADHD-exercise loop.

By no means is all use of computers, laptops, and personal devices harmful. In the previous chapter I outlined some of the ways that computers make life easier or more organized for individuals with ADHD. And many of the experimental neuro-feedback treatments for ADHD that train people to increase activation in certain brain circuits or regions employ video games to elicit and maintain enthusiasm among participants [810, 811]. As with virtually all substances and activities, dosage determines the detriment. We need to find ways to allow healthy amounts of screen time while preventing excessive and unhealthy use, a task that remains particularly difficult for, and yet more crucial to, the well-being of those with ADHD.

People's attitude towards cyber technology presents a barrier to putting limits on our use of computers and smart phones, at both

Feedback Loops in Our ADHD World

individual and societal levels. Telling you to restrict your access to the internet or your devices is likely to leave you feeling deprived, resentful, and resistant. It may be more palatable and helpful to reframe the issue as how to restrict the internet's access to you. This shift creates the potential for you to feel liberated from the intrusiveness and crass capitalism of the internet, by reminding you that all of the delightful imagery, intriguing dialogue, and engrossing games are Trojan horses designed to entice you into directly buying products or services, or are traps to capture and sell *you* and your private information to advertisers and business partners [812, 813].

Like any other successful drug dealer, the cyber tech moguls know that having too many customers overdose is bad for business, and many are already adapting to this awareness by providing choices to make using their products a little less immediately attractive and reinforcing—like having options for grayed-out screens rather than colorful, enticing buttons to click. Use these options! Many systems have alarms to alert you when you have exceeded your scheduled time on the app or device, but these alarms are too easily ignored, especially for people with ADHD. I have had patients use a variety of strategies to deal with alarm fatigue. Some use a specific sound for each app's alarm, so they associate that sound with its linked activity and the specificity of each alarm helps each signal to be more salient and identifiable. Conversely, others use random generators to produce a different alarm for every single alert, to decrease desensitization to any particular signal. Still others use the same alarm sound for all notices, and train themselves to always and immediately attend to their alarms and their calendar in order to direct their activity to whatever task they had actually planned for that specific interval. For those who find themselves perpetually ignoring or overriding alarms, most devices or apps have ways to lock yourself out of the system at a given time rather than counting on your own willpower to remove yourself.

Nature appears to be a healthy antidote to screen time. Immersion in nature can diminish symptoms of ADHD [814]; merely looking out the window at a tree has healthful, calming, and healing effects [815]. To help break the cyber space-ADHD loop, spend more time screening your calls and less time calling your screen.

The ADHD-Private Communication Feedback Loop

The prevalence of texting and social media is making our behavior more ADHD-like, and ADHD-driven behavior encourages us to seek out more extensive and frequent connection through these forums, producing another feedback loop. Extrapolating from internet addiction studies, the intrusion of social media into our lives and our consequent immersion in a miasma of interpersonal information are weakening our executive functions [816]. Multiple streams of data constantly bombard and distract us. Information is fragmented into tinier and tinier quanta, and responses are demanded at faster and faster rates [817]. All of us have passed coffee shops where dozens of people are sitting, tapping on their devices to the exclusion of talking with the human beings sitting nearby—often the very friends or family members they are texting with! Time management and punctuality dwindle in importance when people can check in remotely from wherever they are at any moment. Long-term planning skills wither as cooperative ventures that used to require meticulous considerations and calculations, numerous steps, and long waits, now happen in impromptu and ad hoc ways. Many intelligent, resourceful millennials become completely overwhelmed by the steps needed to write, address, stamp, and post a "snail-mail" letter. The ubiquity of texting, the typos inherent in rapid emailing, and the misguided mangling of auto-correct cause a proliferation of careless mistakes in spelling and grammar, which becomes the new normal. Our behaviors and our standards trend evermore ADHD-like.

This modern environment not only alters our attention, but also contributes to disinhibition of our impulses. I perceive a multitude of factors colluding to foment this increase in impetuousness. The increased speed of interactions leaves us less time to think before we respond. When information arrives so quickly, much of it is transitory, which further reduces the perceived consequences of any given response, because "this too, shall pass." The emphasis on what is interesting rather than what is important also promotes responses that are driven to attract attention or are themselves replies to surface provocations, rather than a consideration of deeper, underlying issues. The triumph (or tyranny) of interest over importance also fosters a spirit of framing responses in terms of how this will affect us personally, rather than considering the other person, or some concept of the greater good. Finally, the anonymity of many of our computer communications and the physical distancing of our online avatars from our flesh-and-blood selves independently promote impulsive reactions by blinding us to the direct personal consequences of our actions or comments, thereby rendering us less likely to feel (much less take) personal responsibility.

Deficits in persistently employing social skills characterize the interactions of many individuals with ADHD. Some research suggests these social problems more often result from a failure to routinely apply the skills, rather than from being completely oblivious of social norms [818]. Another study indicates that those with ADHD, compared to those without it, have a stronger preference for online friends, but actually have fewer social-media friends and derive less support from them [819]. This may actually represent a narrow case of the more generalized observation that those who are more active on Facebook had lower self-reported mental health and felt more negative about themselves than those who are less active [820, 821]. Youth with ADHD, compared to other youngsters, are more hostile, forgetful, and less adept at communicating online when studied in research settings [822]. Taken together, this suggests that people with ADHD, or communities with ADHD tendencies, by favoring online communication over direct human contact, practice their social skills less often, become less socially adept, and thereby promote further cycles of miscommunication and alienation. We have vastly inflated the quantity of communication while deflating the quality, to the detriment of individuals and society.

Having nearly constant and instantaneous access to others can help those with ADHD. They can instantly ascertain lost appointment times or locations, enter responses much closer to a final deadline, or more quickly reconnect interrupted friendships than in the days when all of these tasks required far more effort and planning. However, the constant connectivity with cohorts is often not a panacea for communication. With ADHD, the right kind of structure is important: Too much is overly constraining, too little is frustrating, and either can derail attention and performance.

One patient of mine texts with his wife throughout the day when she goes on frequent business trips, and then they FaceTime at the end of the day. Even though they had ongoing contact during the day, he would feel anxious until their nighttime video communication. Eventually he realized that the texting, because both of them were distracted and multi-tasking, felt tenuous, incomplete, and less genuine than their face-to-face online communication. Even with their ongoing texting, and despite knowing he would connect with his wife sometime in the evening, his anxiety and sense of feeling cut off remained high until we discovered a solution. If he started each day by setting a definite time for that evening's FaceTime session, then that provided enough structure and certainty that he could be more at ease during the day. For many people with ADHD, what is immediately in their presence feels much more real than a nebulous future event; by making the appointment a concrete item he could see on his calendar, it became more real than just imagining that something would happen "later." It is likely that there are many other ways in which having so much ready accessibility to information and to each other, while creating an appearance of permitting spontaneity and impromptu activity, may actually be undermining our sense of security and connection, and contributing to our anxiety.

The solutions to addressing our overuse of social media are similar to those for general cyber use: Find ways to limit time spent online, particularly when in the company of others; shut off devices unless you are an emergency responder; and attend to those who are actually *in* your life.

The ADHD-News Loop: The Medium Is the Message Is the Medium Is the Message Is the....

In a single generation, changes in print and television journalism have dramatically altered how they inform us about our world. When CNN launched in 1980 it was the first 24-hour news channel; the prevailing standard was a dinnertime news show perhaps augmented by briefer early-morning and late-evening condensed versions of the same information. Presentations averaged closer to minutes than seconds, and no chyrons skulked across the bottom of our screens. A multitude of channels now provide round-the-clock "news," usually composed of brief sound bites and snippets repeated over and over. Similarly when *USA Today* began publication in 1982 it was widely derided for being "shallow" and catering to "people's interest in distraction" [823] by featuring a paragraph of clipped commentary for each state. But as of 2014, it was the daily publication with the widest US circulation [824], and a model for reducing in-depth reporting on substantive issues in favor of short items driven by human interest.

We thus receive information about the world in more and more ADHD-like fashion: Complicated stories are chunked into smaller and smaller bits [825], more energy is spent on opinions than factual reporting [826], and images that capture attention are featured more than in-depth exploration of ideas and meaning [827]. The news diet of less information, with less historical, social, and scientific context for the information, and with more emphasis on emotional elements than on rational processing, trains us to reduce our attention spans, to view information as fragmentary and isolated, and to anticipate entertainment rather than education. Once our expectations have been tuned in these directions, we demand the media feed us more of the same, completing the ADHD-media loop.

If we want each day filled with *nuance*, rather than some *new angst*, we must take control of our data streams. Rather than checking Facebook or your Twitter feed dozens of times a day, set aside twenty minutes to actually read online in-depth articles. Get facts, not just opinions. Give yourself time to think about, not just accumulate, the facts. And not all facts are useful information. While it may be interesting to update voting tallies dozens of times a day, or to capture in real time a tit-for-tat exchange between petulant officials, at the end of the day much of that is irrelevant. The real news remains who wins the election, or what policy will be advanced or altered. Opt for reading rather than watching—you control the pace, and the process elicits more thoughts than feelings. Examine your sources. While virtually all of our media have biases, it can be valuable to differentiate news channels from propaganda peddlers. A real news source will actually report when a perceived foe acts in a way to benefit the country, and will also hold their favorites accountable when they do make an error (as all of us imperfect people do), rather than trying to justify it. And real news sources monitor themselves; they correct and publicize their own errors. All of us, not just those with ADHD, will need to work harder to contextualize the information to which the media exposes us today. If we don't want to completely make a mess of this era, we need to attend not just to the content of our messages, but also to how and when they are delivered.

The ADHD-Trump Loop: He Has Thrown *Us* for a Loop

One result of society becoming more ADHD-like was our electing as president a man who would have been implausible in that role to earlier generations. Part of what made Trump attractive as a candidate was how readily he reflected parts of our ADHD-friendly culture back to us. His mastery of only what interests him, his nanosecond attention span, and his infatuation with surface over substance are all traits that match the direction our culture is racing in. And our ADHD-ified culture not only made a Trump presidency possible, but he manages to push our country and world in evermore ADHD-like directions, completing the feedback loop.

Our sound-bite society responds with incredulity that some of the audience for Abraham Lincoln's 275-word Gettysburg Address complained that his speech was too short to be meaningful or memorable [828]; the other orator that day, Edward Everett, spoke for more than two hours [829]. It is hard to imagine Trump articulately expressing himself for two hours; it is highly likely he would quickly become bored listening to the succinct eloquence of Lincoln's brief speech. Of all the societal changes in the direction of ADHD-ification, I believe that the evolution of the news media mentioned in the previous section prepared us most for a Trump presidency. By delivering information in tiny chunks, by instantly moving on to new items before the previous news is digested, by attending to the surface rather than the underlying issues, and by focusing on what was entertaining or controversial rather than addressing what was substantive, current journalism's mode of operation conditioned us to being receptive to a candidate like Trump.

Trump did not arrive *de novo*; the bar had been lowered progressively. Others have identified substantive ADHD-like behavior in both Presidents Bush [830, 831] ranging from their "garbled syntax," difficulty staying on track in speeches, and lack of the "vision thing," among other behaviors. Even some conservative writers felt that the Bushes' ADHD-traits were instrumental in their perceived failures as president [832]. Sarah Palin's word-salad paragraphs, distractibility, and tangentiality were precursors for speech patterns remarkably similar to Trump's. The two also share ADHD-driven propensities for being reactive rather than contemplative, following their guts instead of their brains, elevating their own feelings over the objective world's facts, and blurting out demeaning comments directed at those who have particular knowledge or pertinent experience on a subject. They delight their followers by being "authentic" rather than being politically correct, considerate, or thoughtful. Going back further in time, President Reagan's simplified word choices and sentence structure, and his reliance on slogans rather than expounding on ideas, particularly towards the end of his eight years as president, also foreshadowed these behaviors in Trump. For Reagan, however, these executive function deficits have been ascribed to early dementia, rather than ADHD [833]. America's embrace of previous leaders who displayed an ADHD-like ethos has culminated in electing President Trump, an exemplar of adult ADHD. (I don't believe our recent Democratic presidents and candidates are free of foibles, but as a group they have tended more towards reserved, cautious, contemplative, antithesis-of-ADHD approaches—with perhaps Joe Biden providing a mild counterexample.)

To close this final feedback loop, our ADHD-ified culture not only produced Trump, but he himself continues to push our world in evermore ADHD-like directions. He drives news cycles with controversial, impulsive statements prompted by his ADHD. Although others frame these tangential eruptions as primarily strategic or narcissistic, I believe that while both strategic or narcissistic motivations may drive a few specific incidents, the evidence argues that his ADHD drives the prevailing pattern of outbursts. If his behavior were primarily intentional and strategic, he would silence himself after putative victories, but almost constantly his uninhibited commentary on new topics distracts us at such moments. If he stockpiled these verbal explosions with the plan of purposefully using them as distractions, why would they so often emerge poorly formulated, startling his supporters as well as his adversaries, as was the case with his initial announcements about trusting Russian dictators more than his own security leaders, withdrawing troops from Syria, or depriving immigrants' children birthright citizenship. If one tries to discern a persistent strategic pattern to explain Trump's record-breaking streak of unforced errors, one would have to conclude that his underlying intent must be to convince us all that he has untreated ADHD.

If narcissism were the prevailing motivator for his outbursts and antics, we would expect these incidents to portray Trump in predominately self-flattering ways, whereas, more often his comments demean and diminish himself. An adept narcissist would make sure that an agreement was nailed down before abruptly declaring a second conference with North Korea's leader, and would have a plan in place before abruptly declaring troop withdrawals from Syria. Although the narcissistic elements of Trump's actions are often dramatic and readily apparent, the media would have tired of this aspect long ago; some significant part of our continued fascination with Trump remains his inconsistency and self-contradictory nature in so much of what he does, and which ADHD explains so well. All of his actions sail on a prevailing sea of ADHD-driven behavior. His ubiquitous ADHD antics continue to shorten our attention spans, coarsen the discourse, promote statements of "gut feelings" over truth, emphasize the superficial, and flatten the distinctions between what is interesting and what is important. In short, his own ADHD makes our society more ADHD-like. As the ancient curse says, "may you live in interesting times"; Trump will keep life interesting as long as he remains in power.

Chapter 11 contains a host of approaches for coping with Trump's ADHD-driven behavior and for disrupting the ADHD-Trump feedback loop. To encapsulate that advice, awareness that Trump displays a full range of ADHD symptoms grants permission to all of us to listen to his comments differently than if this were not the case. Even though he speaks from the presidential podium, we do not need to engage with each utterance as if it were a well-thought-out consideration of the facts and options available; it helps to understand that he is usually just spouting what he feels in the moment, which is likely to change depending on what influences him next. Although his organized minions may effectively carry out some of his policies, he himself has not shown any talent for sticking with or executing the ideas he puts forth, resulting in his being far less effective than his bluster would suggest. If one wants to sway his opinion, one should appeal to what interests him, rather than stressing what is important to the world, the country, or oneself. Although an impulsive act of his might catastrophically destroy large parts of our world, hopefully enough structural and personnel constraints remain in place to reduce this likelihood. Short of such catastrophe, America, and the world, will outlast Trump, but we will then be faced with how to address the ADHD-ification of the world, of which he is both a product and a purveyor.

Out of The Loop(s)

Similar to Socrates's complaint in *The Phaedrus* that the advent of writing would cause deterioration of memory, and that the process of writing captures facts but does not imply true understanding or wisdom [834], one could rail against social media and computerization and lament those executive functions and other human capabilities that may continue to shrivel in the years ahead. Or, like the leaders of Silicon Valley, one could promote the optimistic view that these new technologies will make humankind more effective, efficient, or egalitarian [835, 836]. A more balanced stance accepts that there will be both losses and gains as we adopt new technologies, and that we still have some capacity to direct how we will change ourselves and our culture, if we use our awareness of how we are already transforming. Historically and currently, we interact with the world primarily via our brains, but we are altering how we use our brains much faster than evolution can restructure our basic neurobiology. We keep updating the software, but it runs on old hardware that was developed for different demands. As individuals and as a society, we need to examine both what we are gaining and what we are losing by becoming more ADHD-like.

Our society is pushing all of us, from the most ADHD-prone to the least, to move further along the spectrum of ADHD-ness, and the more prevalent ADHD behaviors become, the more these societal templates encourage our brains to engage in more ADHD-like behaviors. Unless we want our society to move further in ADHD-like directions, we need to continue to find alternative ways to use our brains other than the patterns fostered by these technologies and personalities. I hope that this book heightens awareness of ADHD in our social and political spheres. Awareness includes not just realization of the situation we are in, but that we have options for responding. Although the term "mindfulness" saturates our conversations, at a basic level it is the antidote to ADHD-ification. Being mindful of what information we take in, how we respond, how we fuel and rest and train our bodies and our minds, remains the core of resistance to the trend of being more reactive and less reflective. Failing to strengthen mindfulness may contribute to a world where those with more linear, organized, and reserved brain styles are anomalies, and where Trump will have set a precedent as only the first of many presidents dominated by ADHD.

We also need to continue using our awareness of what ADHD entails in order to help identify those with ADHD, and to employ targeted treatments to help these individuals to be less hyperactive, less impulsive, less disruptive, less tangential, and less disorganized. Too many people continue to suffer because of their untreated ADHD and because ADHD afflicts their parents, partners, children, workmates, neighbors, and presidents. Too many creative, vibrant individuals have their dreams diminished and their goals derailed because of untreated ADHD. Hopefully we can use our growing understanding and awareness to help those with ADHD to more fully and harmoniously achieve their aspirations—and help ourselves in the process.

ACKNOWLEDGMENTS

In addition to dedicating this book to my patients, I will start the acknowledgments with them as well, because they inspired me to write this particular book, encouraged me to share my insights about ADHD, and asked me to publicize that ADHD profoundly impairs people and that effective treatment improves lives.

While I have striven for accuracy and clarity, and to promote understanding, I accept responsibility for any errors in facts, tone, or exploring too many tangents. My apologies to the many friends and colleagues who have helped or encouraged me over the last few years, but whose names I have inadvertently omitted from the following paragraphs.

I thank my parents, Alice and Robert Kruse, for inspiring a love of reading and of learning. I am forever indebted to teachers outside of the classroom, including Bob Segedi, Harvey Webster, and Tim White at the Cleveland Museum of Natural History, and, Nell Maloney at Camp Blue Heron, who encouraged detailed observations and precise descriptions. I greatly appreciate several academic mentors, among them Robert Selander, Jack Kampmeier, Carol Kellogg, and Anna Witz-Justice who promoted intellectual curiosity and individual growth. I feel particularly grateful that Coach Buzz Boomer taught me that in swimming, as in most of life, success flows from getting out of your own way.

The San Francisco FrontRunner community has provided positive and nurturing feedback regarding my writing over the last three decades, and I particularly appreciate the kind words and support from Terry Baransy, Chuck Louden, Steve Kotler, and Maureen Bogues. Good conversations, happy meals, and ongoing friendships with Anne Ludwig and Leslie Adams have provided a grounding presence that allowed me to engage in the indulgence of writing a book. I am grateful for the numerous insights and encouragement provided by Randy Weiss, Gary Pfitzer, and Dan Hoffman during numerous walks and runs while fleshing out some of the chapters in *Recognizing Adult ADHD*.

I am very glad that more than a decade ago, Peter Klaphaak, MD, organized, and for many years deftly led, a group of psychiatrists in San Francisco to discuss diagnosis and treatment of adults with ADHD. The group's illuminating and fruitful conversations have both broadened and deepened my understanding of ADHD. I particularly value what I have learned from, and connections I have made with, Josh Israel, MD, John Hensela, MD, Miran Choi, MD and Andrew Klompus, MD.

Gina Pera's kindly, insightful, and articulate advice regarding writing for and about the ADHD community provided invaluable assistance in helping me structure and think about my book. Positive feedback from numerous psychiatric colleagues has buoyed me up over the years and sustained me on this writing project, so I thank Tina Barney, MD, Rob Daroff, MD, and Paul Linde, MD, among others, for their input.

Kristy Lin Billuni, my writing teacher, offered tremendous help and guidance in my progress both as a writer and as an involved and concerned world citizen. Avoidance of the passive voice was also promoted by her.

I feel incredibly fortunate that I found Deanna Wallace Donovan, PhD to help with the scientific citations and popular culture references. She has greatly lightened my load, as well as being unfailingly upbeat and delightful to work with. I have really appreciated her resourcefulness and persistence in tracking down sources and ascertaining that they really said what I thought they said. She turned what could have been an onerous chore into a joyous collaboration.

Acknowledgments

I truly appreciate that Stephanie Chandler, Chela Hardy, and the rest of the staff at Authority Publishing have enthusiastically embraced this book and have been working diligently to help bring it into this world. They have also been hard at work to ensure that *Recognizing Adult ADHD* garners a warm welcome from the world, including introducing me to the amazing team at Wasabi Publicity. Drew Gerber, Michelle Tennant, Shannon Nicholson, Harrison Metzger, and Hannah Coloson have all been generous with their time, knowledge, thoughtful strategies, and good cheer, and kind words.

Members of my extended family constitute some of the most enthusiastic cheerleaders for this book and have also delivered some of the most penetrating discussions about its content. In particular, I enjoyed and learned from conversations with Kelly and Chris Moody, George and Sharon Roth, Laura Roth, Linda Roth, and Cindy Cupples. For relentlessly reviewing untold copies of the manuscript, offering astute suggestions, and delivering unstinting support at all stages of its development, I am grateful for the loving companionship of my husband, Gary Beuschel. I also thank my daughters, Veronica and Zola, for allowing me to spend so much time on this project, for asking smart questions, and for developing into such wonderful young women.

APPENDIX A

OFFICIAL DSM-5 CRITERIA FOR ADHD

DSM-5™ Diagnostic Criteria
Attention-Deficit/Hyperactivity Disorder (ADHD)

A. **A persistent pattern of inattention and/or hyperactivity-impulsivity that interferes with functioning or development, as characterized by (1) and/or (2):**

   1. **Inattention:** Six (or more) of the following symptoms have persisted for at least 6 months to a degree that is inconsistent with developmental level and that negatively impacts directly on social and academic/occupational activities:

   Note: The symptoms are not solely a manifestation of oppositional behavior, defiance, hostility, or failure to understand tasks or instructions. For older adolescents and adults (age 17 and older), at least five symptoms are required.

   a. Often fails to give close attention to details or makes careless mistakes in schoolwork, at work, or during other activities (e.g., overlooks or misses details, work is inaccurate).
   b. Often has difficulty sustaining attention in tasks or play activities (e.g., has difficulty remaining focused during lectures, conversations, or lengthy reading).
   c. Often does not seem to listen when spoken to directly (e.g., mind seems elsewhere, even in the absence of any obvious distraction).

d. Often does not follow through on instructions and fails to finish schoolwork, chores, or duties in the workplace (e.g., starts tasks but quickly loses focus and is easily sidetracked).
e. Often has difficulty organizing tasks and activities (e.g., difficulty managing sequential tasks; difficulty keeping materials and belongings in order; messy, disorganized work; has poor time management; fails to meet deadlines).
f. Often avoids, dislikes, or is reluctant to engage in tasks that require sustained mental effort (e.g., schoolwork or homework; for older adolescents and adults, preparing reports, completing forms, reviewing lengthy papers).
g. Often loses things necessary for tasks or activities (e.g., school materials, pencils, books, tools, wallets, keys, paperwork, eyeglasses, mobile telephones).
h. Is often easily distracted by extraneous stimuli (for older adolescents and adults, may include unrelated thoughts).
i. Is often forgetful in daily activities (e.g., doing chores, running errands; for older adolescents and adults, returning calls, paying bills, keeping appointments).

2. **Hyperactivity and impulsivity:** Six (or more) of the following symptoms have persisted for at least

6 months to a degree that is inconsistent with developmental level and that negatively impacts directly on social and academic/occupational activities:

Note: The symptoms are not solely a manifestation of oppositional behavior, defiance, hostility, or a failure to understand tasks or instructions. For older adolescents and adults (age 17 and older), at least five symptoms are required.

a. Often fidgets with or taps hands or feet or squirms in seat.
b. Often leaves seat in situations when remaining seated is expected (e.g., leaves his or her place in the classroom, in the office or other workplace, or in other situations that require remaining in place).

Appendix A

  c. Often runs about or climbs in situations where it is inappropriate. (*Note:* In adolescents or adults, may be limited to feeling restless.)
  d. Often unable to play or engage in leisure activities quietly.
  e. Is often "on the go," acting as if "driven by a motor"(e.g., is unable to be or uncomfortable being still for extended time, as in restaurants, meetings; may be experienced by others as being restless or difficult to keep up with).
  f. Often talks excessively.
  g. Often blurts out an answer before a question has been completed (e.g., completes people's sentences; cannot wait for turn in conversation).
  h. Often has difficulty waiting his or her turn (e.g., while waiting in line).
  i. Often interrupts or intrudes on others (e.g., butts into conversations, games, or activities; may start using other people's things without asking or receiving permission; for adolescents and adults, may intrude into or take over what others are doing).

B. **Several inattentive or hyperactive-impulsive symptoms were present prior to age 12 years.**

C. **Several inattentive or hyperactive-impulsive symptoms are present in two or more settings (e.g., at home, school, or work; with friends or relatives; in other activities).**

D. **There is clear evidence that the symptoms interfere with, or reduce the quality of, social, academic, or occupational functioning.**

E. **The symptoms do not occur exclusively during the course of schizophrenia or another psychotic disorder and are not better explained by another mental disorder (e.g., mood disorder, anxiety disorder, dissociative disorder, personality disorder, substance intoxication or withdrawal).**

Reprinted with permission from the Diagnostic and Statistical Manual of Mental Disorders, Fifth Edition (Copyright © 2013). American Psychiatric Association. All Rights Reserved.

Specify whether:

314.01 (F90.2) Combined presentation: If both Criterion A1 (inattention) and Criterion A2 (hyperactivity-impulsivity) are met for the past 6 months.

(F90.0) Predominantly inattentive presentation: If Criterion A1 (inattention) is met but Criterion A2 (hyperactivity-impulsivity) is not met for the past 6 months.

(F90.1) Predominantly hyperactive/impulsive presentation: If Criterion A2 (hyperactivity- impulsivity) is met but Criterion A1 (inattention) is not met over the past 6 months.

Specify if:

In partial remission: When full criteria were previously met, fewer than the full criteria have been met for the past 6 months, and the symptoms still result in impairment in social, academic, or occupational functioning.

Specify current severity:

Mild: Few, if any, symptoms in excess of those required to make the diagnosis are present, and symptoms result in only minor functional impairments.

Moderate: Symptoms or functional impairment between "mild" and "severe" are present.

Severe: Many symptoms in excess of those required to make the diagnosis, or several symptoms that are particularly severe, are present, or the symptoms result in marked impairment in social or occupational functioning.

Reprinted with permission from the Diagnostic and Statistical Manual of Mental Disorders, Fifth Edition (Copyright © 2013). American Psychiatric Association. All Rights Reserved.

APPENDIX B

LINKS TO ADHD SELF-ASSESSMENTS

You can choose from many ADHD self-assessments available online. The majority of these, such as the ADHD Self-Report Scale (ASRS), essentially translate the individual DSM-5 criteria into questions. Scales based on DSM- 5 usually contain eighteen questions, one for each DM-5 criteria. Although these tests can provide helpful information to begin sorting out whether you have ADHD, and I occasionally use such tests myself, I prefer questionnaires that cover a broader range of executive function deficits and capture a broader example of ADHD symptoms. *ADDitude Magazine* provides two such tests, and a wide range of other useful information regarding the diagnosis and treatment of ADHD.

https://www.additudemag.com/inattentive-adhd-symptom-test-adults/

https://www.additudemag.com/hyperactive-impulsive-adhd-symptom-test-adults/

BIBLIOGRAPHY

1. American Psychiatric Association: *Diagnostic and Statistical Manual of Mental Disorders, Fourth Edition* 1994, Washington, DC: American Psychiatric Association
2. American Psychiatric Association: *Diagnostic and Statistical Manual of Mental Disorders, Fifth Edition* 2013, Washington, D.C.: American Psychiatric Association.
3. Rubia, K., *Cognitive Neuroscience of Attention Deficit Hyperactivity Disorder (ADHD) and Its Clinical Translation.* Front Hum Neurosci, 2018. **12**: p. 100.
4. Diamond, A., *Executive functions.* Annu Rev Psychol, 2013. **64**: p. 135-68.
5. Sanneh, K., *Intellectuals for Trump*, in *The New Yorker*. 2017.
6. Krugman, P., *Donald Trump's 'Big Liar' Technique*, in *The New York Times*. 2016.
7. Mayer, J., *Donald Trump's Ghostwriter Tells All*, in *The New Yorker*. 2016.
8. Blow, C.M., *Trump: King of Chaos*, in *The New York Times*. 2018.
9. Earle, G., *Trump's screaming fit at size of his inauguration crowd is revealed as Reince Priebus tells how he ordered proof it was bigger than Obama's*, in *Daily Mail*. 2018.
10. News, T.I., *Donald Trump's shocking display of bad* in *The Irish News*. 2018.
11. editors, A., *Could Donald Trump Have ADHD?*, in *ADDitude*.
12. Sachs, G., *Does Trump Have ADHD? My Professional Opinion*, in *Huffington Post*. 2016.

13. Hodgkins, P., et al., *Individual treatment response in attention-deficit/hyperactivity disorder: broadening perspectives and improving assessments.* Expert Rev Neurother, 2013. **13**(4): p. 425-33.
14. Thapar, A., et al., *What have we learnt about the causes of ADHD?* J Child Psychol Psychiatry, 2013. **54**(1): p. 3-16.
15. Capusan, A.J., et al., *Childhood maltreatment and attention deficit hyperactivity disorder symptoms in adults: a large twin study.* Psychol Med, 2016. **46**(12): p. 2637-46.
16. Pond, E., K. Fowler, and J. Hesson, *The Influence of Socioeconomic Status on Psychological Distress in Canadian Adults With ADD/ADHD.* J Atten Disord, 2016.
17. Kranish, M. and M. Fisher, *Trump revealed : an American journey of ambition, ego, money, and power.* First Scribner hardcover edition. ed. 2016, New York: Scribner. x, 431 pages.
18. editors, A., *The Many Faces of ADHD*, in *ADDitude*.
19. Reimherr, F.W., et al., *Types of adult attention-deficit hyperactivity disorder (ADHD): baseline characteristics, initial response, and long-term response to treatment with methylphenidate.* Atten Defic Hyperact Disord, 2015. **7**(2): p. 115-28.
20. Filkins, D., *Rex Tillerson at the Breaking Point*, in *New Yorker*. 2017.
21. Moniuszko, S., *Chris Evans says he knows why 'moronic' Donald Trump has so many spelling errors*, in *USA Today*. 2018.
22. Olberman, K., *COULD DONALD TRUMP PASS A SANITY TEST?*, in *Vanity Fair*. 2016.
23. Schneider, C., *Donald Trump has a sickening fetish for cruelty*, in *USA Today*. 2017.
24. Sharkov, D., *TRUMP IS ACTING 'JUVENILE' AND 'PATHETIC' BY ACCUSING DEMOCRATS OF TREASON, EX-U.S. AMBASSADOR SAYS*, in *Newsweek*. 2018.
25. Pera, G., *Is it you, me, or adult A.D.D.? : stopping the roller coaster when someone you love has attention deficit disorder.* 1st ed. 2008, San Francisco, Calif.: 1201 Alarm Press. xxvii, 369 p.
26. Barkley, R.A., *Taking charge of adult ADHD*. 2010, New York: Guilford Press. vii, 294 p.
27. McCabe, J. *How to ADHD*. 2019; Available from: https://www.youtube.com/channel/UC-nPM1_kSZf91ZGkcgy_95Q.
28. Eakin, L., et al., *The marital and family functioning of adults with ADHD and their spouses.* J Atten Disord, 2004. **8**(1): p. 1-10.

29. Hamed, A.M., A.J. Kauer, and H.E. Stevens, *Why the Diagnosis of Attention Deficit Hyperactivity Disorder Matters.* Front Psychiatry, 2015. **6**: p. 168.
30. Pera, G. and A.L. Robin, *Adult ADHD-focused couple therapy: clinical interventions.* 2016, New York: Routledge, Taylor & Francis Group. xxxi, 236 pages.
31. Geffen, J. and K. Forster, *Treatment of adult ADHD: a clinical perspective.* Ther Adv Psychopharmacol, 2018. **8**(1): p. 25-32.
32. Asherson, P., et al., *Under diagnosis of adult ADHD: cultural influences and societal burden.* J Atten Disord, 2012. **16**(5 Suppl): p. 20s-38s.
33. Ginsberg, Y., T. Hirvikoski, and N. Lindefors, *Attention Deficit Hyperactivity Disorder (ADHD) among longer-term prison inmates is a prevalent, persistent and disabling disorder.* BMC Psychiatry, 2010. **10**: p. 112.
34. Editors, A., *ADHD, By the Numbers*, in *ADDitude*.
35. Wilens, T.E., et al., *Misuse and diversion of stimulants prescribed for ADHD: a systematic review of the literature.* J Am Acad Child Adolesc Psychiatry, 2008. **47**(1): p. 21-31.
36. Schwarz, A., *ADHD nation : children, doctors, big pharma, and the making of an American epidemic.* First Scribner hardcover edition. ed. 2016, New York: Scribner. viii, 338 pages.
37. Ginsberg, Y., et al., *Underdiagnosis of attention-deficit/hyperactivity disorder in adult patients: a review of the literature.* Prim Care Companion CNS Disord, 2014. **16**(3).
38. Das, D., et al., *A population-based study of attention deficit/hyperactivity disorder symptoms and associated impairment in middle-aged adults.* PLoS One, 2012. **7**(2): p. e31500.
39. Solanto, M.V., et al., *Efficacy of meta-cognitive therapy for adult ADHD.* Am J Psychiatry, 2010. **167**(8): p. 958-68.
40. Durell, T.M., et al., *Atomoxetine treatment of attention-deficit/hyperactivity disorder in young adults with assessment of functional outcomes: a randomized, double-blind, placebo-controlled clinical trial.* J Clin Psychopharmacol, 2013. **33**(1): p. 45-54.
41. Biederman, J. and S.V. Faraone, *The effects of attention-deficit/hyperactivity disorder on employment and household income.* MedGenMed, 2006. **8**(3): p. 12.
42. Katzman, M.A., et al., *Adult ADHD and comorbid disorders: clinical implications of a dimensional approach.* BMC Psychiatry, 2017. **17**(1): p. 302.

43. Spencer, T., et al., *Is attention-deficit hyperactivity disorder in adults a valid disorder?* Harv Rev Psychiatry, 1994. **1**(6): p. 326-35.
44. Doyle, R., *The history of adult attention-deficit/hyperactivity disorder.* Psychiatr Clin North Am, 2004. **27**(2): p. 203-14.
45. Mann, H.B. and S.I. Greenspan, *The identification and treatment of adult brain dysfunction.* Am J Psychiatry, 1976. **133**(9): p. 1013-7.
46. Wood, D.R., et al., *Diagnosis and treatment of minimal brain dysfunction in adults: a preliminary report.* Arch Gen Psychiatry, 1976. **33**(12): p. 1453-60.
47. Reimherr, F.W., D.R. Wood, and P.H. Wender, *An open clinical trial of L-dopa and carbidopa in adults with minimal brain dysfunction.* Am J Psychiatry, 1980. **137**(1): p. 73-5.
48. Wender, P.H., F.W. Reimherr, and D.R. Wood, *Attention deficit disorder ('minimal brain dysfunction') in adults. A replication study of diagnosis and drug treatment.* Arch Gen Psychiatry, 1981. **38**(4): p. 449-56.
49. Werry, J.S., *Studies on the hyperactive child. IV. An empirical analysis of the minimal brain dysfunction syndrome.* Arch Gen Psychiatry, 1968. **19**(1): p. 9-16.
50. Lie, N., *Follow-ups of children with attention deficit hyperactivity disorder (ADHD). Review of literature.* Acta Psychiatr Scand Suppl, 1992. **368**: p. 1-40.
51. Goodin, K., *Famous People with ADHD*, in *Parenting*. 2018.
52. Nylander, L., et al., *Attention-deficit/hyperactivity disorder (ADHD) and autism spectrum disorder (ASD) in adult psychiatry. A 20-year register study.* Nord J Psychiatry, 2013. **67**(5): p. 344-50.
53. Magnin, E. and C. Maurs, *Attention-deficit/hyperactivity disorder during adulthood.* Rev Neurol (Paris), 2017. **173**(7-8): p. 506-515.
54. Kolar, D., et al., *Treatment of adults with attention-deficit/hyperactivity disorder.* Neuropsychiatr Dis Treat, 2008. **4**(2): p. 389-403.
55. Polanczyk, G., et al., *The worldwide prevalence of ADHD: a systematic review and metaregression analysis.* Am J Psychiatry, 2007. **164**(6): p. 942-8.
56. Biederman, J., et al., *Further Evidence of Morbidity and Dysfunction Associated With Subsyndromal ADHD in Clinically Referred Children.* J Clin Psychiatry, 2018. **79**(5).
57. Faraone, S.V., J. Biederman, and E. Mick, *The age-dependent decline of attention deficit hyperactivity disorder: a meta-analysis of follow-up studies.* Psychol Med, 2006. **36**(2): p. 159-65.
58. Biederman, J., et al., *How persistent is ADHD? A controlled 10-year follow-up study of boys with ADHD.* Psychiatry Res, 2010. **177**(3): p. 299-304.

59. Faraone, S.V. and J. Biederman, *What is the prevalence of adult ADHD? Results of a population screen of 966 adults.* J Atten Disord, 2005. **9**(2): p. 384-91.
60. Kessler, R.C., et al., *The prevalence and correlates of adult ADHD in the United States: results from the National Comorbidity Survey Replication.* Am J Psychiatry, 2006. **163**(4): p. 716-23.
61. Agnew-Blais, J.C., et al., *Young adult mental health and functional outcomes among individuals with remitted, persistent and late-onset ADHD.* Br J Psychiatry, 2018: p. 1-9.
62. Rowland, A.S., et al., *Attention-Deficit/Hyperactivity Disorder (ADHD): Interaction between socioeconomic status and parental history of ADHD determines prevalence.* J Child Psychol Psychiatry, 2018. **59**(3): p. 213-222.
63. Hechtman, L., et al., *Functional Adult Outcomes 16 Years After Childhood Diagnosis of Attention-Deficit/Hyperactivity Disorder: MTA Results.* J Am Acad Child Adolesc Psychiatry, 2016. **55**(11): p. 945-952.e2.
64. in *Hidden Costs, Values Lost: Uninsurance in America*. 2003: Washington (DC).
65. McIntyre, R.S., et al., *The Efficacy of Psychostimulants in Major Depressive Episodes: A Systematic Review and Meta-Analysis.* J Clin Psychopharmacol, 2017. **37**(4): p. 412-418.
66. Jeffers, A.J. and E.G. Benotsch, *Non-medical use of prescription stimulants for weight loss, disordered eating, and body image.* Eat Behav, 2014. **15**(3): p. 414-8.
67. Rodriguez, J.E. and K.M. Campbell, *Past, Present, and Future of Pharmacologic Therapy in Obesity.* Prim Care, 2016. **43**(1): p. 61-7, viii.
68. Lammers, G.J., *Drugs Used in Narcolepsy and Other Hypersomnias.* Sleep Med Clin, 2018. **13**(2): p. 183-189.
69. Lee, H., et al., *Comparing effects of methylphenidate, sertraline and placebo on neuropsychiatric sequelae in patients with traumatic brain injury.* Hum Psychopharmacol, 2005. **20**(2): p. 97-104.
70. Rabiner, D.L., et al., *Motives and perceived consequences of nonmedical ADHD medication use by college students: are students treating themselves for attention problems?* J Atten Disord, 2009. **13**(3): p. 259-70.
71. Peterkin, A.L., et al., *Cognitive performance enhancement: misuse or self-treatment?* J Atten Disord, 2011. **15**(4): p. 263-8.
72. Hinshaw, S.P. and R.M. Scheffler, *The ADHD explosion : myths, medication, money, and today's push for performance.* 2014, New York, NY: Oxford University Press. xxxii, 254 pages.
73. Prakash, M.D., et al., *Methamphetamine: Effects on the brain, gut and immune system.* Pharmacol Res, 2017. **120**: p. 60-67.

74. Brown, K.A., S. Samuel, and D.R. Patel, *Pharmacologic management of attention deficit hyperactivity disorder in children and adolescents: a review for practitioners.* Transl Pediatr, 2018. **7**(1): p. 36-47.
75. Furczyk, K. and J. Thome, *Adult ADHD and suicide.* Atten Defic Hyperact Disord, 2014. **6**(3): p. 153-8.
76. Jerome, L., A. Segal, and L. Habinski, *What we know about ADHD and driving risk: a literature review, meta-analysis and critique.* J Can Acad Child Adolesc Psychiatry, 2006. **15**(3): p. 105-25.
77. Biederman, J., et al., *Functional impairments in adults with self-reports of diagnosed ADHD: A controlled study of 1001 adults in the community.* J Clin Psychiatry, 2006. **67**(4): p. 524-40.
78. Dalsgaard, S., et al., *Long-term criminal outcome of children with attention deficit hyperactivity disorder.* Crim Behav Ment Health, 2013. **23**(2): p. 86-98.
79. Knecht, C., et al., *Attention-deficit hyperactivity disorder (ADHD), substance use disorders, and criminality: a difficult problem with complex solutions.* Int J Adolesc Med Health, 2015. **27**(2): p. 163-75.
80. Shaw, M., et al., *A systematic review and analysis of long-term outcomes in attention deficit hyperactivity disorder: effects of treatment and non-treatment.* BMC Med, 2012. **10**: p. 99.
81. Saul, R., *ADHD does not exist : the truth about attention deficit and hyperactivity disorder.* First edition. ed. 2014, New York, NY: HarperWave. xviii, 313 pages.
82. Robbins, C.A., *ADHD couple and family relationships: enhancing communication and understanding through Imago Relationship Therapy.* J Clin Psychol, 2005. **61**(5): p. 565-77.
83. Kandel, E.R., Schwartz, J.H., Jessell, T.M., *Principles of Neural Science.* 5th ed. 2012: McGraw-Hill Professional.
84. *PubMed.* Bethesda (MD).
85. Thapar, A., et al., *What causes attention deficit hyperactivity disorder?* Arch Dis Child, 2012. **97**(3): p. 260-5.
86. Frodl, T. and N. Skokauskas, *Meta-analysis of structural MRI studies in children and adults with attention deficit hyperactivity disorder indicates treatment effects.* Acta Psychiatr Scand, 2012. **125**(2): p. 114-26.
87. Sowell, E.R., et al., *Cortical abnormalities in children and adolescents with attention-deficit hyperactivity disorder.* Lancet, 2003. **362**(9397): p. 1699-707.
88. Seidman, L.J., E.M. Valera, and N. Makris, *Structural brain imaging of attention-deficit/hyperactivity disorder.* Biol Psychiatry, 2005. **57**(11): p. 1263-72.

89. Xia, S., et al., *Topological organization of the "small-world" visual attention network in children with attention deficit/hyperactivity disorder (ADHD).* Front Hum Neurosci, 2014. **8**: p. 162.
90. Castellanos, F.X., et al., *Developmental trajectories of brain volume abnormalities in children and adolescents with attention-deficit/hyperactivity disorder.* JAMA, 2002. **288**(14): p. 1740-8.
91. Durston, S., et al., *Magnetic resonance imaging of boys with attention-deficit/hyperactivity disorder and their unaffected siblings.* J Am Acad Child Adolesc Psychiatry, 2004. **43**(3): p. 332-40.
92. Silk, T.J., et al., *White-matter abnormalities in attention deficit hyperactivity disorder: a diffusion tensor imaging study.* Hum Brain Mapp, 2009. **30**(9): p. 2757-65.
93. Cao, M., et al., *Imaging functional and structural brain connectomics in attention-deficit/hyperactivity disorder.* Mol Neurobiol, 2014. **50**(3): p. 1111-23.
94. Monastra, V.J., *Overcoming the barriers to effective treatment for attention-deficit/hyperactivity disorder: a neuro-educational approach.* Int J Psychophysiol, 2005. **58**(1): p. 71-80.
95. Spencer, T.J., et al., *Effect of psychostimulants on brain structure and function in ADHD: a qualitative literature review of magnetic resonance imaging-based neuroimaging studies.* J Clin Psychiatry, 2013. **74**(9): p. 902-17.
96. Zang, Y.F., et al., *Altered baseline brain activity in children with ADHD revealed by resting-state functional MRI.* Brain Dev, 2007. **29**(2): p. 83-91.
97. Munakata, Y., et al., *A unified framework for inhibitory control.* Trends Cogn Sci, 2011. **15**(10): p. 453-9.
98. Abraham, A., et al., *Creative thinking in adolescents with attention deficit hyperactivity disorder (ADHD).* Child Neuropsychol, 2006. **12**(2): p. 111-23.
99. Christoff, K., et al., *Mind-wandering as spontaneous thought: a dynamic framework.* Nat Rev Neurosci, 2016. **17**(11): p. 718-731.
100. Belanger, M., I. Allaman, and P.J. Magistretti, *Brain energy metabolism: focus on astrocyte-neuron metabolic cooperation.* Cell Metab, 2011. **14**(6): p. 724-38.
101. Volkow, N.D., et al., *Methylphenidate decreased the amount of glucose needed by the brain to perform a cognitive task.* PLoS One, 2008. **3**(4): p. e2017.
102. Schweitzer, J.B., et al., *Effect of methylphenidate on executive functioning in adults with attention-deficit/hyperactivity disorder: normalization of*

behavior but not related brain activity. Biol Psychiatry, 2004. **56**(8): p. 597-606.
103. Roman-Urrestarazu, A., et al., *Brain structural deficits and working memory fMRI dysfunction in young adults who were diagnosed with ADHD in adolescence.* Eur Child Adolesc Psychiatry, 2016. **25**(5): p. 529-38.
104. Szekely, E., et al., *Defining the Neural Substrate of the Adult Outcome of Childhood ADHD: A Multimodal Neuroimaging Study of Response Inhibition.* Am J Psychiatry, 2017. **174**(9): p. 867-876.
105. Franke, B., B.M. Neale, and S.V. Faraone, *Genome-wide association studies in ADHD.* Hum Genet, 2009. **126**(1): p. 13-50.
106. Brikell, I., R. Kuja-Halkola, and H. Larsson, *Heritability of attention-deficit hyperactivity disorder in adults.* Am J Med Genet B Neuropsychiatr Genet, 2015. **168**(6): p. 406-413.
107. Jelenkovic, A., et al., *Genetic and environmental influences on height from infancy to early adulthood: An individual-based pooled analysis of 45 twin cohorts.* Sci Rep, 2016. **6**: p. 28496.
108. Gejman, P.V., A.R. Sanders, and J. Duan, *The role of genetics in the etiology of schizophrenia.* Psychiatr Clin North Am, 2010. **33**(1): p. 35-66.
109. Sullivan, P.F., M.C. Neale, and K.S. Kendler, *Genetic epidemiology of major depression: review and meta-analysis.* Am J Psychiatry, 2000. **157**(10): p. 1552-62.
110. Arcos-Burgos, M. and M. Muenke, *Toward a better understanding of ADHD: LPHN3 gene variants and the susceptibility to develop ADHD.* Atten Defic Hyperact Disord, 2010. **2**(3): p. 139-47.
111. Faraone, S.V. and H. Larsson, *Genetics of attention deficit hyperactivity disorder.* Mol Psychiatry, 2018.
112. Kissling, C., et al., *A polymorphism at the 3'-untranslated region of the CLOCK gene is associated with adult attention-deficit hyperactivity disorder.* Am J Med Genet B Neuropsychiatr Genet, 2008. **147**(3): p. 333-8.
113. Ribases, M., et al., *Case-control study of six genes asymmetrically expressed in the two cerebral hemispheres: association of BAIAP2 with attention-deficit/hyperactivity disorder.* Biol Psychiatry, 2009. **66**(10): p. 926-34.
114. Faraone, S.V., et al., *The worldwide prevalence of ADHD: is it an American condition?* World Psychiatry, 2003. **2**(2): p. 104-13.
115. Ghosh, M., C.D. Holman, and D.B. Preen, *Exploring parental country of birth differences in the use of psychostimulant medications for ADHD: a whole-population linked data study.* Aust N Z J Public Health, 2015. **39**(1): p. 88-92.

116. Hinshaw, S.P., et al., *International variation in treatment procedures for ADHD: social context and recent trends.* Psychiatr Serv, 2011. **62**(5): p. 459-64.
117. Clemow, D.B. and D.J. Walker, *The potential for misuse and abuse of medications in ADHD: a review.* Postgrad Med, 2014. **126**(5): p. 64-81.
118. Storebo, O.J., et al., *Methylphenidate for attention deficit hyperactivity disorder (ADHD) in children and adolescents - assessment of adverse events in non-randomised studies.* Cochrane Database Syst Rev, 2018. **5**: p. Cd012069.
119. Lubke, G.H., et al., *Maternal ratings of attention problems in ADHD: evidence for the existence of a continuum.* J Am Acad Child Adolesc Psychiatry, 2009. **48**(11): p. 1085-93.
120. McLennan, J.D., *Understanding attention deficit hyperactivity disorder as a continuum.* Can Fam Physician, 2016. **62**(12): p. 979-982.
121. Esserman, L.J., I.M. Thompson, Jr., and B. Reid, *Overdiagnosis and overtreatment in cancer: an opportunity for improvement.* Jama, 2013. **310**(8): p. 797-8.
122. Nikiforov, Y.E., et al., *Nomenclature Revision for Encapsulated Follicular Variant of Papillary Thyroid Carcinoma: A Paradigm Shift to Reduce Overtreatment of Indolent Tumors.* JAMA Oncol, 2016. **2**(8): p. 1023-9.
123. Whelton, P.K., et al., *2017 ACC/AHA/AAPA/ABC/ACPM/AGS/APhA/ASH/ASPC/NMA/PCNA Guideline for the Prevention, Detection, Evaluation, and Management of High Blood Pressure in Adults: Executive Summary: A Report of the American College of Cardiology/American Heart Association Task Force on Clinical Practice Guidelines.* J Am Coll Cardiol, 2018. **71**(19): p. 2199-2269.
124. Huth, A.G., et al., *Natural speech reveals the semantic maps that tile human cerebral cortex.* Nature, 2016. **532**(7600): p. 453-8.
125. Weitz, E., et al., *Do depression treatments reduce suicidal ideation? The effects of CBT, IPT, pharmacotherapy, and placebo on suicidality.* J Affect Disord, 2014. **167**: p. 98-103.
126. Hetrick, S.E., et al., *Cognitive behavioural therapy (CBT), third-wave CBT and interpersonal therapy (IPT) based interventions for preventing depression in children and adolescents.* Cochrane Database Syst Rev, 2016(8): p. Cd003380.
127. Burcusa, S.L. and W.G. Iacono, *Risk for recurrence in depression.* Clin Psychol Rev, 2007. **27**(8): p. 959-85.
128. Holma, K.M., et al., *Long-term outcome of major depressive disorder in psychiatric patients is variable.* J Clin Psychiatry, 2008. **69**(2): p. 196-205.

129. Tandon, M., et al., *Trajectories of ADHD severity over 10 years from childhood into adulthood.* Atten Defic Hyperact Disord, 2016. **8**(3): p. 121-30.
130. Goldman, L.S., et al., *Diagnosis and treatment of attention-deficit/hyperactivity disorder in children and adolescents. Council on Scientific Affairs, American Medical Association.* Jama, 1998. **279**(14): p. 1100-7.
131. Kramer, P.D., *Listening to Prozac.* 1993, New York, N.Y., U.S.A.: Viking. xix, 409 p.
132. Benson, K., et al., *Misuse of stimulant medication among college students: a comprehensive review and meta-analysis.* Clin Child Fam Psychol Rev, 2015. **18**(1): p. 50-76.
133. Kauffman, R.P., et al., *Impact of the selective serotonin reuptake inhibitor citalopram on insulin sensitivity, leptin and basal cortisol secretion in depressed and non-depressed euglycemic women of reproductive age.* Gynecol Endocrinol, 2005. **21**(3): p. 129-37.
134. Bagot, K.S. and Y. Kaminer, *Efficacy of stimulants for cognitive enhancement in non-attention deficit hyperactivity disorder youth: a systematic review.* Addiction, 2014. **109**(4): p. 547-57.
135. Sinita, E. and D. Coghill, *The use of stimulant medications for non-core aspects of ADHD and in other disorders.* Neuropharmacology, 2014. **87**: p. 161-72.
136. Taylor, R.M., *Ethical principles and concepts in medicine.* Handb Clin Neurol, 2013. **118**: p. 1-9.
137. Biederman, J. and S.V. Faraone, *Attention-deficit hyperactivity disorder.* Lancet, 2005. **366**(9481): p. 237-48.
138. Moffitt, T.E., et al., *Is Adult ADHD a Childhood-Onset Neurodevelopmental Disorder? Evidence From a Four-Decade Longitudinal Cohort Study.* Am J Psychiatry, 2015. **172**(10): p. 967-77.
139. Agnew-Blais, J.C., et al., *Evaluation of the Persistence, Remission, and Emergence of Attention-Deficit/Hyperactivity Disorder in Young Adulthood.* JAMA Psychiatry, 2016. **73**(7): p. 713-20.
140. Caye, A., et al., *Attention-Deficit/Hyperactivity Disorder Trajectories From Childhood to Young Adulthood: Evidence From a Birth Cohort Supporting a Late-Onset Syndrome.* JAMA Psychiatry, 2016. **73**(7): p. 705-12.
141. Sibley, M.H., et al., *Late-Onset ADHD Reconsidered With Comprehensive Repeated Assessments Between Ages 10 and 25.* Am J Psychiatry, 2018. **175**(2): p. 140-149.
142. Gentile, J.P., R. Atiq, and P.M. Gillig, *Adult ADHD: Diagnosis, Differential Diagnosis, and Medication Management.* Psychiatry (Edgmont), 2006. **3**(8): p. 25-30.

143. Miller, C.J., J.H. Newcorn, and J.M. Halperin, *Fading memories: retrospective recall inaccuracies in ADHD.* J Atten Disord, 2010. **14**(1): p. 7-14.
144. Du Rietz, E., et al., *Self-report of ADHD shows limited agreement with objective markers of persistence and remittance.* J Psychiatr Res, 2016. **82**: p. 91-9.
145. Caye, A., et al., *Late-Onset ADHD: Understanding the Evidence and Building Theoretical Frameworks.* Curr Psychiatry Rep, 2017. **19**(12): p. 106.
146. Canela, C., et al., *Skills and compensation strategies in adult ADHD - A qualitative study.* PLoS One, 2017. **12**(9): p. e0184964.
147. Hansson Hallerod, S.L., et al., *Experienced consequences of being diagnosed with ADHD as an adult - a qualitative study.* BMC Psychiatry, 2015. **15**: p. 31.
148. Mueller, A.K., et al., *Stigma in attention deficit hyperactivity disorder.* Atten Defic Hyperact Disord, 2012. **4**(3): p. 101-14.
149. SAVRANSKY, S. *Trump on intelligence briefings: 'I get it when I need it'.*
150. McIntosh, D., et al., *Adult ADHD and comorbid depression: A consensus-derived diagnostic algorithm for ADHD.* Neuropsychiatr Dis Treat, 2009. **5**: p. 137-50.
151. Cillizza, C. *Donald Trump said he would stare down the NRA. Then he blinked.* 2018.
152. Diamond, J. and L. Fox *Trump tells senators 'You're afraid of the NRA'.* CNN Politics, 2018.
153. Leonnig, C.H., Shane and Jaffe, Greg, *Breaking with tradition, Trump skips president's written intelligence report and relies on oral briefings*, in *Washington Post.* 2018.
154. Venkatasubramanian, G. and M.S. Keshavan, *Biomarkers in Psychiatry - A Critique.* Ann Neurosci, 2016. **23**(1): p. 3-5.
155. Beidel, D.C. and B.C. Frueh, *Adult psychopathology and diagnosis.* Eighth edition. ed. 2018, Hoboken, NJ: Wiley. pages cm.
156. Ramsay, J.R., *Assessment and monitoring of treatment response in adult ADHD patients: current perspectives.* Neuropsychiatr Dis Treat, 2017. **13**: p. 221-232.
157. Epstein J, J.D., Conners CK. Conners *Adult ADHD Diagnostic Interview for DSM-IV.* 2001.
158. Fuermaier, A.B.M., et al., *Cognitive impairment in adult ADHD--perspective matters!* Neuropsychology, 2015. **29**(1): p. 45-58.

159. Spencer, T.J., et al., *Further evidence of dopamine transporter dysregulation in ADHD: a controlled PET imaging study using altropane.* Biol Psychiatry, 2007. **62**(9): p. 1059-61.
160. Faraone, S.V., C. Bonvicini, and C. Scassellati, *Biomarkers in the diagnosis of ADHD--promising directions.* Curr Psychiatry Rep, 2014. **16**(11): p. 497.
161. Lenartowicz, A., et al., *Aberrant Modulation of Brain Oscillatory Activity and Attentional Impairment in Attention-Deficit/Hyperactivity Disorder.* Biol Psychiatry Cogn Neurosci Neuroimaging, 2018. **3**(1): p. 19-29.
162. Thome, J., et al., *Biomarkers for attention-deficit/hyperactivity disorder (ADHD). A consensus report of the WFSBP task force on biological markers and the World Federation of ADHD.* World J Biol Psychiatry, 2012. **13**(5): p. 379-400.
163. Colleges, A.o.A.M., *Overview for Applicants: Documenting Learning Disabilities, ADHD, and/or Psychiatric Disabilities.*
164. Barkley, R.A., *Neuropsychological Testing is Not Useful in the Diagnosis of ADHD: Stop It (or Prove It)!* The ADHD Report, 2019. **27**(2): p. 1-8.
165. Culpepper, L. and G. Mattingly, *A practical guide to recognition and diagnosis of ADHD in adults in the primary care setting.* Postgrad Med, 2008. **120**(3): p. 16-26.
166. National Collaborating Centre for Mental, H., *National Institute for Health and Care Excellence: Clinical Guidelines*, in *Attention Deficit Hyperactivity Disorder: Diagnosis and Management of ADHD in Children, Young People and Adults.* 2018, British Psychological Society Copyright (c) National Institute for Health and Care Excellence 2018.: Leicester (UK).
167. Kahle, B. *The Internet Archive, by archive.org.* 2018; Available from: https://archive.org/details/trumparchive.
168. Watkins, E.a.P., A. *Trump decries immigrants from 'shithole countries' coming to US.* 2018 January 12, 2018]; Available from: https://www.cnn.com/2018/01/11/politics/immigrants-shithole-countries-trump/index.html.
169. Parker, A., *'You Have to Brand People,' Donald Trump Says*, in *New York Times.* 2016: NY, NY.
170. Manor, I., et al., *Low self-awareness of ADHD in adults using a self-report screening questionnaire.* Eur Psychiatry, 2012. **27**(5): p. 314-20.
171. Barkley, R.A., et al., *Young adult outcome of hyperactive children: adaptive functioning in major life activities.* J Am Acad Child Adolesc Psychiatry, 2006. **45**(2): p. 192-202.

172. Barkley, R.A., et al., *The persistence of attention-deficit/hyperactivity disorder into young adulthood as a function of reporting source and definition of disorder.* J Abnorm Psychol, 2002. **111**(2): p. 279-89.
173. Lahey, B.B., et al., *DSM-IV field trials for attention deficit hyperactivity disorder in children and adolescents.* Am J Psychiatry, 1994. **151**(11): p. 1673-85.
174. Faraone, S.V., et al., *Psychiatric, neuropsychological, and psychosocial features of DSM-IV subtypes of attention-deficit/hyperactivity disorder: results from a clinically referred sample.* J Am Acad Child Adolesc Psychiatry, 1998. **37**(2): p. 185-93.
175. Gibbins, C., et al., *ADHD-hyperactive/impulsive subtype in adults.* Ment Illn, 2010. **2**(1): p. e9.
176. Willcutt, E.G., *The prevalence of DSM-IV attention-deficit/hyperactivity disorder: a meta-analytic review.* Neurotherapeutics, 2012. **9**(3): p. 490-9.
177. Matte, B., et al., *ADHD in DSM-5: a field trial in a large, representative sample of 18- to 19-year-old adults.* Psychol Med, 2015. **45**(2): p. 361-73.
178. Wang, T., et al., *Prevalence of attention deficit/hyperactivity disorder among children and adolescents in China: a systematic review and meta-analysis.* BMC Psychiatry, 2017. **17**(1): p. 32.
179. VandeHei, J.A., Mike, *Reality bites: Trump's wake-up call*, in *Axios*.
180. Cornwell, S.a.B., Amanda, *Senate Republicans complain of chaos in healthcare effort*, in *Reuters*. 2017.
181. Thrush, G.M., Jonathan, *On Senate Health Bill, Trump Falters in the Closer's Role*, in *New York Times*. 2017.
182. Demirgian, K.D., Josh, *Congress advances bill to renew NSA surveillance program after Trump briefly upstages key vote*, in *Washington Post*. 2018.
183. News, C. *Trump visits with families affected by Santa Fe school shooting*. May 31, 2018]; May 31, 2018: [Available from: https://www.cbsnews.com/news/trump-visits-with-families-affected-by-santa-fe-school-shooting/.
184. Kruse, M., *Donald Trump's Shortest Attribute Isn't His Fingers*, in *Politico Magazine*. 2016.
185. Graham, D., *'President Trump Did Disrespect My Son'*, in *The Atlantic*. 2017.
186. Hirschfeld Davis, J., *Parents and Students Plead With Trump: 'How Many Children Have to Get Shot?'*, in *The New York Times*. 2018.
187. Wolff, M., *Fire and fury : inside the Trump White House*. First edition. ed. 2018, New York: Henry Holt and Company. xiii, 321 pages.
188. Healy, P.P., Ashley; Haberman, Maggie, *New Debate Strategy for Donald Trump: Practice, Practice, Practice*, in *New York Times*. 2016.

189. News, C., *Gary Cohn answers question about future at White House: "I'm here today"*. 2018.
190. Ray, Z., *FORMER TRUMP ADVISER SAYS HE TRIED TO TEACH PRESIDENT THE CONSTITUTION, BUT HIS EYES JUST ROLLED BACK IN HIS HEAD*, in *Newsweek*. 2018.
191. Trump, D.J., *Executive Order Protecting the Nation from Foreign Terrorist Entry into the United States*. 2017.
192. Trump, D.J., *Executive Order Protecting The Nation From Foreign Terrorist Entry Into The United States, 2*. 2017.
193. Schoen, J.W. *After 500 days, hundreds of White House jobs remain unfilled by Trump administration*. CNBC, 2018.
194. Association, A.F.S. *List of Ambassadorial Appointments*. 2018 July 31, 2018; Available from: http://www.afsa.org/list-ambassadorial-appointments.
195. Smith, D.a.J., Ben, *Chaos in the White House: 'There's never been anything like this'*, in *The Guardian*. 2017.
196. Heer, J., *Trump's Chaos Is Becoming America's Chaos*, in *The New Republic*. 2018
197. Walsh, K.T., *A History of Chaos*, in *U.S. News and World Report*. 2018.
198. Becker, B., *Confusion and chaos ahead as new tax rules take immediate effect*, in *Politico*. 2017.
199. Liptak, K., *Trump's go-it-alone immigration strategy ends in chaos, confusion*, in *CNN* 2018.
200. Snell, K.a.D., Susan, *Trump Injects Chaos Into Immigration Debate — Opposing, Then Backing GOP Bill*, in *All Things Considered*. 2018, National Public Radio.
201. Swanson, A., *White House's Nafta Approach Frustrates Businesses, Panicked Emails Show*, in *The New York Times*. 2018.
202. Ackerman, S., *What's Trump's plan for Syria? Five different policies in two weeks*, in *The Guardian*. 2018.
203. Baker, P., *Trump Now Sees Qatar as an Ally Against Terrorism*, in *The New York Times*. 2018.
204. Gomez, A., *What is President Trump's policy on DREAMers? It keeps changing*, in *USA Today*. 2018.
205. Rucker, P., *Trump praises Kim Jong Un's authoritarian rule, says 'I want my people to do the same'*, in *Chicago Tribune*. 2018.
206. Watkins, E., *Trump taunts North Korea: My nuclear button is 'much bigger,' 'more powerful'*, in *CNN Politics*. 2018.
207. Hirschfeld Davis, J.C., Helene, *Trump Says Transgender People Will Not Be Allowed in the Military*, in *The New York Times*. 2017.

Bibliography

208. Defense, S.o., *Memo for the President: Military Service by Transgender Individuals*. 2018.
209. Haltiwanger, J., *How the Trump administration's stance on Russian election interference has evolved since the controversial summit with Putin*, in *Business Insider*. 2018.
210. Estepa, J., *Meet 19 women who claim affairs with Trump or accuse him of unwanted advances*, in *USA Today*. 2018.
211. Gold, M.N., Anu, *Republican committees have paid nearly $1.3 million to Trump-owned entities this year*, in *The Washington Post*. 2017.
212. O'Connell, J., *Trump business dealings raise 'serious concerns,' ethics office says*. 2018.
213. Hakim, D., *New York Attorney General Sues Trump Foundation After 2-Year Investigation*, in *The New York Times*. 2018.
214. Shear, M.H., Maggie, *Foreign Trip Comes at Crucial Time, but Trump Is a Reluctant Traveler*, in *The New York Times*. 2017.
215. Corasaniti, N., *Look at My African-American Over Here,' Donald Trump Says at Rally*, in *The New York Times*. 2016.
216. Hartman, M., *Scouts Dishonor: The 14 Most Inappropriate Moments From Trump's Speech at the Boy Scout Jamboree*, in *New York Magazine*. 2017.
217. Jenkins, A., *President Trump Calls Elizabeth Warren 'Pocahontas' at Event Honoring Native American Veterans*, in *Time*. 2017.
218. Berenson, T., *President Trump Went Way Off Script and Turned His CPAC Speech into a Campaign Rally*, in *Time*. 2018.
219. Page, S., *State of the Union analysis: Trump's speech was remarkable for what he didn't say*, in *USA Today*.
220. Jackson, R.A.D.R., *White House Daily Briefing*, in *C-SPAN*. 2018.
221. Berenson, T., *Trump Says 'Many Black Pastors Endorsed Him After Meeting'*, in *Time*. 2015.
222. Dedaj, P., *Trump talks Dems' memo, guns and border wall in exclusive interview with Fox News*, in *Fox News*. 2018.
223. Howell, T., *Donald Trump questions poll showing Ben Carson ahead in Iowa, calls him 'low energy'*, in *The Washington Post*. 2015.
224. Gebelhoff, R., *Trump got the most airtime during the GOP debate — by a lot*, in *The Washington Post*. 2015.
225. Wilson, C., *Donald Trump Interrupted Hillary Clinton and Lester Holt 55 Times in the First Presidential Debate*, in *Time* 2016.
226. Schwartzman, P.M., Michael E., *Confident. Incorrigible. Bully: Little Donny was a lot like candidate Donald Trump*, in *The Washington Post*. 2016.

227. Chotiner, I., *Why Trump Is Like This*, in *Slate Magazine*. 2017.
228. Editors, A., *Famous People with ADHD: Role Models We Love*, in *ADDitude*.
229. Perrault, S., *Seven Habits of Highly Successful Entrepreneurs With ADHD*, in *Psychology Today*. 2009.
230. Baron, D.A., *The gold medal face of ADHD*. J Atten Disord, 2010. **13**(4): p. 323-4.
231. Resource, T.N.I.o.M.H.I. *Research Domain Criteria (RDoC)*. 2019; Available from: https://www.nimh.nih.gov/research/research-funded-by-nimh/rdoc/index.shtml.
232. Shekim, W.O., et al., *A clinical and demographic profile of a sample of adults with attention deficit hyperactivity disorder, residual state*. Compr Psychiatry, 1990. **31**(5): p. 416-25.
233. Lee, B.Y., *Donald Trump's Sniffling Continues: Here Are The Possible Causes*, in *Forbes*. 2016.
234. Retz, W., et al., *Emotional dysregulation in adult ADHD: What is the empirical evidence?* Expert Rev Neurother, 2012. **12**(10): p. 1241-51.
235. McGill, A., *What Trump Tweets While America Sleeps*, in *The Atlantic*. 2016.
236. Dadomo, H., et al., *Schema Therapy for Emotional Dysregulation: Theoretical Implication and Clinical Applications*. Front Psychol, 2016. **7**: p. 1987.
237. Dodson, W., *How ADHD Ignites Rejection Sensitive Dysphoria*, in *ADDitude*.
238. Bondu, R. and G. Esser, *Justice and rejection sensitivity in children and adolescents with ADHD symptoms*. Eur Child Adolesc Psychiatry, 2015. **24**(2): p. 185-98.
239. Bondu, R., F. Sahyazici-Knaak, and G. Esser, *Long-Term Associations of Justice Sensitivity, Rejection Sensitivity, and Depressive Symptoms in Children and Adolescents*. Front Psychol, 2017. **8**: p. 1446.
240. Safren, S.A., et al., *Mastering your adult ADHD : a cognitive-behavioral treatment program : therapist guide*. Second edition. ed. Treatments that work. 2017, New York: Oxford University Press. xxx, 148 pages.
241. Epstein, T., N.A. Patsopoulos, and M. Weiser, *Immediate-release methylphenidate for attention deficit hyperactivity disorder (ADHD) in adults*. Cochrane Database Syst Rev, 2014(9): p. Cd005041.
242. Ghanizadeh, A., *Sensory processing problems in children with ADHD, a systematic review*. Psychiatry Investig, 2011. **8**(2): p. 89-94.
243. Lane, S.J., S. Reynolds, and L. Dumenci, *Sensory overresponsivity and anxiety in typically developing children and children with autism and*

attention deficit hyperactivity disorder: cause or coexistence? Am J Occup Ther, 2012. **66**(5): p. 595-603.
244. Brus, M.J., M.V. Solanto, and J.F. Goldberg, *Adult ADHD vs. bipolar disorder in the DSM-5 era: a challenging differentiation for clinicians.* J Psychiatr Pract, 2014. **20**(6): p. 428-37.
245. Skirrow, C., et al., *Everyday emotional experience of adults with attention deficit hyperactivity disorder: evidence for reactive and endogenous emotional lability.* Psychol Med, 2014. **44**(16): p. 3571-83.
246. Kim, J.S., et al., *Diagnostic stability of first-episode psychosis and predictors of diagnostic shift from non-affective psychosis to bipolar disorder: a retrospective evaluation after recurrence.* Psychiatry Res, 2011. **188**(1): p. 29-33.
247. Kendler, K.S., *The clinical features of mania and their representation in modern diagnostic criteria.* Psychol Med, 2017. **47**(6): p. 1013-1029.
248. Maté, G., *Scattered minds : a new look at the origins and healing of attention deficit disorder.* 1999, Toronto: Vintage Canada. xix, 348 p.
249. Sprich, S., et al., *Adoptive and biological families of children and adolescents with ADHD.* J Am Acad Child Adolesc Psychiatry, 2000. **39**(11): p. 1432-7.
250. Biederman, J., et al., *Examining the nature of the comorbidity between pediatric attention deficit/hyperactivity disorder and post-traumatic stress disorder.* Acta Psychiatr Scand, 2013. **128**(1): p. 78-87.
251. Chang, Z., et al., *Association Between Medication Use for Attention-Deficit/Hyperactivity Disorder and Risk of Motor Vehicle Crashes.* JAMA Psychiatry, 2017. **74**(6): p. 597-603.
252. Broyd, S.J., et al., *Default-mode brain dysfunction in mental disorders: a systematic review.* Neurosci Biobehav Rev, 2009. **33**(3): p. 279-96.
253. Kirova, A.M., R.B. Bays, and S. Lagalwar, *Working memory and executive function decline across normal aging, mild cognitive impairment, and Alzheimer's disease.* Biomed Res Int, 2015. **2015**: p. 748212.
254. Callahan, B.L., et al., *Adult ADHD: Risk Factor for Dementia or Phenotypic Mimic?* Front Aging Neurosci, 2017. **9**: p. 260.
255. Golimstok, A., et al., *Previous adult attention-deficit and hyperactivity disorder symptoms and risk of dementia with Lewy bodies: a case-control study.* Eur J Neurol, 2011. **18**(1): p. 78-84.
256. Fischer, B.L., et al., *The identification and assessment of late-life ADHD in memory clinics.* J Atten Disord, 2012. **16**(4): p. 333-8.
257. Hamblin, J., *Is Something Neurologically Wrong With Donald Trump?*, in *The Atlantic*. 2018.

258. Manigault Newman, O., *Unhinged: An Insider's Account of the Trump White House*. 2018: Gallery Books.
259. Davis, D.H., et al., *Montreal Cognitive Assessment for the diagnosis of Alzheimer's disease and other dementias.* Cochrane Database Syst Rev, 2015(10): p. Cd010775.
260. Christensen, J. *This is the cognitive test the president passed.* 2018.
261. Mason, J.H.S., *Exclusive: Exercise? I get more than people think, Trump says*, in *Reuters*. 2018.
262. Azouvi, P., et al., *Neuropsychology of traumatic brain injury: An expert overview.* Rev Neurol (Paris), 2017. **173**(7-8): p. 461-472.
263. Damasio, H., et al., *The return of Phineas Gage: clues about the brain from the skull of a famous patient.* Science, 1994. **264**(5162): p. 1102-5.
264. Mez, J., R.A. Stern, and A.C. McKee, *Chronic traumatic encephalopathy: where are we and where are we going?* Curr Neurol Neurosci Rep, 2013. **13**(12): p. 407.
265. Prevention, C.f.D.C.a. *Rates of TBI-related Emergency Department Visits, Hospitalizations, and Deaths — United States, 2001–2010*. 2016 January 22, 2016]; Available from: https://www.cdc.gov/traumaticbraininjury/data/rates.html.
266. Liou, Y.J., et al., *Risk of Traumatic Brain Injury Among Children, Adolescents, and Young Adults With Attention-Deficit Hyperactivity Disorder in Taiwan.* J Adolesc Health, 2018.
267. Bhatia, R., *Rule out these causes of inattention before diagnosing ADHD.* Current Psychiatry, 2016. **15**(10): p. 32-C3.
268. Turner, C., A.D. Handford, and A.N. Nicholson, *Sedation and memory: studies with a histamine H-1 receptor antagonist.* J Psychopharmacol, 2006. **20**(4): p. 506-17.
269. Garland, E.L., et al., *The downward spiral of chronic pain, prescription opioid misuse, and addiction: cognitive, affective, and neuropsychopharmacologic pathways.* Neurosci Biobehav Rev, 2013. **37**(10 Pt 2): p. 2597-607.
270. Broyd, S.J., et al., *Acute and Chronic Effects of Cannabinoids on Human Cognition-A Systematic Review.* Biol Psychiatry, 2016. **79**(7): p. 557-67.
271. Johnson, J., *Trump cites brother's struggle with alcohol in talking about addiction*, in *Chicago Tribune*. 2017.
272. Altman, L., *Donald Trump's Longtime Doctor Says President Takes Hair-Growth Drug*, in *The New York Times*. 2017.
273. Biskin, R.S. and J. Paris, *Diagnosing borderline personality disorder.* Cmaj, 2012. **184**(16): p. 1789-94.

274. Crowell, S.E., T.P. Beauchaine, and M.M. Linehan, *A biosocial developmental model of borderline personality: Elaborating and extending Linehan's theory.* Psychol Bull, 2009. **135**(3): p. 495-510.
275. Kluger, J., *Donald Trump's Very Strange Brand of Narcissism*, in *Time*. 2015.
276. Gartner, J., *Donald Trump's malignant narcissism is toxic*, in *USA Today*. 2017.
277. Timm, J.C. *Tracking President Trump's Flip-Flops*.
278. Kessler, G., *President Trump, the king of flip-flops*, in *The Washington Post*. 2017.
279. Kessler, G.K., Meg, *President Trump's flip-flop on coverage for preexisting health conditions*, in *The Washington Post*. 2018.
280. Cumyn, L., L. French, and L. Hechtman, *Comorbidity in adults with attention-deficit hyperactivity disorder.* Can J Psychiatry, 2009. **54**(10): p. 673-83.
281. Gomez, R. and P.J. Corr, *ADHD and personality: a meta-analytic review.* Clin Psychol Rev, 2014. **34**(5): p. 376-88.
282. Shear, M.D., Julie Hirschfeld, *STOKING FEARS, TRUMP DEFIED BUREAUCRACY TO ADVANCE IMMIGRATION AGENDA*, in *The New York Times*. 2017.
283. Wills, A.L., Alysha. *All the President's tweets*. 2018; Available from: http://www.cnn.com/interactive/2017/politics/trump-tweets/.
284. Cillizza, C. *Donald Trump said 11 false things in just 5 tweets Sunday morning*. 2018 May 20, 2018]; Available from: https://www.cnn.com/2018/05/20/politics/donald-trump-sunday-tweets/index.html.
285. Cillizza, C. *Donald Trump's Twitter feed is getting more and more bizarre*. 2018 June 18, 2018; Available from: https://www.cnn.com/2018/06/18/politics/trump-tweets/index.html.
286. Colby, E., *Donald Trump's noteworthy tweets as president*, in *Newsweek*. 2018.
287. Lee, J.Q., Kevin, *The 487 People, Places and Things Donald Trump Has Insulted on Twitter: A Complete List*, in *The New York Times*. 2018.
288. Pak, J.H., *The good, the bad, and the ugly at the US-North Korea summit in Hanoi*. 2019, Brookings.
289. Volz-Sidiropoulou, E., M. Boecker, and S. Gauggel, *The Positive Illusory Bias in Children and Adolescents With ADHD: Further Evidence.* J Atten Disord, 2016. **20**(2): p. 178-86.
290. Owens, J.S., et al., *A critical review of self-perceptions and the positive illusory bias in children with ADHD.* Clin Child Fam Psychol Rev, 2007. **10**(4): p. 335-51.

291. Menza, K., *16 Things You Didn't Know About Donald Trump's Father, Fred*, in *Town and Country*. 2017.
292. Kelly, K. and P. Ramundo, *You mean I'm not lazy, stupid or crazy?! : the classic self-help book for adults with attention deficit disorder*. 1st Scribner trade pbk. ed. 2006, New York: Scribner. xvi, 460 p.
293. Stocker, T.F., D. Qin, G.-K. Plattner, M. Tignor, S.K. Allen, J. Boschung, A. Nauels, Y. Xia, V. Bex and P.M. Midgley, *Summary for Policymakers. In: Climate Change 2013: The Physical Science Basis. Contribution of Working Group I to the Fifth Assessment Report of the Intergovernmental Panel on Climate Change*, in *Intergovernmental Panel on Climate Change*. 2013.
294. Diaz, D. *Trump looms behind Clinton at the debate*. 2016 October 10, 2016]; Available from: https://www.cnn.com/2016/10/09/politics/donald-trump-looming-hillary-clinton-presidential-debate/index.html.
295. Keneally, M.S., Veronica; Walshe, Shushannah; McGraw, Meridith; Jacobo, Julia. *2nd Presidential Debate: 11 Moments That Mattered*. 2016 October 9, 2016]; Available from: https://abcnews.go.com/Politics/presidential-debate-11-moments-mattered/story?id=42687340.
296. Gajanan, M., *Watch Saturday Night Live's Take on the Second Presidential Debate*, in *Time*. 2016.
297. Jamieson, A. *2016 Presidential Debate: Trump Accused of 'Stalking' Clinton on Stage*. 2016 October 10, 2016]; Available from: https://www.nbcnews.com/storyline/2016-presidential-debates/presidential-debate-trump-accused-stalking-clinton-stage-n663516.
298. Slack, D., *Trump's pacing, lurking turn into a thing*, in *USA Today*. 2016.
299. Filipovic, j., *Donald Was a Creep. Too Bad Hillary Couldn't Say It.*, in *New York Times*. 2017.
300. *New York Senate Debate*. 2000, WNED TV Public Television Station Buffalo, New York.
301. Hillary, T. *SEN CLINTON - " & THIS NEW REPUBLICAN AD USING SOFT MONEY ISN'T A PART OF YOUR CAMPAIGN MR. LAZIO "*. 2000 [cited 2012; Available from: https://www.youtube.com/watch?v=nOySqutXC90.
302. Shamo. *Trump Bullies Jeb Bush & Ted Cruz to The Republican Nomination*. November 15, 2016]; Available from: https://www.youtube.com/watch?v=kO2rZJBtPiM.
303. Reilly, K., *14 Times Donald Trump and Ted Cruz Insulted Each Other*, in *Time*. 2016.
304. Wolf, B.Z. *Presidential name-calling: What 'Little Marco' has to do with 'Rocket Man' (and nuclear weapons)*. 2017 September 23, 2017];

Bibliography

Available from: https://www.cnn.com/2017/09/23/politics/presidential-name-calling/index.html.
305. Clark, D.V., Ali. *Democrats rally behind Gillibrand after Trump's 'sexist smear'*. 2017; Available from: https://www.nbcnews.com/politics/white-house/trump-attacks-kirsten-gillibrand-twitter-after-she-calls-him-resign-n828701.
306. Filipovic, j., *Our President Has Always Degraded Women — And We've Always Let Him*, in *Time*. 2017.
307. Boot, M., *Trump uses xenophobia yet again to rile up his base*, in *Chicago Tribune*. 2018.
308. Finnegan, M.B.M., *Shithole' and other racist things Trump has said*, in *LA Times*. 2018.
309. Heit, E., *Brain imaging, forward inference, and theories of reasoning.* Front Hum Neurosci, 2014. **8**: p. 1056.
310. Gore, M.C. and M.C. Gore, *Inclusion strategies for secondary classrooms : keys for struggling learners*. 2nd ed. 2010, Thousand Oaks, Calif.: Corwin. x, 237 p.
311. Cohen, C., *Donald Trump sexism tracker: Every offensive comment in one place*, in *The Telegraph*. 2017.
312. Wagner, M. *Trump tells Brigitte Macron: 'You're in such good shape'*. 2017; Available from: www.cnn.com/2017/07/13/politics/trump-brigitte-macron-handshake/index.html.
313. Toobin, M., *Trump's Miss Universe Gambit*, in *The New Yorker*. 2018.
314. SAVRANSKY, S. *Trump: 'I'm much better for the gays'*. 2016; Available from: http://thehill.com/blogs/ballot-box/presidential-races/283498-trump-says-he-shamed-clinton-into-saying-radical-islam.
315. Kranish, M.O.H., Robert, *Inside the government's racial bias case against Donald Trump's company, and how he fought it*, in *The Washington Post*. 2016.
316. Forbes, *The Definitive net worth of Donald Trump*, in *Forbes*. 2018.
317. Price, E., *Trump Allegedly Lied About His Wealth to Get on the Forbes 400 List in the 1980s*, in *Fortune*. 2018.
318. Vitali, A. *Trump Threatens to 'Totally Destroy' North Korea in First U.N. Speech*. 2017; Available from: https://www.nbcnews.com/politics/white-house/trump-un-north-korean-leader-suicide-mission-n802596.
319. Ramzy, A., *Trump Threatens Iran on Twitter, Warning Rouhani of Dire 'Consequences'*, in *The New York Times*. 2018.
320. Reifowitz, I., *First-Month Trump Trauma Is A Far Cry From No Drama Obama*, in *Huffington Post*. 2017.

321. Haberman, M., *Donald Trump Says His Mocking of New York Times Reporter Was Misread,* in *New York Times.* 2015.
322. BBC, *Trump mocks Clinton's pneumonia illness.* 2016.
323. Litt, D., *Is Nothing Funny, Mr. President?,* in *The New York Times.* 2017.
324. Sundem, G., *This Is Your Brain on Multitasking,* in *Psychology Today.* 2012.
325. Shute, N., *Health Shots,* in *If You Think You're Good At Multitasking, You Probably Aren't.* 2013, National Public Radio.
326. Bradner, E. *Trump always takes the bait and other debate takeaways.* 2016; Available from: https://www.cnn.com/2016/10/20/politics/presidential-debate-takeaways/index.html.
327. Chozick, A.B., M., *Hillary Clinton, Mocking and Taunting in Debate, Turns the Tormentor,* in *The New York Times.* 2016.
328. Zurcher, A. *Presidential debate: Who won - Trump or Clinton?* 2016; Available from: https://www.bbc.com/news/election-us-2016-37711218.
329. Kentish, B., *Donald Trump says he and Hillary Clinton should take a drugs test after accusing rival of being 'pumped up',* in *The Independent.* 2016.
330. Live, S.N.; Available from: https://www.youtube.com/channel/UCqFzWxSCi39LnW1JKFR3efg.
331. Sansone, R.A. and L.A. Sansone, *Faking attention deficit hyperactivity disorder.* Innov Clin Neurosci, 2011. **8**(8): p. 10-3.
332. Rabiner, D.L., *Stimulant prescription cautions: addressing misuse, diversion and malingering.* Curr Psychiatry Rep, 2013. **15**(7): p. 375.
333. *How to get prescribed ADHD meds.* 2016; Available from: https://www.reddit.com/r/Drugs/comments/44mp3l/how_to_get_prescribed_adhd_meds/.
334. Faraone, S.V. *What can Doctors do about Fake ADHD?* ADHD in Adults 2016; Available from: http://adhdinadults.com/what-can-doctors-do-about-fake-adhd/.
335. Harrison, A.G., M.J. Edwards, and K.C. Parker, *Identifying students faking ADHD: Preliminary findings and strategies for detection.* Arch Clin Neuropsychol, 2007. **22**(5): p. 577-88.
336. Suhr, J.A. and D.T.R. Berry, *The importance of assessing for validity of symptom report and performance in attention deficit/hyperactivity disorder (ADHD): Introduction to the special section on noncredible presentation in ADHD.* Psychol Assess, 2017. **29**(12): p. 1427-1428.
337. Ramachandran, S., et al., *Development of the Subtle ADHD Malingering Screener.* Assessment, 2018: p. 1073191118773881.

338. Groden, C., *Donald Trump Would Be Richer If He'd Have Invested in Index Funds*, in *Fortune*. 2015.
339. Wilkin, S., *How Donald Trump got rich*, in *Business Insider*. 2016.
340. Hafner, J., *Trump on presidential candidates: I'm the most successful*, in *USA Today*. 2015.
341. Trump, D.J., *Trump: I'll choose the best people for my administration*, in *CNBC*, J. Paulson, Editor. 2016.
342. Seabrook, A., *Is Palin's 'Going Rogue' A Good Read?*, in *Talk of the Nation*, R. Roberts, Editor. 2009, NPR.
343. Davidson, J.R., K.M. Connor, and M. Swartz, *Mental illness in U.S. Presidents between 1776 and 1974: a review of biographical sources.* J Nerv Ment Dis, 2006. **194**(1): p. 47-51.
344. Trump, D.J. *Donald Trump Tweet, 4:27AM 6 Jan 2018*. 2018; Available from: https://twitter.com/realDonaldTrump/status/949618475877765120.
345. Novack, J., *Trump Reported $916 Million Tax Loss In 1995, Suggesting He Paid No Income Tax For Years*, in *Forbes*. 2016.
346. *Economy Watch - 1995*. Available from: http://www.economywatch.com/economic-statistics/year/1995/.
347. Barstow, D.C., Susanne; Buettner, Russ; Twohey, Megan, *Donald Trump Tax Records Show He Could Have Avoided Taxes for Nearly Two Decades, The Times Found*, in *New York Times*. 2016.
348. Qiu, L., *Yep, Donald Trump's companies have declared bankruptcy...more than four times*, in *Politifact*. 2016.
349. Penzenstadler, N.R., Steve; et al., *Donald Trump: Three decades, 4,095 lawsuits*, in *USA Today*. 2018.
350. Taylor, K., *Porn star Stormy Daniels is taking a victory lap after Michael Cohen's guilty plea. Here's a timeline of Trump's many marriages and rumored affairs.*, in *Business Insider*. 2018.
351. Criss, D. *A judge has finalized a $25 million settlement for students who claim they were defrauded by Trump University*. 2018; Available from: https://www.cnn.com/2018/04/10/politics/trump-university-settlement-finalized-trnd/index.html.
352. Bagli, C., *Trump Paid Over $1 Million in Labor Settlement, Documents Reveal*, in *New York Times*. 2017.
353. Northam, J., *Trump D.C. Hotel Contractors Say They're Owed Millions*, in *Morning Edition*. 2017, National Public Radio.
354. Mehta, S., *Meet Donald Trump's new campaign managers*, in *L.A. Times*. 2016.

355. Baker, P.H., Maggie, *Reince Priebus Is Ousted Amid Stormy Days for White House*, in *New York Times*. 2017.
356. Lemire, J.L., Catherine, *'Tired of being told no,' Trump freezes out chief of staff*, in *Associated Press*. 2018.
357. Lu, D.Y., Karen, *You're Hired! You're Fired! Yes, the Turnover at the Top of the Trump Administration Is ... "Unprecedented"*, in *New York Times*. 2018.
358. Solanto, M.V., *Cognitive-behavioral therapy for adult ADHD : targeting executive dysfunction*. 2011, New York: Guilford Press. x, 214 p.
359. McGough, J.J. and R.A. Barkley, *Diagnostic controversies in adult attention deficit hyperactivity disorder.* Am J Psychiatry, 2004. **161**(11): p. 1948-56.
360. Irving, G. and M. Lloyd-Williams, *Depression in advanced cancer.* Eur J Oncol Nurs, 2010. **14**(5): p. 395-9.
361. Kavalali, E.T. and L.M. Monteggia, *How does ketamine elicit a rapid antidepressant response?* Curr Opin Pharmacol, 2015. **20**: p. 35-9.
362. Academy, A., et al., *ADHD Parents Medication Guide*, in *Parent Med Guide*. 2018.
363. Low, K. *Non-Stimulant Medications to Treat ADHD*. 2018; Available from: https://www.verywellmind.com/non-stimulant-adhd-medication-20884.
364. Stahl, S.M., et al., *A Review of the Neuropharmacology of Bupropion, a Dual Norepinephrine and Dopamine Reuptake Inhibitor.* Prim Care Companion J Clin Psychiatry, 2004. **6**(4): p. 159-166.
365. Bilodeau, M., et al., *Duloxetine in adults with ADHD: a randomized, placebo-controlled pilot study.* J Atten Disord, 2014. **18**(2): p. 169-75.
366. Kako, Y., et al., *A case of adult attention-deficit/hyperactivity disorder alleviated by milnacipran.* Prog Neuropsychopharmacol Biol Psychiatry, 2007. **31**(3): p. 772-5.
367. Spencer, T.J., et al., *Novel treatments for attention-deficit/hyperactivity disorder in children.* J Clin Psychiatry, 2002. **63 Suppl 12**: p. 16-22.
368. Sharma, A. and J. Couture, *A review of the pathophysiology, etiology, and treatment of attention-deficit hyperactivity disorder (ADHD).* Ann Pharmacother, 2014. **48**(2): p. 209-25.
369. Watch, C., *Strattera New FDA Drug Approval*, in *Center Watch*. 2002.
370. Bardal, S.K.W., Jason E.; Martin, Douglas S., *Noradrenaline and Dopamine Reuptake Inhibitors (NDRIs)*, in *Applied Pharmacology*. 2011.
371. Budur, K., et al., *Non-stimulant treatment for attention deficit hyperactivity disorder.* Psychiatry (Edgmont), 2005. **2**(7): p. 44-8.
372. Berger, S., et al., *Sudden cardiac death in children and adolescents: introduction and overview.* Pediatr Clin North Am, 2004. **51**(5): p. 1201-9.

373. Winterstein, A.G., *Cardiovascular safety of stimulants in children: findings from recent population-based cohort studies.* Curr Psychiatry Rep, 2013. **15**(8): p. 379.
374. *Canada Pulls Adderall After 20 Deaths*, in *Consumer Affairs*. 2005.
375. Rosack, J., *Canada Reverses Ban On ADHD Medication.* Psychiatric News, 2005.
376. Svetlov, S.I., F.H. Kobeissy, and M.S. Gold, *Performance enhancing, non-prescription use of Ritalin: a comparison with amphetamines and cocaine.* J Addict Dis, 2007. **26**(4): p. 1-6.
377. Compton, W.M., et al., *Prevalence and Correlates of Prescription Stimulant Use, Misuse, Use Disorders, and Motivations for Misuse Among Adults in the United States.* Am J Psychiatry, 2018. **175**(8): p. 741-755.
378. Wilens, T.E., et al., *Does stimulant therapy of attention-deficit/hyperactivity disorder beget later substance abuse? A meta-analytic review of the literature.* Pediatrics, 2003. **111**(1): p. 179-85.
379. Biederman, J., et al., *Pharmacotherapy of attention-deficit/hyperactivity disorder reduces risk for substance use disorder.* Pediatrics, 1999. **104**(2): p. e20.
380. Goodman, B. *Experts Warn of Emerging 'Stimulant Epidemic'.* 2018; Available from: https://www.webmd.com/mental-health/addiction/news/20180403/experts-warn-of-emerging-stimulant-epidemic.
381. Harro, J., *Neuropsychiatric Adverse Effects of Amphetamine and Methamphetamine.* Int Rev Neurobiol, 2015. **120**: p. 179-204.
382. Ross, R.G., *Psychotic and manic-like symptoms during stimulant treatment of attention deficit hyperactivity disorder.* Am J Psychiatry, 2006. **163**(7): p. 1149-52.
383. Man, K.K., et al., *Methylphenidate and the risk of psychotic disorders and hallucinations in children and adolescents in a large health system.* Transl Psychiatry, 2016. **6**(11): p. e956.
384. Berman, S.M., et al., *Potential adverse effects of amphetamine treatment on brain and behavior: a review.* Mol Psychiatry, 2009. **14**(2): p. 123-42.
385. Moran, L.V., et al., *Psychosis with Methylphenidate or Amphetamine in Patients with ADHD.* N Engl J Med, 2019. **380**(12): p. 1128-1138.
386. Dube, B., et al., *Neuropsychiatric manifestations of HIV infection and AIDS.* J Psychiatry Neurosci, 2005. **30**(4): p. 237-46.
387. Durvasula, R. and T.R. Miller, *Substance abuse treatment in persons with HIV/AIDS: challenges in managing triple diagnosis.* Behav Med, 2014. **40**(2): p. 43-52.

388. Upadhyaya, H.P., et al., *A review of the abuse potential assessment of atomoxetine: a nonstimulant medication for attention-deficit/hyperactivity disorder.* Psychopharmacology (Berl), 2013. **226**(2): p. 189-200.
389. Popper, C.W., *Antidepressants in the treatment of attention-deficit/hyperactivity disorder.* J Clin Psychiatry, 1997. **58 Suppl 14**: p. 14-29; discussion 30-1.
390. Turner, D., *A review of the use of modafinil for attention-deficit hyperactivity disorder.* Expert Rev Neurother, 2006. **6**(4): p. 455-68.
391. Administration, F.a.D., *Dealing with ADHD: What You Need to Know.* 2018.
392. Nikiforuk, A., *Targeting the Serotonin 5-HT7 Receptor in the Search for Treatments for CNS Disorders: Rationale and Progress to Date.* CNS Drugs, 2015. **29**(4): p. 265-75.
393. Howland, R.H., *Brexpiprazole: another multipurpose antipsychotic drug?* J Psychosoc Nurs Ment Health Serv, 2015. **53**(4): p. 23-5.
394. Naguy, A. and B. Alamiri, *Successful Add-on Vortioxetine for an Adolescent With Attention-Deficit/Hyperactivity Disorder.* J Clin Psychopharmacol, 2018. **38**(4): p. 407-409.
395. Pan, P.Y., A.T. Fu, and C.B. Yeh, *Aripiprazole/Methylphenidate Combination in Children and Adolescents with Disruptive Mood Dysregulation Disorder and Attention-Deficit/Hyperactivity Disorder: An Open-Label Study.* J Child Adolesc Psychopharmacol, 2018.
396. Findling, R.L., et al., *Pharmacokinetics and Safety of Vortioxetine in Pediatric Patients.* J Child Adolesc Psychopharmacol, 2017. **27**(6): p. 526-534.
397. Cappelletti, S., et al., *Caffeine: cognitive and physical performance enhancer or psychoactive drug?* Curr Neuropharmacol, 2015. **13**(1): p. 71-88.
398. Wood, S., et al., *Psychostimulants and cognition: a continuum of behavioral and cognitive activation.* Pharmacol Rev, 2014. **66**(1): p. 193-221.
399. Beck, A.T., *THINKING AND DEPRESSION. I. IDIOSYNCRATIC CONTENT AND COGNITIVE DISTORTIONS.* Arch Gen Psychiatry, 1963. **9**: p. 324-33.
400. Beck, A.T., *The current state of cognitive therapy: a 40-year retrospective.* Arch Gen Psychiatry, 2005. **62**(9): p. 953-9.
401. Anthes, E., *Depression: a change of mind.* Nature, 2014. **515**(7526): p. 185-7.
402. Knouse, L.E. and S.A. Safren, *Current status of cognitive behavioral therapy for adult attention-deficit hyperactivity disorder.* Psychiatr Clin North Am, 2010. **33**(3): p. 497-509.

403. Antshel, K.M., S.V. Faraone, and M. Gordon, *Cognitive behavioral treatment outcomes in adolescent ADHD.* J Atten Disord, 2014. **18**(6): p. 483-95.
404. Solanto, M.V., C.B. Surman, and J.M.J. Alvir, *The efficacy of cognitive-behavioral therapy for older adults with ADHD: a randomized controlled trial.* Atten Defic Hyperact Disord, 2018. **10**(3): p. 223-235.
405. Haberman, M.P., Ashley; Peters, Jeremy W.; Barbaro, Michael, *Inside Donald Trump's Last Stand: An Anxious Nominee Seeks Assurance*, in *New York Times*. 2016.
406. Kludt, T., *Howard Dean under fire for alleging Trump cocaine use at debate*, in *CNN Politics*. 2016.
407. Moritz-Rabson, D., *TOM ARNOLD CLAIMS DONALD TRUMP SNORTED ADDERALL ON 'THE APPRENTICE' SET*, in *Newsweek*. 2018.
408. Scribd. *According to Medical Records Obtained by Newsweek.* 2019; Available from: https://www.scribd.com/document/372716093/According-to-Medical-Records-Obtained-by-Newsweek.
409. Feinberg, A., *Rumor: Doctor Prescribes Donald Trump "Cheap Speed"*, in *Gawker*. 2016.
410. Weisler, R.H. and A.C. Childress, *Treating attention-deficit/hyperactivity disorder in adults: focus on once-daily medications.* Prim Care Companion CNS Disord, 2011. **13**(6).
411. Editors, *Phentermine For ADHD: An Uninvestigated Treatment.* Mental Health Daily, 2016(May).
412. Administration, U.S.F.a.D., *Code of Federal Regulations Title 21, Chapter 2, Part 1308, Schedules of Controlled Substances.* 2018.
413. Staff, E., *Vyvanse: Use, Abuse, and Dangers of Snorting*, A.A. Centers, Editor. 2019.
414. Wainstein, G., et al., *Pupil Size Tracks Attentional Performance In Attention-Deficit/Hyperactivity Disorder.* Sci Rep, 2017. **7**(1): p. 8228.
415. Heiting, G., *Dilated Pupils: Causes and Concerns*, A.A. Vision, Editor. 2019.
416. *2019 State of the Union Address*, CNN, Editor. 2019.
417. *2019 Presidential Address to the Nation*, CNN, Editor. 2019.
418. *Watch live: Trump delivers remarks at Farm Bureau convention*, T.H. Staff, Editor. 2019, The Hill.
419. *Final Clinton-Trump Debate (Full Debate - 10/19/16)*, B. Politics, Editor. 2016.
420. *Presidential Debate - Donald Trump vs. Hillary Clinton*, A. Arizoa, Editor. 2016.

421. *Second 2016 US Presidential Debate October 9, 2016 Donald Trump Vs Hillary Clinton*, C. News, Editor. 2016.
422. Mueller, A., et al., *Linking ADHD to the Neural Circuitry of Attention.* Trends Cogn Sci, 2017. **21**(6): p. 474-488.
423. Rhodan, M., *President Trump Said His Win Was the 'Biggest Since Reagan.' It Wasn't*, in *Time*. 2017.
424. Brown, T.E., *Attention deficit disorder : the unfocused mind in children and adults.* Yale University Press health & wellness. 2005, New Haven: Yale University Press. xxi, 360 p.
425. Hallowell, E., *Hyperfocus: A Blessing and a Curse*, in *ADDitude*. 2018.
426. Jackson, D.M.K., Gregory, *Art of the dodge: The questions Trump didn't answer at his news conference*, in *USA Today*. 2017.
427. Lemire, J.M., Zeke, *Briefing papers warned Trump: 'DO NOT CONGRATULATE' Putin*, in *PBS News Hour*. 2018.
428. Lemire, J.I., Vladamir, *Trump calls Russia's Putin to congratulate him on re-electio*, in *PBS News Hour*. 2018.
429. Blake, A., *The first Trump-Clinton presidential debate transcript, annotated*, in *The Washington Post*. 2016.
430. Hanson, J., *Trump's willingness to walk away at the G7 and North Korea summits shows his foreign policy is working*, in *Fox News*. 2018.
431. Schmidt, M.H., Maggie, *In Russia Inquiry, Lawyers Tell Trump to Refuse Mueller Interview*, in *New York Times*. 2018.
432. Sheth, S., *Some Trump staffers are reportedly afraid to leave Trump alone in meetings with foreign leaders*, in *Business Insider*. 2017.
433. Woodward, B., *Fear : Trump in the White House*. 2018: Simone & Schuster. 448 p.
434. Martin, W.B., Bob, *China hits back at Trump with tariffs on $60 billion of US goods*, in *Business Insider*. 2018.
435. Troianovski, A., *Russia responds to airstrikes in Syria with harsh words but no fire*, in *Washington Post*. 2018.
436. Burleigh, N., *TRUMP SPEAKS AT FOURTH-GRADE LEVEL, LOWEST OF LAST 15 U.S. PRESIDENTS, NEW ANALYSIS FINDS*, in *Newsweek*. 2018.
437. Kruse, M., *The 37 Fatal Gaffes That Didn't Kill Donald Trump*, in *Politico*. 2016.
438. Tobak, S., *Donald Trump's War on Political Correctness*, in *Fox Business*. 2016.
439. Baker, P., *Trump and the Truth: A President Tests His Own Credibility*, in *New York Times*. 2018.

440. Blake, A., *Donald Trump instantly and completely contradicts himself on his great temperament*, in *Washington Post*. 2016.
441. Blake, A., *Transcript: Phone call between President Trump and journalist Bob Woodward*. 2018.
442. Holt, J., *With friends like Trump, who needs enemies?*, in *Chicago Tribune*. 2018.
443. Todd, C.M., Mark; Dann, Carrie, *At NATO summit, Trump again alienates allies and compliments enemies*. 2018.
444. Baker, P.R., Katie, *In Trump's America, the Conversation Turns Ugly and Angry, Starting at the Top*, in *New York Times*. 2018.
445. Erlanger, S., *As Summit Nears, NATO Allies Have One Main Worry: Trump*, in *New York Times*. 2018.
446. Lippman, D., *Trump's diplomatic learning curve: Time zones, 'Nambia' and 'Nipple'*, in *Politico*. 2018.
447. Collinson, S., *Undisciplined Trump disrupts his own tax reform pitch*, in *CNN Politics*. 2017.
448. Jackson, H., *Why is President Trump still talking about a tax bill instead of signing one?*, in *USA Today*. 2017.
449. Barkley, R.M., K.R., *Deficient Emotional Self-REgulation in Adults with ADHD: The Relative Contributions of Emotional Impulseiveness and ADHD symptoms to Adaptive Impairments in Major Life Activities*. Journal of ADHD and Related Disorders, 2010. **1**: p. 5-28.
450. Chan, M., *Donald Trump Says He Has a 'Much Better Temperament' Than Hillary Clinton*, in *Fortune*. 2016.
451. Adler, S.J.M., Jeff; Holland, Steve, *Exclusive: Trump says he thought being president would be easier than his old life*, in *Reuters*. 2017.
452. Liptak, K., *Trump: 'Nobody knew health care could be so complicated'*, in *CNN Politics*. 2017.
453. Benen, S., *Trump: 'Nobody knew that health care could be so complicated'*, in *The Rachel Maddow Show*. 2017.
454. Abelson, M., *On the Rocks: The Story of Trump Vodka*, in *Bloomberg Businessweek*. 2016.
455. Staff, T., *10 Donald Trump Business Failures*, in *Time Magazine*. 2016.
456. Tully, S., *How Donald Trump Made Millions Off His Biggest Business Failure*, in *Fortune*. 2016.
457. Glover, S.R., Maeve; Williams, Brenna, *How Donald Trump sees himself*, in *CNN Politics*. 2016.
458. Markon, J., *U.S. illegal immigrant population falls below 11 million, continuing nearly decade-long decline, report says*, in *Washington Post*. 2016.

459. 6, W.C., *WATCH: `We`re going to build the wall,` Trump says at RIR.* 2016.
460. Lee, D., *Trump likes to talk about steel and manufactured goods. America's better trade hope may lie in exported services.* , in *LA Times*. 2017.
461. Irwin, N., *Most Americans Produce Services, Not Stuff. Trump Ignores That in Talking About Trade.*, in *New York Times*. 2018.
462. Kaczynski, A., *Howard Stern on Trump's misogynistic talk: 'This is who Trump is'*, in *CNN Media*. 2016.
463. Prusher, I., *Opinion: Trump judges women by their bodies. Do you?*, in *CNN Politics*. 2016.
464. *Donald Trump: Billy Bush says infamous Access Hollywood 'grab them by the p***y' tape is real*, in *ABC News*. 2017.
465. Cillizza, C., *Donald Trump's 43 most head-scratching lines from his not-at-all boring West Virginia tax speech*, in *CNN Politics*. 2018.
466. Trump, D.J. *Donald Trump "Boring" Tweets*. 2018; Available from: https://factba.se/topic/twitter?q=boring&f=.
467. Gearan, A.D., Josh, *Bad blood between McCain and Trump lingers, even as the Arizona Republican senator nears the end*, in *Washington Post*. 2018.
468. Radnofsky, L., *Trump Suggests Football Players Who Protest Anthem 'Shouldn't Be in the Country'*, in *Wall Street Journal*. 2018.
469. Dvorak, P., *Trump ignores Puerto Rico's devastation to tweet about the NFL*, in *Washington Post*. 2017.
470. Gleick, P., *Trump's nonsense tweets on water and wildfires are dangerous*, in *Washington Post*. 2018.
471. Belvedere, M., *Trump asks why US can't use nukes*, in *CNBC Elections*. 2016.
472. Kitfield, J., *Tump's Generals Are Trying to Save the World. Starting With the White House.*, in *Politico Magazine*. 2017.
473. Brettschneider, C., *Trump vs. the Constitution: A Guide*, in *Politico Magazine*. 2016.
474. Brown, L., *Government Stumps Trump*, in *U.S. News and World Report*. 2016.
475. Cillizza, C., *Donald Trump's IQ obsession, in 22 quotes*, in *CNN Politics*. 2017.
476. Abadi, M., *Trump jokes about the size of his hands for the second time in 2 weeks at hurricane relief event*, in *Business Insider*. 2017.
477. Sheth, S., *Nearly 100 days into his presidency, Trump is still a voracious consumer of cable news*, in *Business Insider*. 2017.
478. Cillizza, C., *Donald Trump's huge golf hypocrisy*, in *CNN Politics*. 2018.

479. Trump, D. and T. Schwartz, *Trump : the art of the deal*. 1st ed. 1988, New York: Random House. x, 246 p., 16 p. of plates.
480. Segal, D., *What Donald Trump's Plaza Deal Reveals About His White House Bid*, in *New York Times*. 2016.
481. Martin, J., *State Department approves arms sales to Saudi Arabia*, in *DefenseNews*. 2018.
482. Corman, C.A. and E.M. Hallowell, *Positively ADD : real success stories to inspire your dreams*. 2006, New York: Walker. xix, 171 p.
483. Hallowell, E.M. and J.J. Ratey, *Delivered from distraction : getting the most out of life with attention deficit disorder*. Ballantine Books trade pbk. ed. 2006, New York: Ballantine Books. xxxv, 379 p.
484. Ostergaard, S.D., et al., *Teenage Parenthood and Birth Rates for Individuals With and Without Attention-Deficit/Hyperactivity Disorder: A Nationwide Cohort Study.* J Am Acad Child Adolesc Psychiatry, 2017. **56**(7): p. 578-584.e3.
485. Hallowell, E.M. and J.J. Ratey, *Driven to distraction : recognizing and coping with attention deficit disorder from childhood through adulthood*. 1st Anchor Books ed. 2011, New York: Anchor Books. xviii, 382 p.
486. Groen, Y., et al., *Risky behavior in gambling tasks in individuals with ADHD--a systematic literature review.* PLoS One, 2013. **8**(9): p. e74909.
487. Hallowell, E., *A.D.H.D. Is in the American DNA*, in *New York Times*. 2011.
488. Rappenport, A.T., Glenn, *Pentagon Grows, While E.P.A. and State Dept. Shrink in Trump's Budget*, in *New York Times*. 2017.
489. Cama, T.G., Miranda, *Trump moves to roll back Obama emission standards*, in *The Hill*. 2018.
490. Diamond, J.K., Ellie *EPA rolls back Obama-era coal pollution rules as Trump heads to West Virginia.* CNN Politics, 2018.
491. Taylor, A., *Tax cuts, spending to raise U.S. deficit to $1 trillion by 2020, CBO analysis shows*, in *Chicago Tribune*. 2018.
492. Bailey, P.B., Matt; Gonzales, Shelby; Katch, Hannah; Van de Water, Paul, *Health Proposals in President's Budget Would Reduce Health Insurance Coverage and Access to Care.* Center on Budget and Policy Priorities, 2018.
493. Palmer, D., *Trump's global trade war*, in *Politico Magazine*. 2018.
494. Steinbuch, Y., *Trump to present Middle East peace plan in coming months*, in *New York Post*. 2018.
495. News, B., *Trump Kim summit: US and North Korean leaders hold historic talks*, in *BBC News*. 2018.

496. Hahl, O., M. Kim, and E.W. Zuckerman Sivan, *Appendix: Post-Election Survey On Perception Of Trump's False Statement (in, The Authentic Appeal of the Lying Demagogue: Proclaiming the Deeper Truth about Political Illegitimacy).* American Sociological Review, 2018. **83**(1): p. 1-33.
497. Tanner, C., *Study finds Trump voters believe Trump is authentic, even if he appears to lie,* in *USA Today.* 2018.
498. Lucey, C.L., Jonathan, *Donald Trump hopes to follow his instincts more rather than staff's advice,* in *Global News Politics.* 2018.
499. Nakamura, D.P., Damian, *Trump unrestrained: Recent moves show president listening to his gut more than advisers,* in *Washington Post.* 2018.
500. Staff, P., *Full transcript: Second 2016 presidential debate,* in *Politico.* 2016.
501. Lynn, G.T. and J.B. Lynn, *Genius! : nurturing the spirit of the wild, odd, and oppositional child.* Rev. ed. 2006, London ; Philadelphia: Jessica Kingsley Publishers. 271 p.
502. Maynard, S., *How To Soften Blunt Talk,* in *ADDitude.* 2018.
503. Saad, G., *How Often Do People Lie in Their Daily Lives?*, in *Psychology Today.* 2011.
504. Nakamura, D., *Trump boasts that he's 'like, really smart' and a 'very stable genius' amid questions over his mental fitness,* in *Washington Post.* 2018.
505. Rucker, P., *Trump claims 'there is no chaos' in White House, but he warns of future firings,* in *Washington Post.* 2018.
506. Duetch, G., *Full Transcript: Donald Trump at the United Nations General Assembly,* in *The Atlantic.* 2018.
507. Hirschfeld Davis, J., *Trump Repeats False Claim About Canada After Admitting Uncertainty Over Figure,* in *New York Times.* 2018.
508. Prevatt, F., et al., *The positive illusory bias: does it explain self-evaluations in college students with ADHD?* J Atten Disord, 2012. **16**(3): p. 235-43.
509. Dvorsky, M.R. and J.M. Langberg, *A Review of Factors that Promote Resilience in Youth with ADHD and ADHD Symptoms.* Clin Child Fam Psychol Rev, 2016. **19**(4): p. 368-391.
510. Miller, G.J., Greg, *Trump revealed highly classified information to Russian foreign minister and ambassador,* in *Washington Post.* 2017.
511. Miller, G.R., Philip, *'This was the worst call by far': Trump badgered, bragged and abruptly ended phone call with Australian leader,* in *Washington Post.* 2017.
512. Lee, B.X., *The dangerous case of Donald Trump : 27 psychiatrists and mental health experts assess a president.* First edition. ed. 2017, New York: Thomas Dunne Books, St. Martin's Press. xix, 360 pages.

Bibliography

513. Levin, A., *Goldwater Rule's Origins Based on Long-Ago Controversy.* Psychiatric News, 2016.
514. Association., A.P., *The Principles of Medical Ethics With Annotations Especially Applicable to Psychiatry.* 2013.
515. Association., A.P., *APA Reaffirms Support for Goldwater Rule.* 2017.
516. Lilienfeld S, M.J., Lina D, *The Goldwater Rule: Perspectives From, and Implications for, Psychological Science.* Perspectives Psychol Science, 2018. **13**: p. 3-27.
517. Weissman, S., *The Goldwater Rule and free speech, the current 'political morass', and more.* Current Psychiatry, 2018. **17**(5): p. 23,e1-e3.
518. Merideth, P., *The Five C's of Confidentiality and How to DEAL with Them.* Psychiatry (Edgmont), 2007. **4**(2): p. 28-9.
519. Hamedy, S., *Dem lawmaker to introduce 'Stable Genius Act' following Trump tweet*, in *CNN Politics.* 2018.
520. Harrington, R., *After Trump flouts tradition, states introduce bills that would force presidential candidates to release their tax returns*, in *Business Insider.* 2017.
521. Javanbakht, A., *Why psychiatrists should not be involved in presidential politics*, in *Washington Post.* 2018.
522. Leonard, K., *Psychiatric association warns against diagnosing public figures like Trump without medical exam*, in *Washington Examiner.* 2018.
523. Fleming, J., *Neuropolitics: Psychiatrists' responsibility.* Current Psychiatry, 2019. **18**: p. 6-8.
524. Tatarsky, A. and G.A. Marlatt, *State of the art in harm reduction psychotherapy: an emerging treatment for substance misuse.* J Clin Psychol, 2010. **66**(2): p. 117-22.
525. Trump, D., *CNN Late Edition Interview With Donald Trump*, in *CNN Late Edition*, W. Blitzer, Editor. 2004.
526. Effron, L.S., John, *Donald Trump and Family Talk to Barbara Walters About His Presidential Run, What His Kids Think of Their Upbringing, and How He Is Handling the Role of Grandpa Trump*, in *ABC News.* 2015.
527. Scherer, M., *Donald Trump Explains All*, in *Time.* 2015.
528. Kessler, G., *How Trump bobs and weaves to avoid the truth*, in *Washington Post.* 2018.
529. Bort, R., *A BRIEF TOUR THROUGH DONALD TRUMP'S QUESTIONABLE UNDERSTANDING OF AMERICAN HISTORY*, in *Newsweek.* 2017.
530. Fahrenthold, D.A.D., Josh; Helderman, Rosalind, *'He can't get rid of any of this': Trump's wall of secrecy erodes amid growing legal challenges.* 2018.

531. Baker, P.S., Michael D., *Trump's Blasts Upend G-7, Alienating Oldest Allies*, in *New York Times*. 2018.
532. Kessler, G.Y.H.L., Michelle; Shapiro, Leslie, *Trump Promise Tracker*, in *Washington Post*. 2018.
533. Quigley, A., *The 23 people, places and things Donald Trump has attacked on Twitter as president*, in *Politico*. 2017.
534. Rubin, J., *Trump insults Gold Star mom, freaks out U.S. allies*, in *Washington Post*. 2016.
535. Amatulli, J., *Trump Defends Stormy Daniels 'Horseface' Insult: 'Make Your Own Determination'*, in *Huffington Post*. 2018.
536. Berman, R., *The Donald Trump Cabinet Tracker*, in *The Atlantic*. 2018.
537. Hulse, C., *Trump's Twitter Fury at McConnell Risks Alienating a Key Ally*, in *New York Times*. 2017.
538. Tamborrino, K., *White House on GOP senator attacks: Trump hasn't 'alienated anyone'*, in *Politico*. 2017.
539. Stelter, B., *Trump insults Fiorina in Rolling Stone: 'Look at that face!'*, in *CNN Business*. 2015.
540. Sheehan Perkins, M., *A complete timeline of Trump's years-long feud with Rosie O'Donnell*, in *Business Insider*. 2017.
541. Serwer, A., *Trump's War of Words With Black Athletes*. The Atlantic, 2017.
542. Benito, M., *Cajun Navy 'shocked' by President Trump's comments on Harvey rescues*. 2018, WWLTV.
543. Chavez, P.S., Veronica; Keneally, Meghan, *A History of the Donald Trump-Megyn Kelly Feud*, in *ABC News Politics*. 2016.
544. Guardian, T., *'I know you're not thinking': Trump mocks ABC reporter – video*, in *The Guardian*. 2018.
545. Shear, M., *Trump, in Twitter Rant, Revisits Grievances Against Sports Figures*, in *New York Times*. 2017.
546. Hayes, C., *Here are 10 times President Trump's comments have been called racist*, in *USA Today*. 2018.
547. Eltagouri, M., *Most Americans think Trump is racist, according to a new poll*, in *Washington Post*. 2018.
548. Nagourney, A., *In Tapes, Nixon Rails About Jews and Blacks*, in *New York Times*. 2010.
549. Gabbatt, A., *No, over there! Our case-by-case guide to the Trump distraction technique*, in *The Guardian*. 2017.
550. News, B., *Doomsday Clock moved to just two minutes to 'apocalypse'*, in *BBC World News*. 2018.

551. Sanger, D.E.H., Maggie, *50 G.O.P. Officials Warn Donald Trump Would Put Nation's Security 'at Risk'*, in *New York Times*. 2016.
552. Yourish, K.A., Gregor, *The Top Jobs in Trump's Administration Are Mostly Vacant: Who's to Blame?*, in *New York Times*. 2017.
553. Hohmann, J., *The Daily 202: Trump has no nominees for 245 important jobs, including an ambassador to South Korea*, in *Washington Post*. 2018.
554. Stolberg, S.G., *Critics Worry Over How Ben Carson, Lacking Expertise in Public Housing, Will Lead It*, in *New York Times*. 2016.
555. Davenport, C.S., David E., *'Learning Curve' as Rick Perry Pursues a Job He Initially Misunderstood*, in *Washington Post*. 2017.
556. Waldman, P., *Donald Trump has assembled the worst Cabinet in American history*. Washington Post, 2017.
557. Thursh, G.H., Maggie, *Forceful Chief of Staff Grates on Trump, and the Feeling Is Mutual*, in *New York Times*. 2017.
558. Barro, J., *It's no coincidence that Trump is surrounded by criminals*, in *Business Insider*. 2018.
559. Association, A.F.S. *Current U.S. Ambassadors*. 2018; Available from: http://www.afsa.org/list-ambassadorial-appointments
560. Work, C., *Still No US Ambassador in South Korea*, in *The Diplomat*. 2018.
561. Hartman, M., *6 Times Trump Derailed His Own Infrastructure Plan*, in *New York Magazine*. 2018.
562. Tankersley, J.H.D., Julie, *Trump's $1.5 Trillion Infrastructure Plan Is Light on Federal Funds, and Details*, in *New York Times*. 2018.
563. Allen, G., *Trump Says He Will Focus On Opioid Law Enforcement, Not Treatment*, in *All Things Considered*. 2018, NPR.
564. Caminiti, S., *Trump talks tough inState of the Union to end opioid crisis, but high schools get tougher*, in *CNBC*. 2018.
565. Marsh, R.J., Athena, *Inside the confusion of the Trump executive order and travel ban*, in *CNN Politics*. 2017.
566. Landler, M., *North Korea Asks for Direct Nuclear Talks, and Trump Agrees*, in *New York Times*. 2018.
567. Deyoung, K.R., Philip, *Trump's abrupt shifts on NAFTA blindside allies Canada, Mexico*, in *Chicago Tribune*. 2017.
568. Relman, E., *'Hv ur staff brief me': Republicans in Congress are resorting to Twitter to get through to Trump after he blindsided them on near-deal with Democrats*, in *Business Insider*. 2017.
569. Vidal, L., *Trump Blindsides South Korea; Gives Kim Everything He Wanted*, in *PoliticusUSA*. 2018.

570. Reich, R., *ROBERT REICH: TRUMP'S BUNGLING, BITCHY WHITE HOUSE*, in *Newsweek*. 2017.
571. Shear, M., *Trump's Biggest Obstacle to Policy Goals? His Own Missteps*, in *New York Times*. 2017.
572. Depetris, D., *THE TRAGIC IRONY OF TRUMP: HE'S HIS OWN WORST ENEMY*. 2018.
573. Conner, W.R., *A Vacuum at the Center*, in *The American Scholar*. 2018.
574. Soerens, M., *President Trump can solve the immigration crisis with legislation that died in 2013*, in *Fox News*. 2018.
575. Atlas, S.W., *Americans are 'winning' on health care as Trump administration chips away at ObamaCare*, in *Fox News*. 2018.
576. Crowley, M.L., Cristiano; Nelson, Louis, *Trump says Kim meeting will be about 'attitude,' not prep work*, in *Politico*. 2018.
577. Lima, C., *Trump ditches 'boring' tax script for Mexican rapists, illegal voting claims*, in *Politico*. 2018.
578. Semple, R.B., Jr., *KISSINGER TO VISIT CHINA TO PREPARE FOR NIXON'S TRIP*, in *New York Times*. 1971.
579. MacMillan, M., *'Nixon and Mao'*, in *New York Times*. 2007.
580. Editors, H.c., *Reagan challenges Gorbachev to tear down the Berlin Wall*, in *History Channel* 1987.
581. Association., A.P., *Many Americans Stressed about Future of Our Nation, New APA Stress in America™ Survey Reveals*. 2017.
582. Association., A.P., *APA Stress in America™ Survey: US at 'Lowest Point We Can Remember;' Future of Nation Most Commonly Reported Source of Stress*. 2017.
583. Pace, J.B., Bill, *Republican doubts and anxieties about Trump burst into the open*, in *Chicago Tribune*. 2017.
584. Haberman, M.A., Yamiche, *Pelosi and Schumer Say They Have Deal With Trump to Replace DACA*, in *New York Times*. 2017.
585. Logan, B., *'SPITEFUL, POINTLESS SABOTAGE': Democrats excoriate Trump's move to cancel Obamacare payments*, in *Business Insider*. 2017.
586. Parker, A.R., Philip, *'Trump betrays everyone': The president has a long record as an unpredictable ally*, in *Washington Post*. 2017.
587. Reuters, *Trump axes $25m in aid for Palestinians in East Jerusalem hospitals*, in *The Guardian*. 2018.
588. International, T., *CORRUPTION IN THE USA: THE DIFFERENCE A YEAR MAKES*, in *Transparency International*. 2017.
589. Wike, R.S., Richard; Poushter, Jacob; Fetterolf, *U.S. Image Suffers as Publics Around World Question Trump's Leadership*, in *Pew Research Center*. 2017.

590. King, A., *Trump-Putin summit makes US a 'less reliable' partner to its Western allies, former UK official says*, in *CNN*. 2018.
591. Smith, N., *Who Has the World's No. 1 Economy? Not the U.S.*, in *Bloomberg*. 2017.
592. Hsu, S., *How Effective Is Trump's Trade Strategy For China?*, in *Forbes*. 2018.
593. DeYoung, K.W., Joby, *With Trump strategy unclear, U.S. allies turn to Moscow to secure their interests in Syria*, in *Washington Post*. 2018.
594. Tisdall, S., *Turkey's ever-closer ties with Russia leave US lacking key ally on Syria*, in *The Guardian*. 2018.
595. Vinik, D., *138 things Trump did this year while you weren't looking*. Politico, 2017.
596. Calamur, K., *Trump Rips Up a 'Decaying and Rotten Deal' With Iran*, in *The Atlantic*. 2018.
597. Eilperin, J.C., Darla, *How Trump is rolling back Obama's legacy*, in *Washington Post*. 2018.
598. Sang-Hun, C., *A Trump Nobel Peace Prize? South Korea's Leader Likes the Idea*, in *New York Times*. 2018.
599. Bazzi, M., *Saudi Arabia stroked Trump's ego. Now he is doing their bidding with Qatar*, in *The Guardian*. 2017.
600. Lemire, J.C., Jill, *Putin manipulating Trump with flattery, ex-director suggests*, in *Denver Post*. 2017.
601. Landler, M., *In Meeting With Putin, Experts Fear Trump Will Give More Than He Gets*, in *New York Times*. 2018.
602. Keeton, C.P., M. Perry-Jenkins, and A.G. Sayer, *Sense of control predicts depressive and anxious symptoms across the transition to parenthood.* J Fam Psychol, 2008. **22**(2): p. 212-21.
603. Stafford, D., *Trump's previous promises on health care*, in *CNN Politics*. 2017.
604. Nixon, R.Q., Linda, *Trump's Evolving Words on the Wall*, in *New York Times*. 2018.
605. Trump, D., *DONALD J. TRUMP STATEMENT ON PREVENTING MUSLIM IMMIGRATION*. 2015, Donald J. Trump for President, Inc.
606. Green, E., *How Religion Made a Global Comeback in 2017*, in *The Atlantic*. 2017.
607. Kessler, G., *Trump's claim that he, himself, created 1 million jobs as president*, in *Washington Post*. 2017.
608. Fredericks, B., *Trump still says Mexico will pay for the wall*, in *New York Post*. 2018.

609. Gore, D.A.R., Lori. *Trump's 'Travel Ban' Doesn't Affect All Muslims.* 2018; Available from: https://www.factcheck.org/2018/06/trumps-travel-ban-doesnt-affect-all-muslims/.
610. Yen, H.R., Christopher, *AP fact check: Trump's claims on 'record' GDP, jobs and the Russia investigation,* in *PBS News Hour.* 2018.
611. Colvin, J., *Trump backs off call for raising minimum age to buy gun,* in *Denver Post.* 2018.
612. Projects, T.S.F.-O.B.B.S.S. *FAQS: Bay Bridge Info.* 2018; Available from: https://www.baybridgeinfo.org/faq.
613. Nagourney, A.R., Jim, *Palin's Move Shocks G.O.P. and Leaves Future Unclear,* in *New York Times.* 2009.
614. NewsHour, P., *PBS NewsHour.* 2018.
615. Tani, M., *Poll: 78% of GOP Fox News Viewers Say Trump Is Best President Ever,* in *The Daily Beast.* 2019.
616. Liptak, A., *When Is an Offense Impeachable? Look to the Framers for the Answer,* in *New York Times.* 2018.
617. Zhao, C., *TRUMP COULD BE IMPEACHED FOR ATTACKING SESSIONS ON TWITTER OVER GOP INDICTMENTS, TOOBIN SAYS,* in *Newsweek.* 2018.
618. Blinder, A., *How the 25th Amendment Came to Be, by the People Behind It,* in *New York Times.* 2018.
619. Dalsgaard, S., et al., *Mortality in children, adolescents, and adults with attention deficit hyperactivity disorder: a nationwide cohort study.* Lancet, 2015. **385**(9983): p. 2190-6.
620. Parker, A., *Donald Trump's Diet: He'll Have Fries With That,* in *New York Times.* 2016.
621. Diamond, J., *Trump's doctor: Trump 'will be healthiest individual ever elected' president,* in *CNN Politics.* 2015.
622. Editors, H.c. *President Ford survives second assassination attempt.* 1975; Available from: https://www.history.com/this-day-in-history/president-ford-survives-second-assassination-attempt.
623. Jacobson, L.T., Manuela, *Has Donald Trump never 'promoted or encouraged violence,' as Sarah Huckabee Sanders said? (FALSE),* in *Politifact.* 2017.
624. McCarthy, T.B., Lois; Glenza, Jessica, *America's passion for guns: ownership and violence by the numbers,* in *The Guardian.* 2017.
625. Kellison, I., et al., *Assessment of stigma associated with attention-deficit hyperactivity disorder: psychometric evaluation of the ADHD stigma questionnaire.* Psychiatry Res, 2010. **178**(2): p. 363-9.

626. Sowislo, J.F. and U. Orth, *Does low self-esteem predict depression and anxiety? A meta-analysis of longitudinal studies.* Psychol Bull, 2013. **139**(1): p. 213-240.
627. Bennet, C., *Low self-esteem;a disposition that can lead to addiction*, in *Psychology Today*. 2013.
628. Vater, A., et al., *When grandiosity and vulnerability collide: Implicit and explicit self-esteem in patients with narcissistic personality disorder.* J Behav Ther Exp Psychiatry, 2013. **44**(1): p. 37-47.
629. Fredrickson, B.L., *The role of positive emotions in positive psychology. The broaden-and-build theory of positive emotions.* Am Psychol, 2001. **56**(3): p. 218-26.
630. Oquendo, M., *The Golden Goldwater Rule.* Psychiatric News, 2017.
631. Derald, W.S., *Microaggressions: More than Just Race*, in *Psychology Today*. 2010.
632. Dodson, W., *ADHD in Exile: When the Shame of Living with a Disorder Is Worse Than the Disorder Itself*, in *ADDitude*. 2018.
633. Burton, N., *When Homosexuality Stopped Being a Mental Disorder*, in *Psychology Today*. 2015.
634. Center, P.R., *Homosexuality, gender and religion.* Pew Research Center U.S. Politics and Policy, 2017.
635. Harvey, L. *Homosexual Health Hazards and Our Kids.* 2017 March 29, 2017; Available from: http://www.missionamerica.com/article/homosexual-health-hazards-and-our-kids/.
636. You, G.T. *God's Plan for the Gay Agenda.* Grace To You 2018; Available from: https://www.gty.org/library/articles/A170/gods-plan-for-the-gay-agenda.
637. Russell, S.T. and J.N. Fish, *Mental Health in Lesbian, Gay, Bisexual, and Transgender (LGBT) Youth.* Annu Rev Clin Psychol, 2016. **12**: p. 465-87.
638. Lowry, R., et al., *Social Stress and Substance Use Disparities by Sexual Orientation Among High School Students.* Am J Prev Med, 2017. **53**(4): p. 547-558.
639. Raifman, J., et al., *Difference-in-Differences Analysis of the Association Between State Same-Sex Marriage Policies and Adolescent Suicide Attempts.* JAMA Pediatr, 2017. **171**(4): p. 350-356.
640. Hatzenbuehler, M.L., J.C. Phelan, and B.G. Link, *Stigma as a fundamental cause of population health inequalities.* Am J Public Health, 2013. **103**(5): p. 813-21.
641. Banschick, M., *Neurodivergence: Celebrating autism awareness*, in *Psychology Today*. 2017.

642. Luhrmann, T.M., *Living With Voices*, in *The American Scholar*. 2012.
643. Susser, E., R. Moore, and B. Link, *Risk factors for homelessness*. Epidemiol Rev, 1993. **15**(2): p. 546-56.
644. Baillargeon, J., et al., *Psychiatric disorders and repeat incarcerations: the revolving prison door*. Am J Psychiatry, 2009. **166**(1): p. 103-9.
645. Sun, K., *The legal definition of hate crime and the hate offender's distorted cognitions*. Issues Ment Health Nurs, 2006. **27**(6): p. 597-604.
646. Chapman, H.A., et al., *In bad taste: evidence for the oral origins of moral disgust*. Science, 2009. **323**(5918): p. 1222-6.
647. Goff, P.A., et al., *Not yet human: implicit knowledge, historical dehumanization, and contemporary consequences*. J Pers Soc Psychol, 2008. **94**(2): p. 292-306.
648. Drake, S., *Slandering the Jew : sexuality and difference in early Christian texts*. 1st ed. Divinations : rereading late ancient religion. 2013, Philadelphia: PENN/University of Pennsylvania Press. 176 p.
649. Classen, C., D. Howes, and A. Synnott, *Aroma : the cultural history of smell*. 1994, London ; New York: Routledge. viii, 248 p.
650. Tullett, W., *Grease and Sweat: Race and Smell in Eighteenth-Century English Culture*. Cultural and Social History, 2016. **13**(3): p. 307-322.
651. Blissett, J. and A. Fogel, *Intrinsic and extrinsic influences on children's acceptance of new foods*. Physiol Behav, 2013. **121**: p. 89-95.
652. Pettigrew, T.F. and L.R. Tropp, *A meta-analytic test of intergroup contact theory*. J Pers Soc Psychol, 2006. **90**(5): p. 751-83.
653. Hewstone, M. and H. Swart, *Fifty-odd years of inter-group contact: from hypothesis to integrated theory*. Br J Soc Psychol, 2011. **50**(3): p. 374-86.
654. McCormack, M., *The Declining Significance of Homophobia*. 2013: Oxford University Press.
655. Clair, M., C. Daniel, and M. Lamont, *Destigmatization and health: Cultural constructions and the long-term reduction of stigma*. Soc Sci Med, 2016. **165**: p. 223-232.
656. Fortin, J., *James Comey vs. President Trump: How It Came to This*, in *New York Times*. 2018.
657. Press, B., *Donald Trump comes completely unhinged*, in *Chicago Tribune*. 2018.
658. Logan, B., *'Unstable, inept, inexperienced, and also unethical': Former CIA director delivers a brutal assessment of Trump*, in *Business Insider*. 2018.
659. Zumberge, M., *Louis C.K. Compares Donald Trump to Hitler: 'He's an Insane Bigot'*, in *Variety*. 2016.

660. Seipel, A., *FACT CHECK: Trump Falsely Claims A 'Massive Landslide Victory'*, N.P. Radio, Editor. 2016.
661. Bonn, S.A., *John Wayne Gacy: The Diabolical "Killer Clown"*, in *Psychology Today*. 2014.
662. Tithecott, R., *Of men and monsters : Jeffrey Dahmer and the construction of the serial killer*. 1997, Madison: University of Wisconsin Press. xiii, 192 p.
663. Stetson, N., *THE WORLD'S BIGGEST CLOSET?*, in *Chicago Tribune*. 1995.
664. Savage, D., *The Killer That Haunted My Adolescence*, in *The Stranger*. 2018.
665. Jasper, W.F., *The Queering of America*. The New American, 2015.
666. Gamboa, S., *GOP Attack Ads Linking Gangs to Immigration Rankle Latino Advocates*, in *NBC Nightly News*. 2017.
667. Hinojosa, M., *Hate Crimes Against Latinos Increase In California*, in *Weekend Edition*. 2018.
668. Mervosh, S., *Why Do You Hate Us?' He Asked. 'Because You're Mexicans,' She Replied.*, in *New York Times*. 2018.
669. Mosher, D., *Mollie Tibbetts' death is being used to push debunked ideas about illegal immigration and violent crime*, in *Business Insider*. 2018.
670. Davis, K.H., *Stonewall Uprising*, in *American Experience*. 2011, PBS.
671. O'Mahony, N., et al., *Objective diagnosis of ADHD using IMUs.* Med Eng Phys, 2014. **36**(7): p. 922-6.
672. Sridhar, C., et al., *Diagnosis of attention deficit hyperactivity disorder using imaging and signal processing techniques.* Comput Biol Med, 2017. **88**: p. 93-99.
673. Berrouiguet, S., et al., *From eHealth to iHealth: Transition to Participatory and Personalized Medicine in Mental Health.* J Med Internet Res, 2018. **20**(1): p. e2.
674. Morash, M., et al., *The Role of Next-Generation Sequencing in Precision Medicine: A Review of Outcomes in Oncology.* J Pers Med, 2018. **8**(3).
675. Schwartzberg, L., et al., *Precision Oncology: Who, How, What, When, and When Not?* Am Soc Clin Oncol Educ Book, 2017. **37**: p. 160-169.
676. Draper, K., *Madison Square Garden Has Used Face-Scanning Technology on Customers.*, in *New York Times*. 2018.
677. Tabor, N., *Smile! The Secretive Business of Facial-Recognition Software in Retail Stores*, in *New York Magazine*. 2018.
678. Shah, Y., *9 Ways You're Being Spied On Every Day*, in *Huffington Post*. 2014.

679. Pangburn, D., *How—And Why—Apple, Google, And Facebook Follow You Around In Real Life*, in *Fast Company*. 2017.
680. Marks, P., *Apple's smart watch could have us all self-monitoring*, in *New Scientist*. 2014.
681. Bachman, J., *How Random Alcohol, Drug Testing Keep Skies Safe*. Insurance Journal, 2016.
682. Administration, F.A., *Guide for Aviation Medical Examiners*, F.A. Administration, Editor. 2018.
683. Goebel, B., *San Francisco Adopts Alcohol and Drug Testing for Taxi Drivers*, in *KQED News*. 2015.
684. Administration, F.M.C.S., *What CDL Drivers Need to Know*, U.S.D.o. Transportation, Editor. 2018.
685. Administration, F.R., *What You Need to Know About Federal Drug and Alcohol Testing*, D.a.A. Program, Editor. 2018.
686. Baars, B.J. and N.M. Gage, *Fundamentals of cognitive neuroscience : a beginner's guide*. 2013, Amsterdam ; Boston: Academic Press. viii, 463 p.
687. Kim, J.W., V. Sharma, and N.D. Ryan, *Predicting Methylphenidate Response in ADHD Using Machine Learning Approaches*. Int J Neuropsychopharmacol, 2015. **18**(11): p. pyv052.
688. Duda, M., et al., *Use of machine learning for behavioral distinction of autism and ADHD*. Transl Psychiatry, 2016. **6**: p. e732.
689. Duda, M., et al., *Crowdsourced validation of a machine-learning classification system for autism and ADHD*. Transl Psychiatry, 2017. **7**(5): p. e1133.
690. Urban, A., et al., *Understanding the neurovascular unit at multiple scales: Advantages and limitations of multi-photon and functional ultrasound imaging*. Adv Drug Deliv Rev, 2017. **119**: p. 73-100.
691. Albajara Saenz, A., T. Villemonteix, and I. Massat, *Structural and functional neuroimaging in attention-deficit/hyperactivity disorder*. Dev Med Child Neurol, 2018.
692. Yuhas, D., *What's a Voxel and What Can It Tell Us? A Primer on fMRI*. Scientific American, 2012.
693. Bermúdez, J.L., *Cognitive science : an introduction to the science of the mind, Chapter 11.5*. Second edition. ed. 2014, Cambridge: Cambridge University Press. xxxv, 520 pages.
694. Rivers, S., *FDA permits marketing of first brain wave test to help assess children and teens for ADHD*. 2013, FDA News Release.
695. Markowitz, E., *The Tiny Start-up Behind the Brain Wave Test for ADHD*, in *Inc*. 2013.

696. Moisse, K., *Brainwave Test for ADHD: For Patients or Profit?*, in *ABC News*. 2013.
697. Hill, C.P.o.C. *NEBA – A New Biomarker to Assess for ADHD*. 2018; Available from: https://cognitive-psychiatry.com/neba.
698. Institute, R.H. *Neurofeedback for ADHD or Attention Deficit Disorder*. Reintegrative Health Institute - About ADHD St. Louis 2018; Available from: http://www.aboutadhdstlouis.com/about-neurotherapy-st-louis-mo-stress-adhd/.
699. Slaughter, E., *Neurofeedback Therapy Improves Behavior Outcomes in Patients With ADHD*, in *MD Magazine*. 2018.
700. Gloss, D., et al., *Practice advisory: The utility of EEG theta/beta power ratio in ADHD diagnosis: Report of the Guideline Development, Dissemination, and Implementation Subcommittee of the American Academy of Neurology.* Neurology, 2016. **87**(22): p. 2375-2379.
701. Ogrim, G., J. Kropotov, and K. Hestad, *The quantitative EEG theta/beta ratio in attention deficit/hyperactivity disorder and normal controls: sensitivity, specificity, and behavioral correlates.* Psychiatry Res, 2012. **198**(3): p. 482-8.
702. Arns, M., C.K. Conners, and H.C. Kraemer, *A decade of EEG Theta/Beta Ratio Research in ADHD: a meta-analysis.* J Atten Disord, 2013. **17**(5): p. 374-83.
703. Schonenberg, M., et al., *Neurofeedback, sham neurofeedback, and cognitive-behavioural group therapy in adults with attention-deficit hyperactivity disorder: a triple-blind, randomised, controlled trial.* Lancet Psychiatry, 2017. **4**(9): p. 673-684.
704. Editors, A., *The Amen Approach to ADHD*, in *ADDitude*. 2018.
705. Amen, D.G., *Healing ADD from the inside out : the breakthrough program that allows you to see and heal the seven types of attention deficit disorder*. Revised Berkley trade paperback edition. ed. 2013, New York: Berkley Books. xl, 422 pages.
706. Farah, M.J. and S.J. Gillihan, *The Puzzle of Neuroimaging and Psychiatric Diagnosis: Technology and Nosology in an Evolving Discipline.* AJOB Neurosci, 2012. **3**(4): p. 31-41.
707. Shaw, P., et al., *Polymorphisms of the dopamine D4 receptor, clinical outcome, and cortical structure in attention-deficit/hyperactivity disorder.* Arch Gen Psychiatry, 2007. **64**(8): p. 921-31.
708. Vanello, N., et al., *Speech analysis for mood state characterization in bipolar patients.* Conf Proc IEEE Eng Med Biol Soc, 2012. **2012**: p. 2104-7.

709. Spiegel, A., *If Your Shrink Is A Bot, How Do You Respond?*, in *Morning Edition*. 2013, National Public Radio.
710. Rizzo, A., et al., *Automatic Behavior Analysis During a Clinical Interview with a Virtual Human.* Stud Health Technol Inform, 2016. **220**: p. 316-22.
711. Leppanen, J., et al., *Computerised analysis of facial emotion expression in eating disorders.* PLoS One, 2017. **12**(6): p. e0178972.
712. Stockli, S., et al., *Facial expression analysis with AFFDEX and FACET: A validation study.* Behav Res Methods, 2018. **50**(4): p. 1446-1460.
713. Fried, M., et al., *ADHD subjects fail to suppress eye blinks and microsaccades while anticipating visual stimuli but recover with medication.* Vision Res, 2014. **101**: p. 62-72.
714. company, T.T. *The T.O.V.A. Store*. 2018; Available from: https://www.tovatest.com/store-us/.
715. Frye, D., *FDA Clears New Version of Electronic ADHD Assessment Aid*, in *ADDitude*. 2018.
716. McGough, J.J., et al., *Double-Blind, Sham-Controlled, Pilot Study of Trigeminal Nerve Stimulation for Attention-Deficit/Hyperactivity Disorder.* J Am Acad Child Adolesc Psychiatry, 2019. **58**(4): p. 403-411.e3.
717. Hilty, D., et al., *Telepsychiatry: Effective, Evidence-Based, and at a Tipping Point in Health Care Delivery?* Psychiatr Clin North Am, 2015. **38**(3): p. 559-92.
718. Burns, J., *Families In Rural Areas Using Telemedicine For Psychiatric, Specialty Care*, in *Forbes*. 2016.
719. Moss, L., *Virtual therapists are better at getting people to open up*, in *MOTHER NATURE NETWORK*. 2014.
720. Snowdon, D.A., L.H. Greiner, and W.R. Markesbery, *Linguistic ability in early life and the neuropathology of Alzheimer's disease and cerebrovascular disease. Findings from the Nun Study.* Ann N Y Acad Sci, 2000. **903**: p. 34-8.
721. Bennett, D.A., et al., *Overview and findings from the religious orders study.* Curr Alzheimer Res, 2012. **9**(6): p. 628-45.
722. Rumshisky, A., et al., *Predicting early psychiatric readmission with natural language processing of narrative discharge summaries.* Transl Psychiatry, 2016. **6**(10): p. e921.
723. McCoy, T.H., Jr., et al., *Improving Prediction of Suicide and Accidental Death After Discharge From General Hospitals With Natural Language Processing.* JAMA Psychiatry, 2016. **73**(10): p. 1064-1071.
724. Gandhi, T.K., et al., *Outpatient prescribing errors and the impact of computerized prescribing.* J Gen Intern Med, 2005. **20**(9): p. 837-41.

725. Nanji, K.C., et al., *Errors associated with outpatient computerized prescribing systems.* J Am Med Inform Assoc, 2011. **18**(6): p. 767-73.
726. Porterfield, A., K. Engelbert, and A. Coustasse, *Electronic prescribing: improving the efficiency and accuracy of prescribing in the ambulatory care setting.* Perspect Health Inf Manag, 2014. **11**: p. 1g.
727. Simonite, T., *Photo algorithms ID white men fine -- black women, not so much*, in *Wired* 2018.
728. Yang, H., X. Chen, and G.J. Zelinsky, *A new look at novelty effects: guiding search away from old distractors.* Atten Percept Psychophys, 2009. **71**(3): p. 554-64.
729. Estroff Marano, H., *Our Brain's Negative Bias*, in *Psychology Today*. 2003.
730. Kopp, L., C.M. Atance, and S. Pearce, *'Things aren't so bad!': Preschoolers overpredict the emotional intensity of negative outcomes.* Br J Dev Psychol, 2017. **35**(4): p. 623-627.
731. Teoh, E.R. and D.G. Kidd, *Rage against the machine? Google's self-driving cars versus human drivers.* J Safety Res, 2017. **63**: p. 57-60.
732. Gorzelany, J., *Autonomous Car Gets First-Ever Traffic Ticket, In San Francisco*, in *Forbes Magazine*. 2018.
733. Isidore, C., *Self-driving cars are already really safe*, in *CNN Business*. 2018.
734. Affairs, N.P., *USDOT Releases 2016 Fatal Tra.* 2016.
735. America, W.S.o., *Does Your Internet History Effect Google Search Results?* 2018.
736. Meyer, R., *Everything We Know About Facebook's Secret Mood Manipulation Experiment*, in *The Atlantic*. 2014.
737. Bessi, A., et al., *Science vs conspiracy: collective narratives in the age of misinformation.* PLoS One, 2015. **10**(2): p. e0118093.
738. Narayanan, V.B., Vlad; Kelly, John; Kollanyi, Bence; Neurdert, Lisa-Marie; Howard, Philip N. *Polarization, Partisanship and Junk News Consumption over Social Media in the US.* Data Memo 2018.1. Oxford, UK: Project on Computational Propaganda. , 2018.
739. Ma, A., *China has started ranking citizens with a creepy 'social credit' system*, in *Business Insider*. 2018.
740. Simmons, A., *Public Figures, Private Records*, in *The News, Media and The Law*. 2012, Reporters Committee for freedom of the press.
741. Pearce, M., *How much do presidents and candidates need to tell the public about their health?*, in *Los Angeles Times*. 2016.
742. Porter, B., *Is The President Required To Have An Annual Physical?*, in *Forbes*. 2017.

743. Kluger, J., *FDR's Polio: The Steel in His Soul*, in *Time*. 2014.
744. Brown, D., *JFK'S ADDISON'S DISEASE*, in *Washington Post*. 1992.
745. Christakis, N.A. and J.H. Fowler, *Social contagion theory: examining dynamic social networks and human behavior.* Stat Med, 2013. **32**(4): p. 556-77.
746. Datar, A. and N. Nicosia, *Assessing Social Contagion in Body Mass Index, Overweight, and Obesity Using a Natural Experiment.* JAMA Pediatr, 2018. **172**(3): p. 239-246.
747. Wolf, C., *Post-Traumatic Stress Disorder Can Be Contagious.* Scientific American, 2018.
748. Wainberg, M.L., et al., *Curtailing the communicability of psychiatric disorders.* Lancet Psychiatry, 2018. **5**(11): p. 940-944.
749. Merzenich, M.M., *Soft-Wired: How the New Science of Brain Plasticity Can Change Your Life.* 2013, San Francisco, CA: Parnassus Publishing.
750. Merzenich, M.M., T.M. Van Vleet, and M. Nahum, *Brain plasticity-based therapeutics.* Front Hum Neurosci, 2014. **8**: p. 385.
751. Sullivan, E.V., R.A. Harris, and A. Pfefferbaum, *Alcohol's effects on brain and behavior.* Alcohol Res Health, 2010. **33**(1-2): p. 127-43.
752. Boden, J.M. and D.M. Fergusson, *Alcohol and depression.* Addiction, 2011. **106**(5): p. 906-14.
753. Wolitzky-Taylor, K., et al., *Longitudinal investigation of the impact of anxiety and mood disorders in adolescence on subsequent substance use disorder onset and vice versa.* Addict Behav, 2012. **37**(8): p. 982-5.
754. Howard, A.L., et al., *ADHD is associated with a "Western" dietary pattern in adolescents.* J Atten Disord, 2011. **15**(5): p. 403-11.
755. Millichap, J.G. and M.M. Yee, *The diet factor in attention-deficit/hyperactivity disorder.* Pediatrics, 2012. **129**(2): p. 330-7.
756. Sonuga-Barke, E.J., et al., *Nonpharmacological interventions for ADHD: systematic review and meta-analyses of randomized controlled trials of dietary and psychological treatments.* Am J Psychiatry, 2013. **170**(3): p. 275-89.
757. Hawkey, E. and J.T. Nigg, *Omega-3 fatty acid and ADHD: blood level analysis and meta-analytic extension of supplementation trials.* Clin Psychol Rev, 2014. **34**(6): p. 496-505.
758. Lopez-Vicente, M., et al., *Prenatal Omega-6:Omega-3 Ratio and Attention Deficit and Hyperactivity Disorder Symptoms.* J Pediatr, 2019. **209**: p. 204-211.e4.
759. Kotsi, E., E. Kotsi, and D.N. Perrea, *Vitamin D levels in children and adolescents with attention-deficit hyperactivity disorder (ADHD): a meta-analysis.* Atten Defic Hyperact Disord, 2018.

760. Bertin, M., *How ADHD Affects Obesity, Weight and Healthy Eating Habits*, in *Psychology Today*. 2011.
761. Cortese, S. and L. Tessari, *Attention-Deficit/Hyperactivity Disorder (ADHD) and Obesity: Update 2016.* Curr Psychiatry Rep, 2017. **19**(1): p. 4.
762. Chen, Q., et al., *Attention-deficit/hyperactivity disorder and clinically diagnosed obesity in adolescence and young adulthood: a register-based study in Sweden.* Psychol Med, 2018: p. 1-9.
763. Bellisle, F. and A.M. Dalix, *Cognitive restraint can be offset by distraction, leading to increased meal intake in women.* Am J Clin Nutr, 2001. **74**(2): p. 197-200.
764. Long, S., et al., *Effects of distraction and focused attention on actual and perceived food intake in females with non-clinical eating psychopathology.* Appetite, 2011. **56**(2): p. 350-6.
765. Ogden, J., et al., *Distraction, the desire to eat and food intake. Towards an expanded model of mindless eating.* Appetite, 2013. **62**: p. 119-26.
766. Robinson, E., et al., *Eating attentively: a systematic review and meta-analysis of the effect of food intake memory and awareness on eating.* Am J Clin Nutr, 2013. **97**(4): p. 728-42.
767. Mars, M., et al., *Decreases in fasting leptin and insulin concentrations after acute energy restriction and subsequent compensation in food intake.* Am J Clin Nutr, 2005. **81**(3): p. 570-7.
768. Drayer, L., *Weight loss can be tied to when, not just what, you eat*. 2018, CNN.
769. Lustig, R.H., *The hacking of the American mind : the science behind the corporate takeover of our bodies and brains.* 2017, New York: Avery, an imprint of Penguin Random House. 344 pages.
770. Johnson, R.J., et al., *Attention-deficit/hyperactivity disorder: is it time to reappraise the role of sugar consumption?* Postgrad Med, 2011. **123**(5): p. 39-49.
771. Hvolby, A., *Associations of sleep disturbance with ADHD: implications for treatment.* Atten Defic Hyperact Disord, 2015. **7**(1): p. 1-18.
772. Banks, S. and D.F. Dinges, *Behavioral and physiological consequences of sleep restriction.* J Clin Sleep Med, 2007. **3**(5): p. 519-28.
773. Walker, M.P., *Why we sleep : unlocking the power of sleep and dreams.* First Scribner hardcover edition. ed. 2017, New York: Scribner, an imprint of Simon & Schuster, Inc. viii, 360 pages.
774. Xie, L., et al., *Sleep drives metabolite clearance from the adult brain.* Science, 2013. **342**(6156): p. 373-7.

775. Shokri-Kojori, E., et al., *beta-Amyloid accumulation in the human brain after one night of sleep deprivation.* Proc Natl Acad Sci U S A, 2018. **115**(17): p. 4483-4488.
776. Werli, K.S., et al., *Neurocognitive function in patients with residual excessive sleepiness from obstructive sleep apnea: a prospective, controlled study.* Sleep Med, 2016. **26**: p. 6-11.
777. Huang, Y.S., et al., *Attention-deficit/hyperactivity disorder with obstructive sleep apnea: a treatment outcome study.* Sleep Med, 2007. **8**(1): p. 18-30.
778. Marcus, C.L., et al., *Effects of positive airway pressure therapy on neurobehavioral outcomes in children with obstructive sleep apnea.* Am J Respir Crit Care Med, 2012. **185**(9): p. 998-1003.
779. Blesch, L. and S.J. Breese McCoy, *Obstructive Sleep Apnea Mimics Attention Deficit Disorder.* J Atten Disord, 2016. **20**(1): p. 41-2.
780. Yu, Y., et al., *Neuropsychological functioning after adenotonsillectomy in children with obstructive sleep apnea: A meta-analysis.* J Huazhong Univ Sci Technolog Med Sci, 2017. **37**(3): p. 453-461.
781. Hirshkowitz, M., et al., *National Sleep Foundation's sleep time duration recommendations: methodology and results summary.* Sleep Health, 2015. **1**(1): p. 40-43.
782. Foundation, N.S., *2012 Bedroom Poll summary of findings.* 2012.
783. Foundation, N.S., *2006 Teens and Sleep Summary of Findings.* 2006.
784. Knutson, K.L., et al., *Trends in the prevalence of short sleepers in the USA: 1975-2006.* Sleep, 2010. **33**(1): p. 37-45.
785. Keyes, K.M., et al., *The great sleep recession: changes in sleep duration among US adolescents, 1991-2012.* Pediatrics, 2015. **135**(3): p. 460-8.
786. Cooke, R., *'Sleep should be prescribed': what those late nights out could be costing you*, in *The Guardian.* 2017.
787. Krishnan, H.C. and L.C. Lyons, *Synchrony and desynchrony in circadian clocks: impacts on learning and memory.* Learn Mem, 2015. **22**(9): p. 426-37.
788. Rybak, Y.E., et al., *An open trial of light therapy in adult attention-deficit/hyperactivity disorder.* J Clin Psychiatry, 2006. **67**(10): p. 1527-35.
789. Fargason, R.E., et al., *Correcting delayed circadian phase with bright light therapy predicts improvement in ADHD symptoms: A pilot study.* J Psychiatr Res, 2017. **91**: p. 105-110.
790. Rybak, Y.E., et al., *Seasonality and circadian preference in adult attention-deficit/hyperactivity disorder: clinical and neuropsychological correlates.* Compr Psychiatry, 2007. **48**(6): p. 562-71.

791. Baird, A.L., et al., *Adult attention-deficit hyperactivity disorder is associated with alterations in circadian rhythms at the behavioural, endocrine and molecular levels.* Mol Psychiatry, 2012. **17**(10): p. 988-95.
792. BLASZCZAK-BOXE, A., *Night owls and early birds have different personality traits*, in *CBS News*. 2014.
793. Kooij, S., *Are You a Night Owl? About ADHD and Late Sleep*, in *The American Professional Society of ADHD and Related Disorders*. 2016.
794. Coogan, A.N. and N.M. McGowan, *A systematic review of circadian function, chronotype and chronotherapy in attention deficit hyperactivity disorder.* Atten Defic Hyperact Disord, 2017. **9**(3): p. 129-147.
795. Coogan, A.N., et al., *Circadian rhythms and attention deficit hyperactivity disorder: The what, the when and the why.* Prog Neuropsychopharmacol Biol Psychiatry, 2016. **67**: p. 74-81.
796. Hoza, B., et al., *Using Physical Activity to Manage ADHD Symptoms: The State of the Evidence.* Curr Psychiatry Rep, 2016. **18**(12): p. 113.
797. Brownson, R.C., T.K. Boehmer, and D.A. Luke, *Declining rates of physical activity in the United States: what are the contributors?* Annu Rev Public Health, 2005. **26**: p. 421-43.
798. Levine, J.A., N.L. Eberhardt, and M.D. Jensen, *Role of nonexercise activity thermogenesis in resistance to fat gain in humans.* Science, 1999. **283**(5399): p. 212-4.
799. Hussenoeder, F.S. and S.G. Riedel-Heller, *Primary prevention of dementia: from modifiable risk factors to a public brain health agenda?* Soc Psychiatry Psychiatr Epidemiol, 2018. **53**(12): p. 1289-1301.
800. Mandsager, K.H., S.; Cremer, P.; Phelan, D.; Nissen, S.; Jaber, W., *Association of Cardiorespiratory Fitness With Long-term Mortality Among Adults Undergoing Exercise Treadmill Testing.* JAMA Network Open, 2018. **1**(6:e183605).
801. Kietglaiwansiri, T. and W. Chonchaiya, *Pattern of video game use in children with attention-deficit-hyperactivity disorder and typical development.* Pediatr Int, 2018. **60**(6): p. 523-528.
802. Ra, C.K., et al., *Association of Digital Media Use With Subsequent Symptoms of Attention-Deficit/Hyperactivity Disorder Among Adolescents.* Jama, 2018. **320**(3): p. 255-263.
803. Guarino, B., *Prominent gamer died during live-streamed attempt to play 'World of Tanks' for 24 hours*, in *The Washington Post*. 2017.
804. Madigan, S., et al., *Association Between Screen Time and Children's Performance on a Developmental Screening Test.* JAMA Pediatr, 2019.

805. Tamana, S.K., et al., *Screen-time is associated with inattention problems in preschoolers: Results from the CHILD birth cohort study.* PLoS One, 2019. **14**(4): p. e0213995.
806. Wu, L.J., et al., *Prevalence and associated factors of myopia in high-school students in Beijing.* PLoS One, 2015. **10**(3): p. e0120764.
807. Cuellar, J.M. and T.H. Lanman, *"Text neck": an epidemic of the modern era of cell phones?* Spine J, 2017. **17**(6): p. 901-902.
808. Rocha, V., *2 California men fall off edge of ocean bluff while playing 'Pokemon Go',* in *LA Times.* 2016.
809. Chiu, A., *More than 250 people worldwide have died taking selfies, study finds,* in *Washington Post.* 2018.
810. Thomas, K.P., A.P. Vinod, and C. Guan, *Design of an online EEG based neurofeedback game for enhancing attention and memory.* Conf Proc IEEE Eng Med Biol Soc, 2013. **2013**: p. 433-6.
811. Abbasi, J., *Adam Gazzaley, MD, PhD: Developing Prescribable Video Games.* Jama, 2018. **320**(1): p. 16-18.
812. Korosec, K., *This Is the Personal Data that Facebook Collects—And Sometimes Sells,* in *Fortune Magazine.* 2018.
813. Popken, B., *Google sells the future, powered by your personal data.* 2018.
814. McCurdy, L.E., et al., *Using nature and outdoor activity to improve children's health.* Curr Probl Pediatr Adolesc Health Care, 2010. **40**(5): p. 102-17.
815. Keniger, L.E., et al., *What are the benefits of interacting with nature?* Int J Environ Res Public Health, 2013. **10**(3): p. 913-35.
816. Weinstein, A.M., *An Update Overview on Brain Imaging Studies of Internet Gaming Disorder.* Front Psychiatry, 2017. **8**: p. 185.
817. Chun, W.H.K., *Updating to remain the same : habitual new media.* 2016, Cambridge, MA: The MIT Press. xiv, 246 pages.
818. Mikami, A.Y., S. Smit, and A. Khalis, *Social Skills Training and ADHD-What Works?* Curr Psychiatry Rep, 2017. **19**(12): p. 93.
819. Mikami, A.Y., et al., *Online social communication patterns among emerging adult women with histories of childhood attention-deficit/hyperactivity disorder.* J Abnorm Psychol, 2015. **124**(3): p. 576-88.
820. Mehdizadeh, S., *Self-presentation 2.0: narcissism and self-esteem on Facebook.* Cyberpsychol Behav Soc Netw, 2010. **13**(4): p. 357-64.
821. Shakya, H.B. and N.A. Christakis, *Association of Facebook Use With Compromised Well-Being: A Longitudinal Study.* Am J Epidemiol, 2017. **185**(3): p. 203-211.

822. Mikami, A.Y., et al., *Social skills differences among attention-deficit/hyperactivity disorder types in a chat room assessment task.* J Abnorm Child Psychol, 2007. **35**(4): p. 509-21.
823. Ives, N., *USA TODAY: 'MCPAPER' IN MODERN TIMES.* AdAge, 2008(June 02, 2008).
824. Yu, R., *USA TODAY, WSJ, NYT are top three papers in circulation*, in *USA Today*. 2014.
825. Farhi, P., *New Associated Press guidelines: Keep it brief*, in *Washington Post*. 2014.
826. Jurkowitz, M.H., Paul; Mitchell, Amy; Houston Santhanam, Laura; Adams, Steve; Anderson, Monica; Vogt, Nancy, *The Changing TV News Landscape.* Pew Research Center Journalism and Media, 2013.
827. Manjoo, F., *Welcome to the Post-text future*, in *New York Times*. 2018.
828. Garber, M., *Newspaper Corrects 1863 Editorial Calling the Gettyburg Address 'Silly'*, in *The Atlantic*. 2013.
829. Widmer, T., *The Other Gettysburg Address*, in *New York Times*. 2013.
830. Bumiller, E., *White House Letter; Bush Gets 'Vision Thing' And Embraces Big Risks*, in *New York Times*. 2004.
831. Burkeman, O., *You've been a great audience ...The gaffes, the gibberish, the gurning.*, in *The Guardian*. 2009.
832. Prentice, D., *The Bush Family Conundrum*, in *American Thinker*. 2017.
833. Altman, L., *Parsing Ronald Reagan's Words for Early Signs of Alzheimer's*, in *New York Times*. 2015.
834. Balu, *Socrates had objections to Written words*, in *Time For Thought*. 2011.
835. Zuckerberg, M., *Facebook's letter from Mark Zuckerberg - full text.* 2012, The Guardian.
836. Gibbs, S., *Google's founders on the future of health, transport – and robots*, in *The Guardian*. 2014.

CPSIA information can be obtained
at www.ICGtesting.com
Printed in the USA
BVHW041209140819
555870BV00006BA/231/P